More Praise for *The Power of Nice*

"If I had read this book when I began my career, it would not have taken me thirty-five years to arrive at my present position. *The Power of Nice* is a winner!"

> Joel N. Waller
> Chief Executive Officer, Wilsons the Leather Experts

"I have known Ron Shapiro for nearly two decades and I can testify to the high regard in which he is held, as a negotiator and as a person, by me and by many others. In this book, he details for us the approach to negotiations that he uses so successfully."

> Donald M. Fehr
> Executive Director, General Counsel, Major League
> Baseball Players Association

"*The Power of Nice* should be required reading in America's foremost graduate schools of business. Ron Shapiro, who has been lauded as a superb lecturer in his regular assignments at the Wharton School, teaches business people, MBA candidates, and community leaders the essence of effective negotiation. This book is a must read for anyone wanting to improve their negotiation skills."

> Edward B. Shils, JD, PhD, SJD
> George W. Taylor Professor Emeritus of
> Entrepreneurial Studies at the Wharton School,
> University of Pennsylvania

"Read this book and you will learn how to negotiate from the master of negotiation."

> Susan O'Malley
> President, Washington Sports & Entertainment

the POWER of NICE

the POWER of NICE

How to Negotiate So Everyone Wins— Especially You!

Revised Edition

Ronald M. Shapiro and Mark A. Jankowski

with James Dale

JOHN WILEY & SONS, INC.

New York • Chichester • Weinheim • Brisbane • Singapore • Toronto

Published by John Wiley & Sons, Inc.
Published simultaneously in Canada.

This publication is designed to provide accurate and authoritative information in
regard to the subject matter covered. It is sold with the understanding that the
publisher is not engaged in rendering professional services. If professional advice or
other expert assistance is required, the services of a competent professional person
should be sought.

Library of Congress Cataloging-in-Publication Data:
   Shapiro, Ronald M.
      The power of nice : how to negotiate so everyone wins—especially you! /
   Ronald M. Shapiro and Mark A. Jankowski with James Dale.—Rev. ed.
         p. cm.
      Includes index.
      ISBN 0-471-08072-1 (pbk. : alk. paper)
      1. Negotiation in business.   I. Jankowski, Mark A.   II. Dale, Jim, 1948–
   III. Title.
   HD58.6.S5   2001
   658.4′052—dc21

                                                         2001026794

Printed in the United States of America.

10 9 8 7 6 5 4 3 2

To Cathi, for your love and enrichment of my life.

R.M.S.

To my wife, Lori, whose incredible love and support gave me the freedom to let go, tumble down the stream, and embark on this wonderful journey.

M.A.J.

NOTES

· · · · · · · · · · · · · ·

Inspiration for the exercises came from the following sources:

The $10 Game

J. Keith Murnighan, *Bargaining Games: A New Approach to Strategic Thinking in Negotiations.* (New York: William Morrow and Company, Inc., 1992), p. 104–105.

A Listening Test

Patrick Forsyth and Marek Gitlin, *20 Training Workshops for Developing Sales Effectiveness,* (Amherst, MA:HRD Press, 1992) p. 159.

Numbers and Letters Game

John W. Newstrom and Edward E. Scannell, *Games Trainers Play: Experiential Learning Exercises.* (New York: McGraw Hill, Inc. 1980)

Another $10 Game

M. Shubik, The Dollar Auction Game: A Paradox in Noncooperative Behavior and Escalation, *Journal of Conflict Resolution* 15 (1971), 109–11.

FOREWORD

●●●●●●●●●●●●●●●●●●●●●●

Can You Say "Agent" and "Nice" in the Same Sentence?

Some people believe that successful professional athletes are prima donnas, and are only interested in how much money they can make. People may also think agents are aggressive, blood-thirsty sharks, who will promise anything to cut a deal. These stereotypes may be true in some cases but I hope my career proves there are exceptions. I know Ron Shapiro disproves this theory in his profession.

Just because you practice *The Power of Nice,* you listen to the other side, and everybody comes out a winner doesn't mean you're not a good negotiator. In fact, it shows that it is a more involved negotiation, and both sides end up getting what they want—a whole lot more. Ron Shapiro finds out how both parties can come out with a win. He is a real life example of a successful win-win negotiator.

When I first met Ron, I was about 18 or 19 years old. I was an up-and-coming baseball player and a lot of agents were interested in representing me. They wooed me pretty hard, trying to persuade me that they or their agency would represent me the best and the most aggressively, get me to the big leagues faster, get me a more lucrative contract, handle my money better, and get me more endorsements.

These agents had all kinds of not-too-subtle ways of convincing a player they were the best. Some of them would arrive in stretch limousines to take you out to dinner at the finest, fanciest restaurants: great big lobsters and New York strip steaks. They put the emphasis on glitz and glamor.

To tell the truth, I enjoyed it. After all, there were a lot of agents out there, there were a lot of good restaurants, and I like lobster and steak. I would graciously accept the agents' invitation, go out, eat dinner, and listen. I referred to it as "the agent game."

One day, Mr. Shapiro called. Okay, I admit it, I'd heard of him and I called him. But he did call me right back. I now know his name is pronounced "Shap-eye-ro" but I called him Mr. "Shap-ear-o" and he called me "Carl." My parents and I made an appointment to hear his presentation so I could determine if I wanted him to represent me.

Right away, it was obvious that he was different from all the other agents. He said, "Let's meet at my office." So I thought, "This is okay. He'll show me his office and it's probably really posh, rich leather sofas, mahogany paneling, marble floors. Then he'll buzz for his driver and we'll go out to the fancy restaurant."

I arrived at his office and he introduced me to his staff. We talked baseball and what his approach would be for me. In some ways, it was similar to what others had said, but in a different atmosphere. The office wasn't posh. It was, what's the word—plain; no leather, no paneling, no marble. Eventually, it was lunch time and I was getting hungry and I was anticipating that expensive restaurant. Ron had tuna sandwiches brought in and we ate at the conference table (which was oak, not mahogany).

In the end I chose Ron Shapiro. Why? Maybe it was everything he *didn't* do that told me how he'd act on my behalf. Maybe it was not living up to the myths of his profession but clearly being successful. Maybe it was that he asked me what I wanted and needed and actually listened to me instead of telling me what he was going to do. Maybe it was trust.

Or maybe I just guessed right. Now it's many seasons and All-Star games and contracts later and I think I made the smartest decision any 18-year-old could make.

Over the years, I've seen every kind of deal maker there is. I'll take Ron's kind everytime. You can get what you want *and* you can live with yourself. You build relationships, so instead of making one-time deals, you make deals that lead to more deals. Make no mistake, you'll out-negotiate the other side. In fact, Ron taught me how to be a better deal maker so well, I'm not sure I need him anymore. It was just a joke, Ron. Nothing serious. See, I'm nice, too.

Seriously, while I've enjoyed a record-setting streak of consecutive games played, Ron has been on a streak of his own. I've seen him use his Power of Nice for over 15 years. My career, and many others, are testimony to its impact. The stories and lessons he and his partner, Mark Jankowski, tell in this book really work in real life, whether it be in everyday business deals or the hard-nosed negotiations of the big leagues.

CAL RIPKEN, JR.

ORIGINAL EDITION PREFACE

· · · · · · · · · · · · · · · · · ·

A Philosophy Is a
Name for What Works

Did you ever wonder how a philosopher comes up with a philosophy? Does someone just sit down one day and say, "Today's the day I create the Socratic approach" or "Hey, I have an idea—Capitalism?" No. They don't decide to *invent* a code and then live or work by it. The *way* they live or work, by virtue of its longevity and success, *becomes* a code or philosophy. A philosophy is what works. You don't know you have one until you've been practicing it a long time. That's just what happened to us.

I was very busy being a corporate lawyer, athlete's representative (that's a euphemism for sports agent), teacher, and a civic activist, but hardly a philosopher. By virtue of my vocations and interests, I was frequently asked to address various groups: talks to city leaders, talks to young athletes, talks to the Scouts, talks at corporate retreats, talks at fund-raisers, and talks to law students. In 1991, I asked a young associate, Mark Jankowski, to help me write those presentations.

I was fresh out of Harvard undergrad and Virginia Law and a habitual people-watcher. I studied who was good at interaction, how they did it, and started to form my own thoughts on effective relations. I had seen Ron Shapiro, the head of the firm, in action. I'd observed his highly successful approach to dealing with people in business and on a personal level. Naturally, I jumped at the chance to work with him.

One day, I was asked to give a three-hour presentation on negotiation. "Tell us how you make deals. Help us understand your philosophy of negotiation." I accepted. But when it came time to script the program, I thought, "Do I really have a *way* of making deals? Is there a *Shapiro approach*? I'm not a philosopher, am I?"

I asked Mark if he'd like to help me put the presentation together. "Sure," he said, never questioning whether or not I was a philosopher. I also asked him to join me, not just in the writing, but in making the presentation.

Making deals? That was the field of my unofficial self-administered doctorate. When Ron told me we were going to talk about negotiation, I thought this was a speech just waiting to be delivered.

I had talked many times about deals I'd made. I'd told stories. I had even developed what I called the Three Ps—Prepare, Probe, and Propose, but I wasn't sure I'd call it a philosophy.

I said, "Ron, you do have a negotiation philosophy. You've been practicing it for years. That's why clients come to you."

Perhaps Mark was right. I didn't do things like a lot of other deal-makers. I wasn't a shark but I had been getting results for my clients for over 20 years. (If I didn't, they'd have left long ago.) Mark served as a sounding board for the philosophy I'd been practicing and perfecting through the years. Together, we put into words the techniques I had been employing by instinct.

"People fear negotiation. They don't want to be bad guys. They want to like themselves in the morning. But they still want to get what they want."

We took what I believed and had been practicing and distilled it to its essential elements:

"There's more power in being nice than in being an s.o.b."

"Building relationships is more important than making one-time deals."

"Listen to the other side."

We created that three-hour presentation. We covered how I go about dealing with people, whether it's the person I am getting a deal *from,* offering one *to,* or partnering *with.* We examined successes and failures, all of which had contributed to shaping my style, my feelings, and eventually, my axioms. Mark prodded me to re-live the *so-and-so deal,* or the *you-know-who contract.* From his own observations, analysis of key elements, breaking the process down into additional steps and identifying critical practices, he and I began what was to evolve into our approach to teaching negotiation.

At first I thought I hadn't made many deals compared to Ron Shapiro. Then I realized, I had had my share of sports negotiations. Ron made deals for baseball players. When I was a kid, I made deals for baseball cards. Ron negotiated real estate leases. I cut a deal on my apartment. Ron settled a symphony strike. In law school, I mediated familial disputes. (It was all a matter of scale.) And, as I said, I'd been a rapt observer. We constructed that first program by writing down the ways Ron had lived and worked, the ways others who were successful lived and worked, and the ways to avoid the common but misguided methods that too many people use and often back-fire. We identified the lessons and we backed them up with stories, real events that proved the practice or improved it. Then we gave the presentation.

It was one of the most gratifying moments I can recall. We told the audience, "The best way to get what you want is to help the other side get what they want." We talked about "making short-term deals versus building long-term relationships." We realized, at the end, that we'd had a real impact on our audience. They listened. They laughed. They took notes. They came up afterwards and asked questions. "What would you do in this situation or that?" They liked the Shapiro (Jankowski) Philosophy of Negotiation, the one that I had practiced for years before it ever had a name.

As a result of that speech, we got more invitations to speak. But now, more and more often, we were asked to address one topic—negotiation. Ron and I polished the presentation, adding more elements that we'd been living but didn't realize, involving the audience, making it as actionable and practical as possible.

Pretty soon, these speeches were becoming a second career. Seeing the impact we had on people, it was time to take these talks on negotiation to the next level.

We formed the Shapiro Negotiations Institute, the focal point of our negotiation education activities, and began putting on seminars across the country—to big corporations, nonprofit organizations, police departments, schools, professional and trade associations. Everywhere we go, we find we make an impact. We make people better negotiators. And everywhere we speak, audiences are so enthused that participants invariably come up at the end and ask if we have a book so they can give it to their boss, their friend, their husband, their son or daughter.

I said, "Ron, we ought to write a book."

So we did.

P.S. You'll find, as we have, that a philosophy, whether it's political, scientific, or interpersonal, changes and evolves with experience. You'll be a better negotiator with *The Power of Nice*. And you'll be better not only in your business or profession, but in your personal relations, as well. Remember, negotiation isn't something that only occurs from nine to five. It's life.

RONALD M. SHAPIRO
MARK A. JANKOWSKI

REVISED EDITION
PREFACE

If you look back at the postscript to our original preface, we said, a philosophy evolves. That certainly has been true of *The Power of Nice.* Now that we've delivered our programs to over 100,000 people, we've continued to refine and perfect our approach to negotiation. And we've been directly involved in some dramatic, real-life challenges that have proven the power of nice. I said to Mark one day, there's actually more to *The Power of Nice* today than when we wrote the book three years ago.

He responded, "Ron, we've got to share these lessons. Let's revise and update our book."

So we did.

We revised, revamped, honed, polished, and updated. We even added a whole new chapter.

In teaching the 3Ps, we found we should re-examine and enhance the Preparation Planner, from the seven prep steps to the Planner Form, itself. Not only our seminars, but also real-world experience showed us that this tool is invaluable in getting ready—especially under pressure—for any kind of deal making. We have personally used the preparation planner to guide, among others, the negotiations of a major broadcast entity, the sales force of an international bank, and the management team of a multibillion dollar recruiting and staffing firm. We have sharpened each step and made the planner more thorough, preparing the negotiator for more eventualities.

We reconstructed tools such as W.H.A.T.—the probing technique, expanding the methods for digging out key data before going into a negotiation. We observed participants in our seminars and saw new opportunities to assist in gathering more information. We therefore added more probing tools to the Negotiator's Toolbox.

We even checked to see how well our teachings withstood the test of time by getting updates of on-going negotiations such as Cal Ripken, Jr.'s most recent Orioles contract extension. Did the techniques applied during his previous contract talks lead to subsequent success at the negotiating table? Did the methods for dealing with difficult negotiators pay off in the long run? Did the principles of *The Power of Nice* endure?

We updated stories and exercises, taking real events and turning them into negotiation lessons. For example, we took a leap into the future when retired politicos Al Gore and George W. Bush decide to collaborate on a nostalgic book about their famous election battle back in the year 2000. You, the reader, have to act as agent and make the book deal with a publisher.

And then we put virtually every lesson of *The Power of Nice* to a real-life test. In the fall of 1999, I was asked to help the Major League Umpires Association out during a brutal negotiation challenge. Not only had they lost their bargaining leverage with the Major League Baseball Owners, but due to an ill-advised negotiation strategy, the umpires' solidarity had been decimated in the process. We've added an entire chapter to the book that retells the eyewitness story of how *The Power of Nice* was employed, principle-by-principle, meeting-by-meeting, to rebuild the umpires' unity. This one chapter calls upon every lesson we teach and demonstrates how those lessons work in the most daunting of real-life situations.

So, our book and negotiation philosophy is up to date. . . . For now.

RONALD M. SHAPIRO
MARK A. JANKOWSKI

ACKNOWLEDGMENTS

We are grateful to Jim Dale for helping us turn our efforts to capture the Power of Nice into words that can now truly be called a book; and to Skip Connor for his guidance in launching and developing the Shapiro Negotiations Institute.

We also wish to thank the extraordinarily committed people who work with us at SNI, as well as other dedicated professional advisors including Charles Baum, Larry Fox, Larry Gibson, Michael Maas, George Mister, and our Executive Assistant, Gloria Dausch.

We also appreciate the efforts of our agent, David Black, in connection with this revised edition, and those of Joe Spieler, as well as the people of John Wiley & Sons for believing in the project originally.

For the past six years we have been privileged to teach over 100,000 people from the corporate and professional world the power of being "nice" negotiators, and they have reciprocated with appreciation and encouragement, urging us to *Do the book!* and to keep it current.

Many others, too numerous to mention, assisted us during the long process. We thank them. In connection with this revised edition, we thank the leaders of the World Umpires Association for practicing *The Power of Nice* and making Chapter 12 possible.

And finally, this book is also the product of loving relationships—without the love of our families, *The Power of Nice* would never have been so powerful.

R.M.S.
M.A.J.

CONTENTS

"We're going to try to negotiate first."

(Dana Fradon © 1992 from *The New Yorker Collection*. All Rights Reserved.)

Negotiation

"I'LL BURN THAT BRIDGE WHEN I COME TO IT"

Early in my career, I had a law partner who loved his work. He was smart. He knew the law. He always had his clients' best interests at heart. And he liked nothing better than the challenge of negotiation. He had no fear of the other side. In fact, he relished confrontation. He paced outside a conference room like a blitzing linebacker. He had that same hungry look in his eyes, pacing and revving himself up for the kill. He couldn't wait to charge in and nail the quarterback (or the other lawyer) to the Astroturf (or the deal he was after). If a few bones were broken along the way, so be it...or so much the better.

He often got what he and his client wanted. But he only got it once. Nobody wanted or could afford to deal with him twice because he left nothing on the table. *Winner take all. Why take a share of the profit when you can take all of it? Why have investors when you can have sole control? Why pay commissions? Why give concessions to a union when you can break the union? Why not squeeze all suppliers to rock bottom? Why not drive all offers up to the last dollar? Why negotiate when you can dictate?* My partner literally destroyed the other side, and he reveled in it.

One day he strutted out of yet another of his "eat-the-opposition-for-lunch-meetings," fresh blood dripping from his teeth, having dismembered yet another adversary in the name of deal-making. Instead of congratulating him, I asked him a question that took him by surprise. "What did the other side want?"

He looked at me with a combination of curiosity at my naiveté and astonishment at the irrelevance of the question. "I don't know, but they didn't get it," he answered.

I persisted, "Maybe they could have gotten what they wanted *and* you could have gotten what you wanted. What would have been wrong with that?"

Then he sighed like a wise old tobacco-chewing veteran and laid it out for the rookie who just didn't understand how to play the game. "Don't you get it? We won."

"Yeah," I protested, "but what if, sometime in the future, the tables turn and the other side gains the upper hand and then they're in a position to change the deal?"

That's when my wise old veteran partner put his arm around me, took a long, dramatic pause, and said, "I'll burn that bridge when I come to it." That wasn't just his snappy comeback. He meant it. It was the embodiment of his negotiation philosophy.

That's the way a lot of people look at negotiation. Two s.o.b.s locked in a room trying to beat the daylights out of each other and may the biggest s.o.b. win. Even way back then, I thought there was a better way to make deals.

* * * * * * * *

Over the years I practiced and perfected what made sense and worked for me: You can be "a nice guy" and still get what you're after. In fact, you often get better results, achieve more of your goals, and build longer term relationships with even greater returns.

> ### THE POWER OF NICE
>
> The best way to get what you want is to help the other side get what they want.

YOUR FIRST DEAL

What matters in negotiation is results. Everything else is decoration. To get results you must have parties who *want* to make a deal, each of whom has something to *gain*. Never forget, everyone who sits down at a negotiating table is there for one simple reason: They want something the other side has.

You picked up this book, so you must feel you have something to gain. My co-author and I have already gained by making the book sale. So, have we won and you lost? Hardly. As you'll learn, we don't want a one-time deal; we want an ongoing relationship (your recommendation of our book to others, visiting our web site, attending our programs, and buying our next tape or book). You don't want a one-time deal either. You want to learn to negotiate every deal well. Therefore, reader and authors have a common interest (another point I'll be making later) and that is *to make you a better negotiator.*

To achieve that end, we each have to make a commitment. Yours is to answer *two questions* with complete candor (even if it hurts). Ours is to deliver on four objectives that will make you an effective negotiator.

• What negotiation have you handled recently that has not gone or is not going well? [*Remember what I said about candor. Write out your answer and then show it to someone you can't fool (husband, wife, partner, friend, boss, client, mother).*]

_____

_____

_____

• What would you like to be able to do differently after reading this book? *(Be honest, but aim high.)*

_____

_____

_____

Write down your answers and save them. You're going to want to look back at them at the end of the book.

FOUR OBJECTIVES YOU CAN EXPECT

1. Displaying Confidence

The most effective negotiators tend to be the most confident negotiators. Conversely, negotiators who are less confident are less effective. So, how do you get confidence and become a better negotiator? Get smart.

Lack of confidence is mostly lack of knowledge. Knowledge is power. You will be armed with the knowledge it takes to deal from strength. You won't be cocky; you'll be confident. The former is imitating someone who knows what he's doing; the latter is who the cocky person is imitating.

2. Achieving WIN–Win

Today, everybody talks about win–win negotiation. Both sides win. Both get what they want. Both are equally happy. How delightful. How unrealistic.

If we negotiators were seeking truly equal terms and deals, like King Solomon, we'd simply divide everything in half. In reality, we're out to achieve *all* (or most) of *our* goals, to make *our most desirable deal.* But the best way to do so is to let the other side achieve *some* of *their* goals, to make their acceptable deal. That's **WIN–win:** big win for your side, little win for theirs.

The most common approach to deal-making is I Win–You Lose, the pound-of-flesh school—the only good deal for me is a bad deal for you. The unfortunate fate of too many negotiations is:

We both lose

or,

If I can't win, nobody can.

We'll show you how to avoid both of these negative categories.

3. Using the 3 Ps

There's an old saying, "If all you have in your toolbox is a hammer, then every problem looks like a nail." The same holds true for negotiation. More tools enable you to solve more problems. Better tools enable you to find longer lasting, more enriching solutions. *Prepare, Probe,* and *Propose* are the first of the tools that we'll put in your negotiator's tool box.

There is no secret formula that will enable you to get what you want every time you negotiate. But we have created a systematic approach—a step-by-step program—that, if repeated and mastered, will maximize your results. Like all good systems, this one is simple:

Prepare, Probe, and Propose.

That's it. Close the book, you've learned it. Well, it's not quite that simple. We'll show you how to *prepare* better than the other side; how to *probe* so you know what they want and why; and how to *propose* without going first and revealing too much, to avoid impasses or getting backed into a corner, but still achieving what you want. As you'll see, negotiation is a process, not an event.

4. Handling Tough Negotiations

Welcome to the real world of deal-making. Unfortunately, it's full of tough negotiators and tough negotiations. Some people think you have to be a bad guy to be a good negotiator. So, they act the part. Some aren't really so awful but have to answer to an awful boss who demands that they act the part. Sometimes, the negotiation itself may be brutal. The time, terms, or goals may be so difficult to meet that the *process* turns loathsome, even if the person opposite you isn't.

The tools in your negotiator's tool box will enable you to deal with the toughest people and situations, from neutralizing animosity to breaking deadlocks to knowing when the best deal is no deal. You'll learn how to out-negotiate the bad guys without becoming one of them.

One more thing. If you've been around sports long enough, you know the value of a good pep talk—whether it's Vince Lombardi to Bart Starr, Babe Ruth to a kid in the hospital, or Pat O'Brien invoking the memory of the Gipper (Ronald Reagan in his second most famous role) in *Knute Rockne, All American.* It can make players play harder, forget their shortcomings, and literally change the fate of the game. This pep talk isn't just about getting your adrenaline going; it's about putting **PEP** into learning the lessons of negotiation.

> **PEP**
>
> *Participate*   Be open to change. Read. Reread. Question.
> *Engage*   Throw yourself into this endeavor. Challenge yourself.
> *Personalize*   Relate what you learn to your career and your life.

If you read this book passively, you'll be cheating yourself. If you *Participate, Engage,* and *Personalize,* you'll become a better negotiator, faster. Do the exercises in the book. Ask others to help you practice. Role play. Don't skip over parts you find difficult or unpleasant.

> *What I hear, I forget. What I read, I remember.*
> *What I do, I understand.*
>
> Confucious

No, this isn't a normal textbook approach. But that's the point. To be more effective in negotiation, you have to stop using the same old "normal" approach. To harness **The Power of Nice,** you have to want change, accept change, and throw yourself into that change. The results will be worth it.

WHAT NEGOTIATION ISN'T

> *People who fight fire with fire usually end up with ashes.*
> Abigail Van Buren

Think of the word "negotiation." Quick, what images come to mind? Conflict? Confrontation? Battle? War? Or maybe: Debate? Logic? Science?

These are common interpretations. (Both have fueled the negative approach to negotiation.) Both are dead wrong.

Contrary to the novelized, fictionalized, and Hollywoodized version of mythic moguls and the big-bucks business world, from J.P. Morgan to Daddy Warbucks, from *The Man in the Gray Flannel Suit* to *Duddy Kravitz*, from *Dallas* to *Dynasty*, from the investment bankers of Goldman Sachs in *Barbarians at the Gate* to Gordon Gekko in *Wall Street*, deal-making shouldn't be a stare-down in a stud poker game, a shoot-out at the OK Corral, hand-to-hand combat, a high-tech military maneuver, or an all-out atomic war. Despite the macho, swaggering, in-your-face lingo—winner take all, out for blood, call their bluff, raise the stakes, battle-scarred, make 'em beg for mercy, first one to blink, an offer they can't refuse, nuke 'em, meltdown, go for the kill, last man standing—negotiation isn't about getting the other side to wave a flag and surrender. *Negotiation is not war.*

Despite all the clinical, logical, rational, psychological, data-sifting analysis, graphs, pie-charts, methods, and techniques from MBAs, CPAs, CEOs, shrinks, mediators, mediums, gurus, and astrologers *negotiation is not a science.*

The problem is that war stories tell well. Wars have heroes and enemies and simplistic lessons: *Take no prisoners. To the victor belong the spoils.* (But war, you may have noticed, can lead to more war.) And science sounds like a formula. *If you do A, he'll do B, and you'll arrive at C.* Maybe. Unless he does D and then what do you do?

Negotiation as war and negotiation as science have each contributed to the popularity of the negative image of deal-making, one by perpetuating the myth that the biggest, toughest thug wins and the other by way of the equally erroneous proposition that the coldest, least human calculator prevails.

Cultural conditioning (magazines, TV, movies, best-selling books, infomercials) has reduced deal-making to images of brutal combat—often making great entertainment on film but lousy negotiation in reality. Remember Gordon Gekko, the consummate tough guy negotiator from the movie, *Wall Street?* Remember how he played business hardball and never lost? (After all, this was the movies, not life.) You may recall one scene where Gekko showed an adversary how the game is played (or Hollywood's version, anyway). It went something like this:

WALL STREET*

INVESTMENT COMPANY MEETING ROOM—DAY

The well-dressed and self-impressed Sir Larry Waldman tries to bully Gekko into selling his shares of stock cheap so Waldman can pull off a takeover deal. Gekko's protégé, Buddy Fox, watches and learns.

WALDMAN   I'm announcing a tender offer at 65 dollars a share tomorrow. I'm expecting your commitment.

GEKKO   (with a smirk) Showdowns bore me, Larry. Nobody wins. You can have the stock. In fact, it's going to be fun to watch you and your giant ego trying to make a horse race out of it.

(Waldman tries not to reveal his worries about the takeover.)

GEKKO   (as if he doesn't know) Buddy, what is the fair price for that stock?

(Buddy flips through papers.)

BUDDY   The breakup value is higher. It's worth 80 dollars a share.

(Waldman sneers.)

GEKKO   (with a slow grin) Well, we don't want to be greedy. So what do you say to . . . 72?

(Waldman is furious, his own bluff being called.)

WALDMAN   (losing it) You're a two-bit pirate and a green-mailer—nothing more, Gekko. Not only would you sell your mother to make a deal, you'd send her COD.

(Gekko goes eyeball to eyeball with Waldman.)

GEKKO   My mail is the same color as yours, pal—or, at least it was until the Queen started calling you "sir." (cool) Now, if you'll excuse me before I lose my temper . . .

(Gekko heads for the door. Buddy follows. Waldman waits as long as he can, finally stops Gekko.)

WALDMAN ... 71.

(Gekko pauses at the door with a slightly self-satisfied smile.)

GEKKO Well now, considering you brought my mother into it ... 71.50.

(Silence. A stare down. Waldman blinks.)

WALDMAN Done. You'll hear from my lawyers tomorrow, 8 A.M. Goodnight.

(Not happy, Waldman exits. Gekko turns slowly to Buddy to explain the victory.)

GEKKO You know, he's right. I had to sell. The key to the game is your capital reserves. You don't have enough, you can't piss in the tall weeds with the big dogs.

(Buddy listens to his mentor as he delivers the lesson of battle.)

BUDDY In *The Art of War*, Sun Su wrote, "All warfare is based on deception." If your enemy is superior, evade him. If angry, irritate him. If equally matched, fight. If not, split and re-evaluate.

(Gekko puts his arm around his student and leads him out.)

GEKKO (proud) He's learning. My Buddy is learning.

* * * * * * * *

The Hollywood version of deal-making makes good entertainment; it just doesn't make for good deals. The person on the other side of the table doesn't have to stick to the script.

Now, think of the word "negotiation" again. In order to practice **The Power of Nice,** start by wiping out everything you knew, thought, or felt about negotiation. Forget about winners and losers. Forget about verdicts. Forget about survivors and victims. Forget about keeping score. Forget about statistics. Forget about science. Forget about war.

Going into negotiation and counting on scientific results is like betting on the weather. If the forecast calls for a 20 percent chance of rain and you leave your umbrella home and it rains, you won't get 20 percent wet; you'll get soaked.

If you go into negotiation expecting war, bring a flak jacket. If you're armed for combat, the other side will be, too. If you have to

---

NEGOTIATING A PHONE CALL

Imagine your car has broken down. You need to make a phone call for help and you have no cell phone. In the distance, you see a phone booth. You run to the booth but see there's a gentleman talking on the phone. How do you negotiate the man out of the booth? Do you wait patiently? Do you tap on the glass? How long is long enough to wait? Do you reach in and drag the man out?

Okay, change the facts. You had a car accident and your friend is near death in the passenger seat. You have to call 911. Now how do you negotiate? Do you wait patiently? Bang on the door? Throw the man out?

Change the facts again. You still have to call 911, but the man in the booth is Hannibal the Cannibal Lechter from *Silence of the Lambs*. Do you ask politely? Do you try to throw him out? Do you invite him to have dinner with your friend? Do you run for your life? As situations change, negotiation strategies must change. Negotiation isn't a science—there's no laboratory-proven answer. And negotiation isn't war—you don't attack Hannibal the Cannibal. Negotiation is a human interaction; it must be adapted and modified to fit the situation.

---

win at all costs, so do they. Both sides attack, both sustain casualties. Neither side gives in, neither side gets what they want.

I WIN–YOU LOSE BECOMES WE LOSE

Remember, if one party destroys the other, there's no one left to carry out the agreement. (Exacting exorbitant rents, punitive penalty clauses, or unrealistic noncompete terms often defeat their own purposes by creating disincentives; in other words, deals that are so good, they're bad.) The negotiation doesn't end when the contract is signed. If the other side is crippled by the deal, they will have every incentive to break the terms, literally having nothing to lose. You just made your first and last deal, instead of the first of many in a long-lasting relationship.

Nothing proves the point like history.

THE LAST DAY OF WORLD WAR I WAS
THE FIRST DAY OF WORLD WAR II

It was 1919 and the Allies had defeated Germany. The story goes that the Allied representatives sat the vanquished German leaders down in a railroad car outside of Compiegne, France, to dictate the settlement that would eventually become the Treaty of Versailles. "Dictate" was the appropriate word. President Wilson had warned the Germans that the terms of armistice would be harsh—and they were.

German troops had to withdraw to a line six miles east of the Rhine River. Allied troops would occupy the evacuated territory. The German naval fleet was surrendered. Virtually all military supplies were given up to the Allies, including 5000 cannon, 25,000 machine guns, 5000 locomotives, and 150,000 railroad cars.

But the toughest demands were political and economic. Germany was ordered to pay huge reparations to the Allies in the form of cash and the removal of German assets and capital goods. France, which had been devastated by the German forces, regained Alsace-Lorraine and took over several German colonies. France was also given a 15-year lease on the Saar coal mines which, along with Lorraine, provided coal, iron, and potash to the development of heavy industry.

With a crippled post-war economy, it was soon clear that Germany could not sustain the burden of the payments. In 1923, the Dawes Plan was conceived to create a payment plan that Germany could meet. As a result of German reparation defaults, Belgium and France occupied the Ruhr district. By 1928, with Germany further behind, the Young Plan was a second effort to collect payments. Again, Germany was unable to pay. President Hoover called for a moratorium on reparations (and the United States forgave all debts from other Allied countries that were going to be repaid with monies they were to have received from Germany).

The Allies had won, Germany had lost. It was a classic I Win–You Lose negotiation. The Allies got to set all the terms. But the terms were unrealistic. *They made a deal that could not be carried out.* Instead of creating peace, they created further resentment. The loss of the Ruhr, the devastation of the German economy, the sacrifice of natural resources, all contributed to a latent, seething desire for revenge. Many historians feel that it was the ideal atmosphere for the rise of Adolph Hitler.

The deal that ended World War I, in effect, helped start World War II. In fact, when the Nazis invaded France, Hitler ordered that same railroad car, then housed in a museum, be the site where he would "dictate" the terms of the German occupation of France. I Win–You Lose became We Lose.

* * * * * * * *

I Win–You Lose and its negative consequences seem obvious when the stakes are high and you have the historical benefit of hindsight. But the principle applies to even the simplest deal. In our seminars, we often begin with this game. You can try it yourself.

The $10 Game

Take 10 one dollar bills. Find two people—two partners, husband and wife, people in your office, your kids. Tell them, "If you two can negotiate a deal in 30 seconds on how to divide the $10 between you, you can have the money. But there are three rules:

1. You can't split it, $5 and $5.
2. You can't say $7 and $3 or $6 and $4 and make a side deal to adjust the division later.
3. If you don't make a deal in 30 seconds, I take all $10 back."

Chances are, both parties will have a hard time resisting the urge to "win" and not "lose."

You'll hear the hard sell:

It's better for one of us to get it than neither of us so let's make it me.

I agree. As long as the one is me.

The soft sell:

> *Oh, gosh, whatever you think is fair.*
>
> **Golly, how about $7 for me and say, $3 for you?**
>
> *No way!*

The sympathy ploy:

> *I need the $10. I just ran out of gas.*
>
> **At least you have a car.**

The so-called logic ploy:

> **We've only got 30 seconds so you take $4, I'll take $6, and we'll both come out ahead.**
>
> *Yeah, but you're more ahead.*

The trust-me ploy:

> *Give me all $10 and I'll make it up to you later. Trust me.*
>
> **I've got a better idea. Give it all to me and you trust me.**

BZZZZ! Time's up!

Not only is it likely you'll keep your $10 with this game, but you can learn a lot about why negotiations *don't* work:

- When you have no preparation time, you don't think; you react.
- When you have time pressure *and* no preparation time, you revert to habits—usually bad ones. (When someone else is watching and judging your negotiations, it just adds to the pressure.)
- Most people revert to the habit of *I Win–You Lose*. Each one wants to win so much, is so convinced one can win *only* if the other loses, that they both lose.
- Sometimes *I Win–You Lose* turns to *I Lose–You Win*. "I'll take $2, you take $8." In the quest to make a deal, any deal, people sometimes give away too much. Never forget, the goal

should still be *WIN–win*—big win-little win and ideally, the big one is yours.

How Can You Achieve WIN–Win in the $10 Game?

Start with this premise:

Maximize your interests. Determine what is the most you can come away with. Don't give away more than you have to. Get the most of a good deal, not the least of a bad deal. (That's another way of expressing WIN–win.)

Here are some interesting solutions we've seen in the seminars:

- **Find ways to agree.** Rather than leaping into battle over who gets the most money, look for an idea upon which you both can agree. For example, "If we don't make a deal in 30 seconds, we both get nothing. So, let's start by splitting $8 of the money, $4 for me and $4 for you. Now let's just negotiate over the last $2." Once you've found one basis for agreement, you may well find more.
- **Remove ego.** Take subjectivity out and replace it with objectivity. Use a coin flip. "Heads, I get $6 and you get $4. Tails, you get $6 and I get $4." Both sides now have an equal chance to "WIN" or "win." And, regardless, it happened "fair and square."
- **Be creative.** Look at the rules. They're limiting but not totally restricting if you're really creative. No one said you can't make change. Split the money $4.99 and $5.01. That's only a 2-cent windfall for the supposed winner.
- **Increase the pie.** Again, the rules allow for imaginative solutions. No one said you can't add to the total. Let's say, you put in an extra dollar. Now you're dividing $11. You take $6 and the other side takes $5. Both sides "WIN" by increasing the pie before dividing it.

Unfortunately, most people don't reach these solutions. They fall into the conventional traps of win-lose negotiation.

The Real or the Apparent Adversary?

What most people lose sight of in dividing the money is, who they're up against. Each of the two negotiators generally sees the other as the opponent. They're wrong. In reality, they're up against the person holding the money. If the two negotiators don't succeed in making a deal, the one holding the money keeps the money. Before negotiators can find solutions, they have to identify their real obstacles, not just the apparent ones.

FILLING THE NEGOTIATOR'S TOOL BOX

How do you avoid the pitfalls of negotiation? Don't revert to the same old methods to solve your problems. If your only tool is a hammer, all problems look like nails; if the only tool in your negotiator's toolbox is **I Win–You Lose,** then everything turns into an I Win–You Lose situation. Negotiating becomes a battle of wills and/or egos. It isn't a good deal unless you defeat the other side in the process.

Conversely, if the only tool you have is **I Lose–You Win,** every negotiation will look like you have to give in, sacrifice, or settle for less in order to appease the other side's appetite.

Turn a mirror on yourself and ask, "What tools am I using in my negotiations?" The goal here is to put more tools in your negotiator's tool box. By giving you the appropriate tools *and* an understanding of how and when to use them, you can become a more confident, and ultimately more successful, negotiator. Instead of dreading negotiation, you may even look forward to it.

WHAT NEGOTIATION IS

> *Knowledge is power.*
>
> Francis Bacon

If negotiation isn't a laboratory science or a bloody war, if it isn't the macho drama portrayed in the movies, what is it?

Negotiation Is the Commerce of Information for Ultimate Gain

Let's take that definition apart. First, **"the commerce of information . . . "** Commerce is the business of trading. It's the stock market in New York, the commodities floor in Chicago, the street
vendors in Tangiers. The difference here is that you're not ex-
changing corn futures for sow bellies or Moroccan francs for Persian rugs. *You're trading what you know for what you need to know.* In
the negotiation market, information is the commodity. And in a negotiation, nothing is more valuable than information, whether it's
two countries trying to make peace, two companies merging, two
workers trading office gossip, or two kids swapping baseball cards.
Is one veteran's card worth three unknowns? It all depends on information: What one kid wants and how bad. What the other kid
has and is willing to give up.

BUZZ   I'll give you a Dan Wilson. What'll you give me?

BOB   I'll give you a B. J. Surhoff. But I won't give you my Ken
    Griffey, Jr.

BUZZ   That's okay, my cousin's got a Ken Griffey he'll trade me.

BOB   This one's in mint condition.

BUZZ   Well, all I got is a whole mess of rookie cards.

BOB   Really? I got a rookie collection. Which ones you got?

BUZZ   Let's see. I've got a Jeff Nelson and a Michael Tucker.

BOB   Not bad, but not enough for a mint Griffey.

BUZZ   Okay, see ya.

BOB   You sure you don't have any others?

BUZZ   Well, my little brother has this Dante Bichette.

BOB   Too bad it's your brother's.

BUZZ   He's only five and he says I can do whatever I want.

BOB   Really? Well, I have to think about it.

BUZZ   I gotta go in for dinner.

BOB   Deal.

* * * * * * * *

Kids swapping cards are no different than grown up deal-makers. The commerce of information determines whether there can be a deal at all. Does one side have something of possible or real value to the other side, and vice versa? Do the sides want to make a deal or are they fishing? Is there competition? How deep are the buyer's pockets/resources? What are the terms of the deal? Who has decision-making power? Does either side have a deadline?

After feeling each other out with two players' cards either side would give up *(fishing)*, Bob revealed he had the Ken Griffey card *(possible value)*. Buzz wisely explained that he already could get a Griffey from his cousin *(competition)*, which led to getting the information that Bob's Griffey card is in excellent condition *(real value)*. Then, Buzz gave up information again, this time admitting he only had rookie cards *(limited resources)*. Very smart move by Buzz. Either way, he learns. If Bob doesn't want rookies, there's nothing to talk about. But if he does, then there's plenty to talk about. It turns out Bob collects rookies *(value for both sides)*. Buzz offers two rookies but Bob wants a third *(terms of the deal)*. The third belongs to Buzz's brother, but Buzz can speak for his brother *(decision-maker)*. So now it's up to Bob to ponder whether it's a good deal. But Buzz has to go in for dinner *(deadline)*.

Each side obtained information. Each side gave information. But one side got more than it gave. Each piece of information given out garnered key feedback, which better equipped that side for negotiation.

And that leads to the second half of the definition of negotiation, "**. . . for ultimate gain.**" You enter a negotiation with a goal or goals—to get what you came for—to gain. A piece of land, a client, a lease, an option, a contract. You want to win but it *doesn't* mean the other side has to lose. In fact, it may not matter what the other side gains, as long as you achieve your goal. (You should even be willing to *help* the other side get what they want, *if* it enables you to realize your goal.) That's WIN–win or GAIN–gain. Big gain–little gain.

But you're not just after gain; you want ultimate gain. That means two things. One, it may take a while. Be patient. Be ready to exchange as much information as possible. Let it sink in. Wait. Each deal has its own pace. (They can be sped up or slowed down, but not without affecting the results.) Allow each side to absorb the information, modify positions, evolve goals, adjust expectations, even save face. Ultimate gain also means down the road, well past today's deal. It means the next deal that comes out of the first one or a renewal of a contract, or forgiveness for late shipping, or offering a reference to your next prospect, or even making you a partner in their next deal. You never know when ultimate is coming but you can be sure it will arrive. That's when you find out just how good that deal was in the first place.

Now put the definition back together:

Negotiation is the commerce of information for ultimate gain.

Or in shorthand, *negotiation is using knowledge to get what you want.*

EVERYTHING WORTHWHILE IN LIFE HAPPENS AFTER 10:00 P.M.

Some deals seem to come up over and over again. You face the same guy on the other side, who uses the same techniques to get the same results. He knows what he wants and you know what he wants. So you have lots of opportunities to do the deal until you get it right. But you never get it right.

You know the kind of guy I mean. He trades in the commerce of information better than you do. He attains ultimate gain better than you do. He's one of those shrewd but patient types, armed with dogged determination and relentless pursuit. Everybody has a negotiating nemesis like him. Mine is my stepson, William, now a teenager but only 11 and already a skilled deal-maker at the time of this scene:

It's dinner time and William is perfect. "Mm, these lima beans are delicious." By 7:30 P.M. he's doing homework. He's quiet, he's studious, he's a model child at 8:00 ... 8:30 ... 9:00 ... 9:30, right up until the minute hand creeps across the hour mark of 10:00. That's when William the Cooperative becomes William the Conqueror. Because 10:00 is his bedtime. Theoretically. (Call our house at 10:25 any night and see who answers the phone.)

On weekdays, 10:00 is primetime, the start of NYPD Blue, ER, or Law and Order. Sometimes 10:00 is the bottom of the sixth inning with the score tied, Orioles 3—Yankees 3. But 10:00 is always when William engages in "the commerce of information for ultimate gain."

* * * * * * * *

WILLIAM   "My science teacher says kids my age only need 6 hours of sleep."

ME   "I thought it was more like 8 hours, William."

WILLIAM   "Well, if you think I shouldn't believe my science teacher . . ."

ME   "Of course, I think you should believe your science teacher."

WILLIAM   "Me, too. So, then I guess I should get to stay up later."

* * * * * * * *

WILLIAM   "If this was a playoff game, would you let me stay up?"

ME   "I guess if it was a playoff, maybe."

WILLIAM   "This game could turn out to be the key game that decides if the Orioles make it to the playoffs. So it's really a playoff game for the playoff game."

* * * * * * * *

WILLIAM   "Have you ever seen *Law and Order?*"

ME   "No, I haven't."

WILLIAM   "It's about lawyers, so it might help you do your job better. I'll stay up and watch it with you."

* * * * * * * *

William knows that if he can get me interested in what he's interested in, I'll forget what time it is. Pretty soon, I'm caught up in Law and Order *and I'm asking William why the cop is lying to the DA. Or it's the eighth inning, the Orioles are up by two runs, and New York has the bases loaded.*

* * * * * * * *

(William fishes with information until he hooks me.)

WILLIAM   "The judge is in love with the woman who's accused of the murder."

(He waits for the information to penetrate.)

ME   "But the cop said the woman just moved from Boston."

(William builds on it.)

WILLIAM   "The cop is a bad guy, too. He and the woman are partners."

(William works me slowly, patiently. Meanwhile, the clock is ticking. He's already getting what he wants, even in the process of negotiating.)

ME   "How do you know?"

WILLIAM   "You'll see when the trial starts."

(I modify my position.)

ME   "Okay, just until the next commercial."

(He trades more info.)

WILLIAM   "The DA has a secret witness."

ME   "Really? Who?"

WILLIAM   "They won't tell you until the very end."

(He's got me!)

* * * * * * * *

By now, it's close to 11:00 and I'm yawning. William, whose bedtime is absolutely, positively, without exception 10:00 P.M., is up, wide awake. So, at my house, it's clear who's best at using "the commerce of information for ultimate gain." William, age 11, skilled negotiator.

* * * * * * * *

WHAT NEGOTIATION CAN BE

> *Success is finding the right Customers and keeping them.*
> MBNA corporate motto
>
> *It's not the sale, it's the relationship that counts.*
> MBNA's Joe Gatti

Negotiation seems like a finite activity, with a beginning and an end: *You're selling and I'm buying. You set a price, I offer, you counter-offer, I counter your counter, you modify, I accept, we sign, deal's done.* Not necessarily.

Negotiation can be the initial step toward lasting business arrangements. It can yield clients, not just buyers. It can lead to repeat business, added business, referrals, even loyalty. Negotiation can result in partnership instead of one-upsmanship. But it rarely does.

Most people act as if the deal they're making is the last one they'll ever make with the other side. In fact, the opposite is generally the case. Banks want to lend money to people who pay it back. People like to borrow from banks who give terms they can live with. Shopping centers try to retain good tenants. Tenants wish to remain where business is good. Sports teams want to hold on to their stars. Stars like to keep playing for good teams. Husbands who hate cleaning the bathtub hope their wives will trade for sweeping the garage. Most deals are just daily or monthly or yearly pieces of an overall deal. . . . or they should be.

Name five of your negotiations that were truly one-time deals, with no ramifications, no chance for future deals, no openings for repeat business or for an on-going relationship. Those five represent *lost opportunities* for long-term deals. The point is, you have nothing to lose by assuming you might do business again.

MBNA: THE CREDIT CARD COMPANY THAT STARTED IN AN ABANDONED A&P SUPERMARKET

This company didn't even exist before 1982. That's when a gentleman named Charles Cawley opened a fledgling credit card company in an old A&P store that A&P didn't want anymore.

MBNA had a simple philosophy: *"Success is finding the right Customers and keeping them."* It wasn't brilliant as much as it was sensible. The company didn't have many customers—and customers were hard to get. So, management figured when they found a good customer, they should hang on. Once they had one customer, they went after two and kept two, and then three and ten and a hundred.

In an industry that had become too complacent about the word churn (constant customer turnover), MBNA went on a crusade for retention. Throughout the office was posted one of the company's mantras, *"Think of yourself as the customer."* When a cardholder called with a billing question or complaint, the goal was no more than two rings until a customer service representative answered. The staff was educated to be fanatically polite and knowledgeable. Good customers were automatically rewarded with higher credit limits without having to request the increase. Management often personally responded to customer inquiries.

Further, MBNA found new ways to bond with customers. The company pioneered affinity cards, credit cards tied to professional groups, universities, or other organizations to which the customer had loyalty. A University of North Carolina graduate could feel good that every time he made a purchase with his Tarheel Master-Card, he was supporting his alma mater. And he'd be far less prone to cancel his Tarheel card than he might be to cancel a card from an impersonal credit card company. MBNA soon became the industry leader in affinity marketing, with endorsements ranging from the American College of Surgeons to the Chicago Bulls. Needless to say, the company outgrew that original A&P store.

Today, MBNA, headquartered in Wilmington, Delaware, is one of the top three credit card issuers in the world. MBNA has almost $50 billion in net asset loans (which, in the credit card business, is a good thing) and annual profits in excess of $500 million (which, in most any business, is a good thing.) More important, the company has more than 14 million customers it serves loyally and services tenaciously (and, not surprisingly, has a very low churn rate).

There are no short-term, one-time deals at MBNA. Every customer is a potential customer for life, whether it's an affinity group, a partner bank, or the ultimate consumer/card-holder. In every town where MBNA does business, the company is determined to be the best corporate citizen. MBNA comes to a community to stay and wants the communities to want MBNA to stay. Employees are taken care of the same way. MBNA recognizes effort and dedication. The company doesn't just give raises; it gives awards. It promotes from within. So there's a very low churn rate of employees as well.

In fact, MBNA's business philosophy is so deeply ingrained that the employees are walking ads for the corporate culture. One of the top MBNA performers, Joe Gatti, came up to me in the parking lot, before our first MBNA seminar even began, and like the scene in *The Graduate* where the family friend offers Benjamin Braddock that memorable career-counseling wisdom ("I have one word for you, Ben. Plastics..."), this executive looked at me and said, "It's not the sale, it's the relationship that counts."

At MBNA, it's not the bottom-line of any one deal. It's the cumulative reward over the life of the relationship. No wonder the company has become so successful, so fast.

* * * * * * * *

As you'll read in Chapter 4, negotiation can and should be a *process,* not an *event.* But one aspect of that idea is, when you live from sale to sale, each sale becomes a measure of success or failure. If a competitor undercuts your price, you lose. If you over-promise and can't make good, you lose. Even if you make the sale, it pays a one-time profit and you have to start over with the same customer tomorrow. When you have a relationship with a customer, prices, promises, and results are measured in total return.

Sales pay one-time profits. Relationships pay dividends. It's a simple matter of economics. Which do you prefer?

R·E·F·R·E·S·H·E·R
CHAPTER 1
NEGOTIATION
What it isn't, is, and can be

Four Objectives

1. Display confidence. Confident negotiators negotiate better.
2. Achieve WIN–win. Both parties win, but you win bigger.
3. Use the 3 Ps: Prepare, Probe, Propose.
4. Handle tough negotiations.

PEP

Participate Be open to change, read, re-read, question.

Engage Throw yourself into the process of learning ne-gotiation.

Personalize Relate what you learn to your career and your life.

Lessons from the $10 Game

- Find ways to agree—create momentum.
- Remove ego—break deadlocks.
- Be creative—look for new approaches.
- Increase the pie—before splitting it.

Negotiation *is not* war.
Negotiation *is not* a science.
Negotiation *is* the commerce of information for ultimate gain.

I Win-You Lose becomes We Both Lose

With the Power of Nice you can:
1. Make deals.
2. Build relationships.
3. Make more deals.

P.S. Don't negotiate with kids. Chances are, you'll lose.

"They're offering a deal—you pay court costs and damages, they drop charges of breaking and entering."

I Win–You Lose Negotiation:

An Exercise in Flawed Logic

The winning team, like the conquering army, claims everything in its path and seems to say that only winning is important. Yet, like getting into the college of your choice or winning an election or marrying a beautiful mate, victory is fraught with as much danger as glory. Victory has very narrow meanings and, if exaggerated or misused, can become a destructive force.

Bill Bradley, *Life on the Run*

ENEMIES AND ENTRENCHED POSITIONS

I Win–You Lose is probably the most common (and least productive) approach to negotiation. Victory, not the achievement of goals, is the only acceptable outcome. And the counterpart of victory is defeat. In order for one side to *gain* what it wants, the other side must *give up* what it wants. There is no winner unless there's a loser. This is negotiation as war. The other side is the enemy. The success rate is about as good as that of war—seldom and rarely long-lasting—the opposite of **The Power of Nice.**

> *I love the smell of napalm in the morning—it smells like victory.*
>
> Lt. Col. Kilgore, *Apocalypse Now*

ENEMIES

In I Win–You Lose negotiation, one side assumes the other is an adversary. Sometimes both sides assume so. They couldn't possibly each be business people or neighbors or siblings or even fellow human beings. They couldn't share wants or needs or fears or hopes. They have nothing in common. They're enemies.

And as enemies, there's no goodwill, no open mindedness, no willingness to learn about each other's pressures, priorities, and goals in the negotiation. There is no trust.

> *I hate to lose more than I like to win. I hate to see the happiness on their faces when they beat me.*
>
> Jimmy Connors

Therefore, there is no opportunity for mutual interests, creative solutions, and least of all, building a relationship:

- The two parties may never learn that one party could have a delayed payout for tax purposes and the other party can meet a high price only if allowed to pay over time. Or that both sides must get the deal done by the end of the calendar year. Or that a third player has been talking to both.

- They may never experiment with shared profits instead of fixed payments. Or open books on both sides. Or lending each other talented employees. Or joining forces instead of trying to drive each other into oblivion.

- And they will certainly never explore how this deal might lead to others. Or joining forces instead of one buying out the other. Or one giving the other a "first look" or "second chance" on the next opportunity.

They are not at the table to reach their goals; they're at the table to defeat the enemy. And the assumption (usually erroneous) is that they will never encounter this same "enemy" again.

They conveniently forget the cliché, "It's a small world," which got to be a cliché because it's true.

ENTRENCHED POSITIONS

If you believe there's no victory unless there's defeat, if you assume the other side is your enemy, then the negotiation process itself is nothing but taking a position, stating it, and restating it (sometimes louder for emphasis):

"My price is $1,000,000."
"Is there any room for negotiating . . . ?"
"My price is $1,000,000."
"We don't have that much but . . ."
"Too bad. We'll have to go to your competitor."
"If we could have some time . . ."
"The offer ends at midnight."
"Maybe we could . . ."
"My price is $1,000,000."

I Win–You Lose negotiators don't determine the individual circumstances, needs, or particular interests of the other party. They simply arrive at their offer or their price or their terms or all of the above. Take it or leave it. (Their idea of an offer.) And, by the way, there's a deadline. (Their idea of an incentive.)

The one thing they don't do is listen. There's a cynical expression that describes the entrenched approach of the win–lose negotiator perfectly: *Don't confuse me with the facts.* Why learn when I've already made up my mind? Why compromise? Why meet halfway? Why try give and take? Why look for common ground? Why find an innovative answer, creative terms, or a new route? You're the enemy. You're only trying to get the better of me. (After all, that's what I'm trying to do to you.)

Entrenched negotiators have a great deal of trouble completing deals. It's no wonder. They have so fixed their position, they have nowhere to move. Only a perfect coincidental match will work. You must need *exactly* what they have to offer, at the price they're offering, on the terms they're offering.

Meanwhile, deals are being made all around them and they wonder why.

HIT AND RUN

Don't Win–Lose negotiators ever make deals? Sure, it happens. In fact, there isn't a seminar we do where someone doesn't come up and say, "Hey, I know somebody who fits that win–lose description and I've seen them make great deals." Okay, it's true. How and why? When the quick-hit, I Win–You Lose negotiator is in an advantageous deal-making position (i.e., desirable property, best talent, available space, an attractive client list, ready cash, an anxious buyer), he or she tends to opt for *Instant Deal Gratification*—get it all and get it now. Take cash, not an earn-out. If you get a higher offer, take it. Promises are nice, cash is better. How can they do it? They're *Hit-and-Run negotiators*. They get in, score, and get out, scoring one-time deals that make a fast buck and have a short life. No long-term relationships and very little repeat business.

But when their transactions are examined closely and over time, their apparent grand successes are often matched with equally grand failures. The sports agency business seems to have more than its share of Hit-and-Run negotiators. They're the agents who make headlines by bad-mouthing ball clubs, constantly making their players hold-outs, and shamelessly shopping their players to get one-time, record-breaking contracts rather than life-fulfilling, career-making deals. They love to "leak" their big-dollar deals and their own prowess to the press.

What the Hit-and-Run negotiators don't like to mention, though, are the numerous times their strategies lead to the loss of as many or more millions of dollars for their clients over the long-term, wasted years of a player's potential professional development, or worse, threaten or end a client's career.

I've Never Been on the Cover of Sports Illustrated

A case in point was the July 15, 1996, *Sports Illustrated* cover story. From every newsstand in America, the front of the issue blared a color photo of a 29-year-old sports biz wunderkind and, in 24-point type, this self-description, *"I am a ruthless warrior. I am a hit man. I will move in for the kill and use everything within my power to succeed for my clients."*—Agent Drew Rosenhaus. Beneath his name was the article's title, "The most hated man in pro football."

Inside, the article described Rosenhaus' negotiation style. "Deceit is part of his job. He will not only lie, he will also scream, cajole, threaten, and whine to defend his clients' interests." "He has been described as slithering and blindly ambitious." The story quotes other agents on Rosenhaus, "When you look up sleazeball agent in the dictionary, there's a picture of Drew," are the words of Craig Fenech and, according to Peter Schaffer, "Drew is the biggest scumbag in the business."

Pretty strong words. He may even sound effective with all that hype. But bloody victories that leave a trail of carnage do not necessarily make a successful negotiator. The ability to make deals and build relationships that lead to more deals is the definition of an effective negotiator. Will the Drew Rosenhauses, who have one-shot, headline-making wins, continue to have them, one after another, in the long run? Maybe. But after reading the *Sports Illustrated* article, I said to myself, "Give it a couple of years and there'll be stories about how the Win–Lose approach blew up in his and his clients' faces."

I didn't have to wait a couple of years, only a few months. On October 25, 1996, *USA Today** columnist, Bryan Burwell, ran a story about Errict Rhett, a well-known Rosenhaus client, headed, "Rhett's holdout turns out to be big bucks mistake." This is how Burwell described the situation:

> Say hello to Errict Rhett, poster child for the *really, really, really big, gigantic, jumbo, super-sized mistake.* As the Tampa Bay Bucs running back finally ended his 93 day-long holdout Wednesday, halfway through the NFL season, a few minor questions ran across my mind, such as: What was he thinking?
>
> To review: The two-time, 1,000 yard rusher insisted he would not play for the $336,000 he was scheduled to earn this

season. He rejected a six year, $14.1 million offer from the Bucs during training camp, claiming the deal had most of the money back-loaded, then launched a lengthy holdout to force the Bucs to give him a better deal.

But when he finally showed up in camp on Wednesday, Rhett still had no new deal. Instead, this is what he did have: A bill for $5000 a day in fines. Let me do the math for you—$5000 a day at 93 days = $465,000. I'm no math whiz . . . But, if you're only making $336,000 and you've already rung up $465,000 in fines, you might have what I might call a slight cash flow problem. . . . There are migrant farm workers who have a better deal than this, and the last time I checked, they didn't have . . . The Most Hated Man in Football representing them.

Player agent, Drew Rosenhaus, a rather colorful, amusing, self-absorbed fellow who was given that title in a recent *Sports Illustrated* cover story, is the genius who navigated Rhett through this disastrous holdout. But let's be fair. In the history of ill-advised, bubble-headed plans, Rhett's three-month long holdout was not the worst of all time. (Let's not forget these) 1. That little boat ride in Deliverance. 2. Christopher Darden saying, "Here, O.J., try on these gloves." 3. The CEO who said, "Hey, how about New Coke!"

Rosenhaus lost a client. Rhett lost millions of dollars, his starting position, and has possibly damaged his career irreparably.

Hit-and-Run negotiators tend to leave victims in their wake, that is, customers, clients, investors, buyers, and sellers who've ended up on the lousy end (temporarily) of the Hit-and-Runner's abusive, short-sighted strategy. Rather than negotiators, they're opportunists. There's nothing wrong with opportunity. When it knocks, you should answer. But if that's all you do, you may miss out on the bigger rewards of deals that last years, renew, and lead to other deals (as well as the intangible benefits of long-term relationships.)

I'M NOT ONE OF THEM (AM I?)

Okay, readers, right now you're saying, "I don't have to worry about being a Win–Lose negotiator. I never beat up on the other side. I don't need to read this book. Everyone who I negotiate with needs to read it."

None of us likes to think of ourselves as Win–Lose negotiators, but there are times when we give in to the temptation of the moment, when we hold the cards, or want to get (just a little bit) even with the other side, and we give in to the dark side and go for the kill.

We've all been there. Truth be told, we all speak from experience. There are three situations that arise when even the most dedicated WIN–win negotiators may be tempted to cross over to Win–Lose:

1. When you've been hit (hurt, damaged, taken advantage of) and have the urge to hit back.
2. When you allow principle (I'm going to teach them a lesson) to cloud vision or become a rationalization.
3. When you think you have the upper hand and underestimate the other side.

The stories that follow are each examples of giving into the temptation of Win–Lose negotiation and the negative outcomes that inevitably result. The first illustrates that even though I've tried to take a WIN–Win approach throughout my career, I, too, have fallen victim to the lure of Win–Lose.

OPRAH BEFORE SHE WAS OPRAH! (OR, I WAS HIT AND WANTED TO HIT BACK)

Okay, it's humility time. I'm the guy who represented Oprah Winfrey before she became so big she only needed a first name. I was her agent in Baltimore and I did my best to get her what she was worth as her talent began to manifest itself. I offered my counsel and advice. I urged her to move fast without moving too fast: the right mix of patience and ambition. As she embarked on her climb up the major market ladder toward Chicago, I helped navigate the journey.

Oprah was hot. You could sense it. And getting hotter. She really came into her own at the ABC affiliate in Chicago. She was magnetic. Audiences were drawn to her. Magic was happening. The magazines and tabloids picked it up. There was, as they say, a buzz.

Not surprisingly, as her star ascended, she re-examined many things, including her career management. It happens to Triple A ballplayers who are brought up to the majors and have a red-hot rookie season. It happens to repertory actors who toil anonymously and suddenly win the lead in a Broadway show, to state governors plucked by their party to be national candidates, to painters, authors, and rock musicians. Are they being managed as they reach for the top as well as they were managed on the way up? Certainly, it's a legitimate question, one over which I've gained a few clients, but never lost one. This proved to be the exception.

I could argue all I want about what a good job I was doing, but ultimately it wasn't my decision; it was hers. She had to do what she thought best. It wasn't long before I got a call from Oprah. She started with, "Ron, this is really hard to say, but . . ." She went on to tell me how much she appreciated everything I'd done for her, how much she respected me, and how she hoped we could stay friends and maybe even work together again someday. I was hurt, but I wished her well.

Sometime later, I read that Oprah thought she no longer wanted a "nice-guy agent." If that's so, I can't argue with the label. Naturally, there are different styles of negotiation. Some clients are comfortable with one type, some with another, and some change from time to time. I believe you can be a nice guy and get what you and/or the client want at the negotiation table. (Hence, this book.)

I lost Oprah Winfrey. But that's not the humbling part of the story. I had a contract with Oprah. According to my partners, she still owed us commissions. Even though she was no longer a client, he said we were entitled to the revenue. On a strictly legal basis, he was probably right. My instinct told me, legal basis or not, drop it. But I didn't follow my instinct. *I had gotten hit and I wanted to hit back.* I said, "Okay, go after the money." Our firm explored legal action. Both sides retained attorneys. Eventually, we settled and got our money, the short-term gain. But we lost the long-term good will. Maybe we'd never have done business with Oprah again. But maybe we would have. After we sued, it wasn't even a question.

IF IT'S A CIRCUS, HOW COME NO ONE IS SMILING? (OR, WHEN PRINCIPLE CLOUDS VISION)

For years, Ringling Brothers and Barnum & Bailey Circus performed in the Baltimore Arena. And every year was a sellout.

But in the late 1980s, the Arena, previously owned by the City, was privatized. The new operators and Ringling Brothers management had a history of bad relations. Neither side trusted the other. Both sides accused the other of bad faith dealings in the past and now stood their ground as a matter of "principle." As a result, each could only see their own side and could not yield. Each was convinced they had to make the other back down, and each was convinced the other couldn't live without them. So what had been a profitable endeavor for both performer and venue was now jeopardized.

Without going into the ugly details, the negotiations were not "entertainment for the whole family." The Arena wouldn't budge. Ringling Brothers wouldn't budge. I was asked to intercede. I tried to mediate and actually made some headway. But the progress was only temporary. The talks broke down. Ringling threatened to pull out. The Arena called Ringling's bluff, figuring that Ringling would come to its senses and call back in a few days. Or, the Arena thought it could bring in another, equally appealing circus. But there were no calls from Ringling and no other circus matched Ringling's market appeal.

Ringling, for its part, was sure the Arena management would think it over and make a better offer. No offers came. Both sides waited longer. Nothing.

Finally? No deal. Two principle-driven devotees became entrenched I Win–You Lose negotiators who set out to out-macho each other, each wanting a win that came out of the other's hide. What they got was nothing at all. "The Greatest Show on Earth" wasn't the greatest show in Baltimore. The circus didn't come to town.

P.S. It took a few years, but wisdom and mutual gain finally overcame overblown principles. With the specific goal of starting a fresh relationship, the CEO of Ringling went to his counterpart at the top of the company that manages the Baltimore Arena and other venues. In contrast to prior dealings between their companies, the two men put that I Win–You Lose history behind them; they made a deal on a handshake in all of thirty minutes and have since agreed to work together at other venues. Some stories, even those with a rocky middle, have a happy ending.

THE BASEBALL STRIKE, SCORE 0–0 (OR, WHEN YOU THINK YOU HAVE THE UPPER HAND AND UNDERESTIMATE THE OTHER SIDE)

There is probably no better lesson in I Win–You Lose than the negotiations over the Major League Baseball strike of 1994 and 1995. The subtleties, nuances, and techniques of deal-making are all here. And all wrong. The Baseball Strike is a *"How-Not-To"* case study for anyone negotiating anything.

During 1994, the Major League Baseball Players Association and the team owners had been talking—I wouldn't even call it negotiating—for months. Both sides were talking, but neither side was listening. And both were convinced they had the upper hand.

The owners said payrolls were getting out of control. They wanted a salary cap. Not surprisingly, the players, who were on the receiving end of those escalating salaries, wanted no such hard-and-fast limit on their earnings. Maybe something more creative, but nothing that resembled a cap. The owners wanted a cap, nothing more creative, hard-and-fast, just the way the players didn't want it.

I talked with representatives of both sides throughout. I can only say that they were equally unrealistic. My contacts among the owners made it clear that there was one thing they were positive the players wouldn't have the guts to do: Strike. I cautioned the owners not to be so sure.

In late summer of 1994, the players struck. The surprised, but unmoved, owners responded with their favorite refrain. They wanted a salary cap. By now, that was fairly clear.

There was another other thing the owners told me they were sure the players wouldn't do: Stay on strike. The owners followed a strategy based on the premise that those "greedy" ballplayers would miss their inflated paychecks, break ranks, and return to the field. Again, I offered my doubts about the owners' outlook. Again, the players surprised the owners. The players stayed out for 10 games, 20, 50, and still didn't give in.

My contacts in the players' union were just as sure (and just as wrong) as the owners. The players were positive that those "greedy" owners would miss all that advertising and attendance money, the TV revenue, souvenir sales, the hot dogs, beer, and pretzel profits, the parking fees, the licensing deals and that they would cave in on the salary cap. I offered a similar caution to the players as I had to the owners. "Don't be so sure." But they didn't want to hear it (at least not yet).

Game after game was missed. All told, 668 regular season games were canceled in 1994. (Eventually, another 261 games were wiped out in the spring of 1995 for a total of 929.)

Even the unthinkable happened. The national despair of the Great Depression wasn't enough to stop the World Series. The second World War couldn't interrupt the World Series. The San Francisco earthquake of 1989 didn't thwart the Series.

But in September, 1994, acting Commissioner Bud Selig announced that the World Series was canceled.

The owners and players had stopped their own game. If they hadn't killed the golden goose, they certainly had their hands wrapped around its throat. It was classic I Win–You Lose negotiation. The only thing both sides agreed on was that the other side was dead wrong (and would have to back down.)

Fay Vincent, the Commissioner of Major League Baseball who had been forced by the owners to resign prior to the showdown, recalls, "I could not talk these people out of having that battle. I didn't have the political skill or the ability not to have this war, and I regret that."

While the two parties were battling to a standstill, both were forgetting the third party, the one neither could live without—the fans, AKA, consumers. With every missed game, they became less attached, less devoted to their favorite pastime, a dangerous disaffection. Without consumers, there is no game—no fans in the stands, covered in logos, inhaling hot dogs and beer, nobody at home in front of the TV or glued to the radio, exposed to all those ads, buying all that stuff the ads hawk.

A good negotiation is about dividing the pie so that both sides get a satisfactory piece. A better negotiation is one that finds a way to grow the pie (increase revenues, add market share, strengthen resources) so both sides get a bigger piece. But baseball was playing out the worst scenario possible. What had been a 2.5 billion dollar pie was actually shrinking. It had taken decades for it to reach that size and, in a matter of weeks, it was losing revenue by the millions.

If the battle kept up, the two sides might be fighting not over slices of the pie, but crumbs. Even now, the economic impact of the strike is hard to fully assess. It wasn't just the teams, the sponsors, and the media: every major league city lost revenue from people *not* stopping for dinner before the game, restaurants *not* ordering extra food and beverages from suppliers, *not* hiring extra help for game nights, the help *not* earning extra tips, fans *not* buying gas to drive to the games, *not* parking in lots by the stadium, *not* fueling the local economies from Boston to San Diego. Spring training cities held their breath for fear of suffering the same fate.

Finally recognizing that more than playing the game was at stake and that simple reason had failed, as had government mediators, President Clinton stepped in. He suggested turning to a distinguished private mediator and asking both sides to enter into voluntary mediation.

If ever there was a well-intentioned effort, this was it. Maybe, just maybe, the intervention of the President of the United States could move both parties in the right direction. The President asked William Usery, a former Secretary of Labor, and a highly respected man, to mediate. Hope turned to whispered optimism. Mr. Usery and his staff met with both sides in early November 1994. Each party opened up to Mr. Usery. The meetings appeared to go well. But appearances were deceiving.

Mr. Usery telephoned me a few weeks later to ask my views of the parties and their positions. He was searching for clues to opportunities for compromise, where he could find common ground, what might open a closed mind. He had been asking the players and the owners these same questions since November and he was getting nowhere. He said, "In order to walk on water, you have to know where the rocks are, and I'll be damned if I can find them."

So, William Usery, distinguished former Cabinet member and statesman, had run into the wall of distrust that had been building for years. It was a power battle and each side thought they had more clout and it was time to show it. From the perspective of the majority of the owners, it was a game of "Break Don Fehr and his union." To say they were hard-liners doesn't do justice to their resolve. On the other side, the union was built on a rock-solid ideology of a free market economy and a deep-seated mistrust of the owners dating back to their illegal collusion in the 1980s. In the past, with the game making record profits, Commissioners of Baseball had managed to persuade the owners to accede to the players on several controversial issues. By now the union had begun to feel that compromise wasn't necessary. But unfortunately for both sides, times had changed.

More weeks passed. The winter wore on. The public relations game, which both sides always played, now seemed to be the World Series of the baseball strike. Who could score with the politicians? Who could come across better with the press? Who could play better to the public on a talk show? They went "off the record" and "on the record." They pitched and they spun. The union made a serious effort to persuade Congress to repeal baseball's long-standing anti-trust exemption, a long shot at best. Ballplayers lobbying members of Congress did nothing but sap energy from the process of negotiation. The owners were no less guilty. They leaked their versions of each story, provided their named and unnamed sources, did their spinning, wooing, and pitching. And the fans were getting weary of it all. If we were getting nowhere slowly before, now we were getting nowhere fast. Spring wasn't far off.

In late 1994, a White House contact and I were lamenting the shrinking baseball revenue, the impending disaster of canceling spring training, and the immeasurable damage being done to a national icon. He asked me if I held out any hope for the mediation process.

I wanted to say "yes." But honestly, I was losing faith. As we talked, I recalled memories of another White House-orchestrated mediation: Jimmy Carter brokering the Israeli-Egyptian peace treaty of 1978. By no means am I comparing baseball to Middle East peace, but I am comparing the dynamics of two seemingly intractable parties. The Camp David peace process demonstrated how confidentiality—knowing that what was said would go no further—enabled discussions to take place that could never have occurred in a public forum. Why not offer a similar safety shield to the players and owners? Why not get away from the press, the klieg lights, the microphones, and the tape recorders?

An interesting thought, but it was never to be. In fact, the opposite atmosphere prevailed. On a Sunday evening in early 1995, I walked into Washington's Mayflower Hotel (the collective bargaining headquarters) and found the lobby had been turned into a media war room. Interviews and exclusives, hot lights, writers on laptops, reporters on cell phones, producers shouting to cameramen. You couldn't get to the elevators without tripping over cables. Hardly the setting for confidential talks.

Then I saw how bad it really had become. Across the room, I spotted Mr. Usery and his press assistant giving a press briefing. The man whom the President had asked to be mediator now apparently had a full-time press assistant. And, the two of them gave regular press briefings. He had fallen prey to the same media promiscuity as the players and the owners. Now the circus had three rings.

Instead of moving the parties out of the spotlight to where they might be able to let their respective guards down, Mr. Usery had done the opposite. This wouldn't lead to settlement. It would lead to a ratings war: Who was getting the best coverage?

As the mediation effort was heading to a close, things got downright embarrassing. The President had requested a meeting with Mr. Usery and representatives of each side. He also asked the mediator for a recommendation. I spoke to the representatives of each side that day and I realized that each side's perception of what was going to occur was diametrically opposed to the other's. Evidently, they had each been told different stories, led to believe different recommendations would be made, in order to get them to come to the meeting. Perhaps, the thought was, if they both showed up in front of the President of the United States, they'd almost have to agree to some kind of settlement. It was a naive plan at best.

Word got out (because word always gets out) that the mediator was going to make a recommendation to the President that would ignore the union position (by supporting a luxury tax plan; in effect, a salary cap.) The union wasted no time in making sure that the White House got the message that if the President supported this proposal, he would be publicly repudiated by the Players Association. In simple political terms, a Democratic President was about to be snubbed by a labor union. Not good politics.

On the flip side, when the owners heard that the President was leaning toward the notion of binding arbitration, they sent a clear message back: "Don't." The unstated part of the message concerned alienating potential big contributors. After all, there was an election coming up.

Baseball visited the White House that evening, but it was a night to forget. Oh, there was hand-shaking and some photo ops, but behind every smile were gritted teeth. The players felt mistreated and so did the owners. No one trusted the mediators. The President was host to a No—Win situation. The mediation effort died right there in the White House.

What are the lessons of the strike? Everything that could be done wrong was done wrong.

1. Each side perceived it had the upper hand and underestimated the other side. Each side was determined to make the other side back down. All the other "wrongs" stemmed from that premise.

2. What should have and could have been handled with delicacy, privacy, and confidentiality, was allowed to deteriorate into the worst sins of *Win—Lose* negotiation. There's no victory without defeat. My gain is your pain.

3. It was a negotiation between enemies. Royalty and Peasants. Labor and Management. North and South.

4. It was a battle of entrenched positions. Over the course of the entire year, neither side materially modified nor compromised its stance. Every meeting was an echo of the last. Repetition replaced innovation.

5. Despite how long it took, it was a hit-and-run deal. Baseball finally resumed on a delayed basis in 1995. But it wasn't the result of negotiation; rather, it was, by virtue of a judge's ruling, a short-term solution. Though the strike had ended, the issues remained.

6. The parties differences were not resolved. Both parties walked away dissatisfied. The distrust did not abate, it festered.

7. *I Win–You Lose* turned to *We Lose.* The players and owners both dealt from *I Win–You Lose* postures. Who won? Nobody. Who lost? Everybody.

And baseball's constituency—the media partners, the advertisers, and the fans—remained skeptical. Even now they fear the game could again come to a halt. And these fans are vulnerable to other suitors—football, hockey, basketball, golf, or any form of entertainment that captures their fancy and won't let them down.

The great American pastime struck out.

AT LEAST ONE DISSATISFIED PARTY

In I Win–You Lose negotiation, one thing you can count on is that somebody will walk away unhappy. The approach practically demands it. If the winner really wins what he or she set out to win, then it was at the expense of the loser. The loser goes home with nothing, except maybe a long memory. If these two ever sit down again, you can bet the loser will be out for more than a deal. The loser will want revenge: *Wait until it's my turn to be the tough guy.*

Because of the nature of I Win–You Lose negotiation, its adversarial, nonaccommodating approach, the impasses it creates, there's a good chance that *at least* one party will not only walk away without the deal they sought, but will come away with practically nothing.

R·E·F·R·E·S·H·E·R
CHAPTER 2
I Win–You Lose Negotiation

I Win–You Lose Negotiators

- Treat each other as enemies.
- Stake out entrenched positions.
- Adopt hit-and-run philosophy.

> Hit-and-run negotiators' successes are usually matched by equally or more devastating failures.

Win–Lose Negotiators

1. Leave a trail of victims.
2. Miss out on deals that last, renew, and lead to more deals.
3. Lose the intangible benefits of long-term relationships.

Even if You Mean to Be WIN–Win, You May Give in to the Temptation of Win–Lose When

- You've been hit and have the urge to hit back. (Oprah)
- You allow "principle" to cloud vision. (The Circus and the Arena)
- You think you have the upper hand and underestimate the other side. (The Baseball Strike)

"Sorry, honey, I can't talk now. I'm in the midst of some very intense negotiations with Bill Gates on the electronic rights to you and the kids."

WIN–win Negotiation

....

When you win, nothing hurts.

Joe Namath

....

MYTH AND REALITY

THE MYTH OF WIN–WIN

Negotiation experts (and amateurs) have been preaching win–win for some time. The trouble is, it's unrealistic. The expression win–win has become more of a pop cliché than a negotiating philosophy. It's either a winner's rationalization for lopsided triumph, a loser's excuse for surrender, or both sides' phrase for when everybody is equally unhappy. There's no such thing as both parties winning identically, that is, both getting all of what they want. One party is bound to get more and one less, *even if both sides are content with the outcome.* The latter is possible. Both parties can be satisfied, but both cannot win to the same degree.

THE REALITY OF WIN–win

If someone is going to come out ahead, our aim is to make sure that someone is you. That's WIN–win. Both parties win, but you win bigger.

WIN–win is realistic. It isn't easy—it requires focus and discipline but it is achievable. And it doesn't turn negotiation into war.

45

Because it's not WIN–lose, WIN–clobber, or WIN-ransack-pillage-and obliterate. You don't have to destroy the other side. On the contrary, you want them to survive, even thrive, in order to make sure the deal lasts and leads to future, mutually beneficial, deals. That's *The Power of Nice* and WIN–win is what that power delivers.

HOW TO WIN–win

Know What You (Really) Want– Know What They (Really) Want

To achieve WIN–win, the first order of business is to identify your own interests, what you really need to achieve from a potential deal. You may say, "Hey, I do that automatically." But that's the problem. What you automatically assume to be your goal may not be what you really require to make the deal worthwhile. For example, you may assume you must get a certain price for a piece of real estate. Do you make the assumption because you hear that's the current market value? Or because another seller supposedly got that price? Or because you promised your partners a given return? Is your price really engraved in stone? Will you take less if it's a cash offer but insist on more if paid out over time? How about the emotional aspects of the deal? Are you trying to get out from under a burdensome property? Are you saddled with nervous investors? Perhaps you need peace of mind more than money. Or vice versa.

You can't satisfy your interests until you know what they are. And they're never as obvious—or simplistic—as you might assume. But, if you force yourself to think through your priorities, your interests will clarify. You will learn the true parameters of your needs, what you can sacrifice, and what you can't.

Before you go into a negotiation, ask yourself what you want out of it. Then challenge your own answers. Take apart your demands. Make hypothetical offers to yourself, each with different terms. Rank your needs. Force yourself to give up goals from the bottom of the list up, until you're left with the one most important goal of the deal. Now you know what you want.

But you're only halfway there. You have to do the same for the other side. Try to determine their needs and interests. Just as you can make the mistake of assuming your goals, you could make the mistake of assuming theirs: *You want to get as a high price as possible so they must want to pay as low a price as possible.* What if you learned that they might pay substantially more if you let them push the deal into their next fiscal year? Or that while you have investors clamoring for a return, they have shareholders who are in an acquisitive mode? Or that they need volume more than they need return on investment?

Honestly determining someone else's needs isn't easy to do alone. Get someone to play the devil's advocate, thinking on behalf of the other side. By role-playing, the advocate will look out for and reveal to you, real interests of the other side, instead of your having to rely on your assumptions.

Chances are, their interests are as complex as yours. The earlier you know what their interests are, the greater your leverage will be. Some of their goals may become apparent as you negotiate. But that may be too late to react or counter.

MARK'S NIECE, ADRIENNE, THE WIN–WIN 2-YEAR-OLD

Adrienne, my 2-year-old niece, displayed one of the more effective uses of the WIN–win maxim: "The best way to get what you want is to help them get what they want." Adrienne likes nothing better than being carried around, all day long, every day, but her parents, wanting her to realize that when you grow up, you don't get carried around, wanted to break her of this habit. When her pleading, "Pick me up!" began to go unanswered, she modified her approach. In no time, she was looking up at her parents, offering her outstretched arms, saying, "Hug. Hug!" Who could ignore that affectionate request? Then, when her father bent down to give his little princess a hug, Adrienne would latch onto his neck, he'd straighten up, and guess what?—she was being carried around. She got what she wanted—being carried—by giving him what he wanted—a hug.

The chapter that follows this one deals with the 3 Ps, one of which is prepare. It means, among other things, learn all you can about the people with whom you're negotiating, what motivates them, and importantly, what they must achieve in a given deal. Find out as much of what they need as you can *before* you sit down at the bargaining table. You will discover even more once you're at the bargaining table, during the probe phase, which follows prepare.

Satisfy Your Interests Well– Satisfy the Other Side's Interests Acceptably

Once you know what the other side needs, you can determine how their interests conflict and/or mesh with yours. You can find areas of mutual benefit: Your price and their terms; their divestiture and your expansion; their capital needs and your investment strategy.

You each have strengths and weaknesses. But, if you do your homework, (and if you probe effectively) you have an advantage. You know what you want *and* you know what they want. You may be tempted to fulfill all of your own needs and to disregard theirs. Believe it or not, that's not in your best interests. No matter now much stronger your position may be, make sure they achieve some of their goals. That's what enables a deal not just to be made, but carried out.

Let's say you're negotiating with three suppliers for a season's worth of embroidered NBA logos for hats—in round numbers say, 24 million logos. Your goal is to lower the cost by .017 cents per logo, but to maintain the quality of those little woven Bulls, Knicks, Jazz, Timberwolves, Pistons, and Magic. (Ideally, you'd like this season's 24 million hats in your warehouse by tip-off of the first game.) You've had multiple logo suppliers in the past but now you're willing to give the entire 24 million logo order to one company if they can meet your specs.

The first supplier, Econo-Emblems, comes in with the lowest price, but only on the condition that they can sew logos with a slightly lower thread-count-per-centimeter. The second supplier, Logo-Motion, can meet the thread-count quality standards but at a cost of .003 cents more per logo, which really adds up when you multiply it by 24 million. The third supplier, Sew-What Ltd., meets the lowest price and the thread-count but they ask for staggered delivery dates. They'll deliver 8 million logos a month, feeding fan demand as the season goes on. You could reject their request for staggered delivery. And they might give in. After all, this is the biggest order in the industry.

But you know their needs, their real interests. By staggering the delivery dates to you, they'll fill factory capacity over several months, eliminating down time, keeping the best workers employed throughout the year, thereby increasing profits on other, previously unprofitable jobs, all of which enables them to give you both the price and quality you want. If you force them to meet the original schedule, you run the risk of sacrificed quality to make the dates or missed dates to maintain quality. And even if they make the dates and maintain the quality, their overall operation will likely lose money and never be able to meet the same specs again.

Remember the one goal at the top of your list. Lower the price without sacrificing standards. You WIN, in capital letters. Now let them win on the delivery schedule. Their win assures your WIN. It enables them to carry out the agreement. Instead of what might be, at best, a one-time, one-sided win, or at worst, a one-time disaster, you now have the makings of a long-term relationship. Remember, the essence of negotiation is not just making a deal; it's building relationships.

GOOD DEALS ECHO, THEY LEAD TO MORE DEALS

Often, the best way to get what you want is to help the other side get what they want. There are very few deals in business or life, in general, that are truly one-time, never-again transactions. The world of negotiation is a small one. How often have you:

- Done business again with someone with whom you did business what seems like a lifetime ago?

- Awarded a job to a supplier who was the runner-up last time you bid them?
- Discovered a familiar name as a reference on a resume?
- Called on an old acquaintance for an opinion?
- Hired a competitor?
- Invested in a rival?
- Found yourself a seller to the same party to whom you were once a buyer?

Too many people negotiate as if they'll never again see or do business with the person across the table. That was the modus operandi of my ex-law partner, the bridge-burner. In fact, the opposite is true. Chances are, you will associate and do business with the same people again. More leases are renewed than written from scratch. More suppliers are retained than replaced. More contracts are extended than begun. More shipments go to old customers than new ones. There's an old business adage that says, it takes five times the time/effort/money to win a new client as it does to keep an existing one. The same, with varied multiples, applies to anyone on the other side of a transaction.

If you treated your last deal as your final deal with that party and left them with a bad taste, or worse, bad business results, next time they'll either come to the table with revenge on their minds or not come at all. But, if you did your best to make sure they got some of what they wanted; if you made sure they achieved a win (lower case), you have the potential of making mutually beneficial deals ad infinitum.

WIN–win IS NOT WIMP–WIMP

We've established that WIN–win is not win–win. It's clearly, unashamedly designed to tilt the scale in your favor. It's not pretending that both sides go away with separate but equal smiles. But, importantly, it also stands in sharp contrast to win–win's mutated relative, Wimp–Wimp. That's where you want to make a deal so bad, you make a bad deal. You give in, give up, and give away; anything to get the deal done.

We've identified five notorious Wimp–Wimp negotiator types. Here's how each would negotiate the purchase of an automobile:

Wimp–Wimp Negotiators: Buying a Car

- **Addicted Wimp.** The addicted negotiator walks into the dealership, falls in love with the red sports utility vehicle, and decides he or she wants it and wants it now. Addicted negotiators don't really care about the terms of the deal, the financing, the extras, or even the undercoating. They will concede all of it and pay full list price, as long as they can drive it home today. These negotiators want to do a deal, any deal, so badly that they make unnecessary and harmful concessions just to get the deal done.

- **Anxious Wimp.** The anxious negotiator walks into the dealership and thinks, *"I hate doing this. All these salespeople know how to play the game, and I always lose. I don't want to look bad. I don't want to look stupid. I just want to get this thing over as quickly as possible. Next time I'm going to buy a Saturn so I can avoid this whole negotiation thing."* These negotiators will accept the first offer put onto the table just so they can get the process over with.

- **Apathetic Wimp.** The apathetic negotiator thinks that negotiating is not worth the hassle. They know they could get a better deal, but they also know it means shopping around to different dealerships, reading *Consumers Report,* and even going back to the same dealer several times to work the price down. They know they could get a better price using this strategy, but they just don't want to put in the time or the energy to make it happen. This negotiator justifies that the time and energy *saved* in *not* negotiating makes up for the higher price they inevitably pay.

- **Aristocratic Wimp.** The aristocratic negotiator walks into the dealership, refuses to speak with any of the salespeople and demands to see the manager. They tell the manager they're going to spend top dollar and do not want to get into a haggling scene over the price. *"Just give me a price and I will tell you whether or not I will buy the car."* The aristocratic negotiator rationalizes that negotiation makes them feel "cheap" and therefore, they claim to be "above petty haggling." They do not want to engage in the game of negotiation and often leave plenty of lost money on the table.

- **Amiable Wimp.** The amiable type walks in and immediately gets into a long conversation with the salesperson about their families. Before you know it, the amiable knows everything about the life history of the salesperson, including the fact that he or she is one car away from getting that bonus that will help to pay for Junior's braces. In the end, the amiable just takes the deal that is offered because he knows that it will help the salesperson out and really feel that they and the salesperson can become good friends—and he would not want to negotiate with a friend. In the end, it is more important to be liked than to get the best deal.

Regardless of variety, the Wimp Negotiator becomes a Wimp in the quest for a deal. This isn't disastrous if the other side is also a Wimp. The real danger is when you become a Wimp and the other side doesn't. Then you become something worse than a Wimp; you become a Loser. The process turns to Lose–Win.

Each of us has a potential Wimp type inside us, just waiting to appear the moment a deal intimidates us. Your goal should be to identify which type you're vulnerable to becoming and look for the warning signs so you can avoid the pitfalls.

Not long ago, we had a participant in our seminar—a broker with a prominent national investment firm who specialized in retirement plans. He asked us to help him unlearn his own Wimp–Wimp approach. Mark became his personal coach and tells the story which illustrates the old maxim, "Old habits are hard to break."

THE MAN WHO SOLD RETIREMENT PLANS

The broker told me, he had all the business he could handle, in fact, maybe more than he could handle. But, his problem was, a lot of his business wasn't profitable. When I asked why he took on unprofitable business, he explained that the industry had become ferociously, even blindly competitive. Winning clients at all costs had become the goal. Score-keeping and body counts had replaced bottom-line results. He wasn't about to lose a client to another broker. So, he bid lower and lower, cutting his own commission to the point where there was virtually no profit left. He'd do anything to win the client. Even make a bad deal.

Guess what. He was willing to lose and he did. He lost time and money on more and more clients. (He was living out the old auto dealer sales pitch. *"We lose money on every car but we make it up in volume."* Huh?)

Naturally, he didn't have time to service his low-commission clients as well as he should have. So, even though they were paying him very little, they weren't happy. And he resented what service he did give them because he was losing money with every extra minute he spent. Eventually, many of the client victories he had "bought," left him anyway, thereby turning into losses. Yet, he kept on underbidding, low-balling, and losing (money) in order to win (clients).

Despite my coaching, the broker had difficulty breaking the Wimp–Wimp cycle. It took an ice-cold slap in the face to snap him out of it. Our broker had an opportunity to bid on what could have been a very good piece of business. Out of habit, he assessed the situation, arrived at a reasonable bid, then lowered it to rock-bottom, to *assure* his winning it. Then he sat back and waited for the call from the client saying, "You win."

He never got that call. Two weeks later, he got a different call altogether. The potential client called to say, "Sorry, you didn't get my business."

Our broker was stunned, *"Wasn't I the lowest bidder?"*

The client said, "Yes, by far."

"But, but, but . . ."

The client went on, "My policy is to throw out the highest bid and the lowest bid because neither is likely to be the right bidder. One is overcharging, the other is underdelivering."

That stopped our broker cold. Imagine, it took a buyer's insight to show the seller how self-defeating a Wimp–Wimp or lose-in-order-to-win approach can be.

From then on, with our assistance, the broker began to assess each prospect differently. He used his own experience and judgment, coupled with a projection of future potential, to arrive at a bid he could live with in the short-run and which had promise of long-term return. His track record of client wins has gone down. His profits have soared. In fact, his entire definition of winning has changed. He's not counting clients anymore. He's counting results.

* * * * * * * *

ROADBLOCKS, MINEFIELDS, AND WISDOM

Okay, it's simple, right?

1. Know what you want.
2. Find out what they want.
3. Let them win some, so you win more.
4. Don't wimp into a bad deal.

What could go wrong? Nothing. If the path to a WIN–win deal was a straight shot. But it isn't. It's almost always littered with barriers, hurdles, detours, potholes, hazards, and all manner of obstacles to keep you from getting to where you want to go. Here's what they look like.

INSUFFICIENT PLANNING

When we harp on the need to prepare, it applies to both sides, yours and the other party. Unfortunately, we can only influence your side. The more prepared you are—the more you know about your goals and their goals, your absolutes and theirs, flexibilities, time limits, creative alternatives, pressures—the greater the opportunity to make a good deal.

As for the other side, the less prepared they are, the more difficult it may be for you to make a deal. The process will surely go slower. They're likely to be skeptical of even the most reasonable offer. Unlike you, they have not thought through various scenarios, in advance. They're worried about what they don't know, even paranoid, and therefore, less willing to compromise. They may obsess on issues of contention (whether they're meaningful or not) instead of focusing on the bigger issues (on which you could be in agreement.)

Why would they let this happen? It's natural. Planning is not fun. Doing is fun. Planning is tedious. (Even if it makes the doing better.) Vacations are fun. Packing isn't. Arriving without socks is not fun. Eating is fun. Flossing isn't fun. Root canals are as un-fun as it gets. Spending is fun. Saving isn't. Bankruptcy is only fun if you're a bankruptcy lawyer.

What can you do about their lack of preparation? Be that much better prepared. Have the answers they lack. Be patient. Walk them through the process carefully, methodically, non-threateningly. Use what you know to educate both sides.

Ineffective Communication

Many negotiators think they're outstanding communicators because they're good talkers. They have big vocabularies, are never at a loss for words, always have a snappy comeback. The problem is, most negotiators aren't good listeners.

When they talk, they're saying what they want to say, instead of answering the concerns and needs of the other party. They're not communicating their ideas clearly; they're uttering words they want to hear themselves say. Or worse yet, the communication takes place through legal representatives and documents, rather than face to face, human to human.

Often, if the other side doesn't communicate effectively, they don't listen well, either. They may listen through a negative filter. They suspect what is being said; they're skeptical of motives. It can't be good; it's someone trying to get the better of them. In the end, both parties end up in disagreement, not necessarily over issues, but over the manner in which the issues and positions were expressed.

In the next chapter, we'll talk about the big L: Listening. We'll show you that listening is more than waiting to speak. It's an art and a science. You can practice it and get better. Listening may be the single most powerful tool in achieving WIN–win, because it tells you what the other side really wants and needs to make the deal.

INEXPERIENCE

It seems like too many negotiators' jobs are filled by the following help wanted ad: "No experience necessary." Because too many perfectly good deals go bad simply as a result of inexperienced negotiators.

Novice negotiators just haven't made enough deals to know what matters and what doesn't. In their quest to avoid a bad deal, they often avoid making a deal at all. They sometimes take a hard line when it isn't necessary. They offend the other party either accidentally or because someone told them that negotiators are supposed to be tough guys. They believe, out of naiveté, in win-lose negotiation. If they can't win, they'd rather walk away. They react emotionally instead of rationally. All of which can be the undoing of an otherwise promising deal.

The experienced negotiator should know how to handle an inexperienced counterpart. Don't take it personally (no matter how offensive). Don't get hung up on tactics (no matter how crude). Do exercise patience. Let the novices make mistakes, say the wrong thing, back themselves into corners, rant, rave, and demand. While they're ranting, you're thinking. When they're demanding; you're strategizing. They are actually giving you time to calmly assess (or reassess) your position, your method, and your priorities.

PUTTING IT TOGETHER

When you can put all the elements together, get past positions, when you can identify what you really want, what the other party really wants, when you can satisfy your interests well and the other side's interests acceptably, that's when you can make a WIN–win deal. Here's a case in point:

CAL RIPKEN'S FIVE-YEAR CONTRACT (THAT TOOK ALMOST A YEAR TO NEGOTIATE)

When we began to negotiate Cal Ripken, Jr.'s 1992 contract, we and the Orioles were a mere $30 million apart. The team wanted a four-year deal and they cited as their precedent, the salaries of the top shortstops in the game. They proposed almost $20 million over the four years. We wanted a five-year contract and we cited, as our precedent and benchmark, the top players in the game, regardless of position. Our proposal approached $50 million (which holds its own with the uppermost pay even in today's game).

Over the next 250 to 300 days, most of the negotiation was about the money/time ratio. The Orioles slowly edged toward five years (fully justified by the trends in the game) and the dollars worked their way north of $25 million over the life of the contract. Our position moved down to the $35 million range. The key to coming together was recognizing each other's interests.

Throughout the talks, the Orioles negotiator was Larry Lucchino, former tough trial lawyer turned baseball executive under then team owner, Edward Bennett Williams and subsequent owner, Eli Jacobs. Larry was one of the prime movers behind the creation of Camden Yards and today is president and a part-owner of the San Diego Padres. He's a good friend but (unfortunately) he never let that stand in the way of saying "no" to me and the ballplayers I represented. Similarly, I didn't let our friendship get in the way of my asking for an aggressive, market-value contract for my client.

We were in the position phase—that is, I said, "This is why it's right for Cal Ripken to get at least $35 million" and he said, "This is why it's right that the Orioles only pay $25 million"—wherein both parties utter and repeat high-minded statements of belief and make very little practical movement. Our pronouncements were impassioned and sincere. Our verbal exchanges were heated and not always what you'd expect from friends. We each had clients and/or employers to represent.

How did we move from this phase to discovering each other's real interests? We changed locations from our offices, usually my conference room—jackets on, jackets off, sleeves rolled up, ties pulled down, crumpled yellow papers, cold coffee dregs in Styrofoam cups and a lineup of Diet Coke cans, and still little or no progress. We moved to my farm—outside, breeze blowing, overlooking a quiet pond, birds chirping in place of car horns. (Not everyone has a farm or a retreat, but a change of location can do wonders when you're stuck. From a cold, serious office to a hotel lobby, someone's den, or a comfortable restaurant.) On the day in early summer when we sat at the farm, I thought another change might help: A deadline, not a threat, just a date we could all aim for. It was Cal's birthday, later in the summer, in August. It was far enough in the future that we both thought it was a good idea.

It was then that we started to hear each other, began to understand the other side's issues and interests. Cal wanted a contract that acknowledged the totality of his accomplishments to date and took into account his contributions to community projects, his outside business ventures, and his future security. The team wanted a figure that acknowledged his recent decline in offensive statistics (though it was short-lived) and met the team's interests—fiscal responsibility, setting future contract precedents, yet still retaining one of the game's all-time greats. Larry was finally beginning to hear us. We were finally beginning to hear Larry and the Orioles.

We started to talk about ways to recognize Cal's contribution to the team in ways other than standard salary. For example, the Orioles eventually agreed to give Cal post-career compensation guarantees which added dollars to the overall contract but did not raise his pay for active years. (Interestingly, these very dollars were later traded for during-career compensation in his next contract.) They gave him merchandising rights in the stadium, another way to provide additional revenue for what Cal had come to represent but not pay for performance, per se. This helped Cal provide funding for his recently created Kelly and Cal Ripken, Jr., Charitable Foundation. The team offered special hotel accommodations on the road, designated parking, seats and a sky box for his family (which he paid for) all in an effort to provide added security as his increased visibility brought increased vulnerability.

Each of these creative solutions answered Cal's "interests." They provided the compensation he felt he had earned for his unflagging performance to the team and the town. At the same time, this form of reward allowed the club to maintain what it wanted, fiscal responsibility. They could hold his annual pay to a level they could live with.

On his birthday, August 24, 1992, Cal signed the biggest contract of his career, 333 days after negotiations began. It was classic WIN–win. Both sides won. We felt Cal won a little more. The Orioles wanted only a four-year deal. Cal wanted five years. Cal got his five. The Orioles didn't want to pay the highest salary of the day. They didn't. Cal would have been eligible for free agency a month and a half after the contract was signed. The bidding would have easily passed the $35 million mark, heading for $40 million. Instead, Cal got $32.5 million; he netted a top contracts (albeit briefly) by getting a combination of revenue streams; and he got something else he truly wanted—to stay in the city he called home.

* * * * * * * *

It doesn't usually take 11 months to get past the impasses. But regardless of the length of negotiation, in order to get over, under, and around deal barriers, you need to employ a systematic approach. That's what the next chapter is all about.

R·E·F·R·E·S·H·E·R
CHAPTER 3
WIN–win Negotiation

Myth of win–win: Both parties may benefit, but there's no such thing as truly equal deals or wins.

Reality of WIN–Win: One side always gets more than the other. Make sure it's you.

How to WIN–Win

1. Know what they want. Find out, dig, ask, learn.
2. What you want. Assess your needs and wants, *before* negotiating.
3. Satisfy your interests well.
4. Satisfy theirs acceptably.

> The best way to get most of what you want is to help the other side get some of what they want.

Good deals echo—they lead to more deals.

WIN–Win Is Not Wimp–Wimp

- Don't turn into a negotiating wimp.
- Don't lose in order to win.
- Don't give in just to get the order.

Five Wimp–Wimp Types

1. Addicted—anything to make the deal.
2. Anxious—accepts the deal to get it over with.
3. Apathetic—time saved is worth over-paying.
4. Aristocratic—negotiating is beneath them.
5. Amiable—more important to be liked than to get a good deal.

Roadblocks to WIN–win

- *Insufficient planning:* One or both parties isn't ready—prepared—negotiate.

- *Ineffective communication:* Someone isn't listening.

- *Inexperience:* The novice is negotiating the way they do it in war or in the movies. Makes the process hard for both sides.

"I do have a fallback position, but it involves firearms."

The Three Ps:
And the Big L

You need to take a systematic approach in order to become a better negotiator. Why is a systematic approach better? Mark's story about skydiving makes the point best. (It's Mark's story because I won't go skydiving no matter how good a point it makes.)

WHY A SYSTEMATIC APPROACH IS PARTICULARLY HELPFUL WHEN YOU'RE HURTLING THROUGH SPACE TOWARD THE EARTH OR NEGOTIATING

I have five friends and once a year we do an "adrenaline rush" thing. We've done bungie jumping, white water rafting, swimming with sharks. One year, we decided, "Here's something we haven't done. We've never jumped out of an airplane." So, it was time to go skydiving.

The five of us went to an airfield in Delaware. Once you get there, the skydiving company trains you for six straight hours. From 6:00 A.M. until noon, they train you and then, after noon, you finally start jumping. We had declined the tandem jump and the static line jump and chosen the most advanced jump they'd let us learn, the free-fall from 10,000 feet. (We wanted to get our money's worth.)

From 6:00 A.M. until noon, there were only five things they taught us.

1. How to step out on the wing of the plane and let go.

2. How to arch your back so you maintain your aerodynamic.

3. How to pull your rip cord so you remain in your aerodynamic.

4. How to get your lines untangled if they get tangled.

5. And very important, how to land.

There were only those five things they told us. The good news was, they were pretty simple. The bad news was, we had to practice each one for over an hour.

We did every single step, over and over. They had me suspended from a hanger, with white cords leading down to blue straps, simulating a parachute. They spun me around and purposely tangled up all the white cords. Then they'd say, "If your white cords get tangled, grab hold of your blue straps and kick like a bicycle." So, I'm up there, doing this exercise for 30 minutes, then 45 minutes and I say, "I get it, I get it." The instructor says, "Nope. We're going to do this for an hour. We're going to spin you around and tangle up the cords. You grab the straps and kick like a bicycle. Just kick like a bicycle." Finally, it's 12:00. That's enough. We got it. It must be time to jump.

The skydiving company owned one small prop plane which could only take one skydiver up at a time. My friend, Brad, had arranged the whole trip, so he got to go up first. The rest of us were on the ground, watching.

It took about 20 minutes for that little prop plane to climb to 10,000 feet. Finally, we see a little dot in the sky. It's Brad. He jumps. We're watching him and thinking, this is going to be great. We can't wait to get up there. Meanwhile, Brad is coming down 10,000 feet...8,000 feet...6,000...4,000. Then his chute opens up. We're watching and feeling like this is going to be the best of all our adrenaline rush things. This is going to be great!

As Brad is floating through the atmosphere, he's receiving ground instructions through a walkie-talkie strapped to his harness. We were told, in advance, to do whatever your walkie-talkie guide tells you to do—steer left, steer right, and, most important, put on the brakes. The walkie-talkie guide that day was Gus, who was about 89 years old and looked like he flew with the Wright Brothers. The very veteran Gus was talking Brad down. "You're looking good, Brad. Yep, a little left, now a little right. Looking good. Looking good. You're coming in, you're coming in, you're coming in . . ." BOOM! Brad hits the ground at about 40 miles per hour. Gus forgot to tell him to put on the brakes. Brad stands up. Brad falls down. He had a spiral fracture from his ankle all the way up to his knee. Fortunately, the paramedics were nearby. They stabilized Brad's leg, gave him something for the pain, and loaded him into the ambulance.

As the ambulance pulled away, Gus turns to us and says, "Okay, which one of you guys is next?" Pointing to each other, we all said, "Him!"

I was the last one to go up. Everybody else before me had some kind of problem. One guy blacked out up there. One missed the landing area. Another person jammed his ankle. Literally, every single person had a problem. As I was putting on my parachute, I heard two young instructors talking. One says to the other, "Get Gus off the walkie-talkie. He's killing these guys." I immediately started thinking of graceful but still semi-macho ways to back out. "Gee guys, I just remembered, ever since the Gulf War, I've had recurrent mortophobia—fear of death." Just then, another instructor puts his arm around me and said, "Mark, I'll be talking you in today." I think, "Thank God, no Gus!"

I confidently strode over to the plane, got on, and who do I see is flying the plane? Gus! Oh boy. I rationalize, maybe he's a better pilot than walkie-talkie guide. We go up; I have my parachute on; I feel good. We get to 10,000 feet and it's time to jump. I wave goodbye to Gus and jump out of the plane.

Wow! This is great. I'm thinking, "I knew I'd be the one who would not screw any of this up." 10,000 feet . . . 6,000 feet . . . 4,000.

It's so easy. Time to pull my rip cord. I pull my rip cord. One problem. They told us to pull it straight out to maintain aerodynamic. But I made the mistake of reaching *across* my body to grab it. I started to spin in the air like a top. My chute opened, thankfully, but when I looked up, all my white lines were tangled *and* all my blue straps were tangled, too. They never told us what to do on the ground if your blue straps got tangled. But one thought popped into my mind: Kick like a bicycle! And I did. I was riding the stationary bike from hell up there! I kicked like a bicycle and kicked and kicked. Slowly, finally, my straps untangled. I grabbed them and then got my cords untangled. I put on the brakes and landed.

What was the lesson I learned from this experience (besides never going skydiving with Gus again)? The key to learning how to skydive was not memorizing 45 different ways to get on the wing of the plane or 75 ways to get your lines untangled. I learned only five basic things—it was simple. They taught us a sequence—it was systematic. They made us simulate each step in the sequence over and over. It was practiced until it was mastered.

* * * * * * * *

When people are under pressure, they revert to habits. In order to create new habits, you need a simple, systematic approach that you can practice and master. I learned that lesson through skydiving, and I learned it again and again in negotiation. We do not teach people the 45 best opening lines or the 75 greatest closing tactics. Instead, we opt for a simple, systematic approach to negotiation. If you learn it—that is, practice and master what we preach—when the pressure hits, you'll revert to your new, learned habit and you'll be a more effective negotiator.

PREPARE, PROBE, AND PROPOSE

Many people view negotiation as an event—haggling or trading offers at the bargaining table. To be an effective negotiator, that view must change:

Negotiation is a process—not an event.

That is the essence of the 3 Ps. Prepare, Probe, and Propose. You prepare for the negotiation *before* it occurs. You probe for information *before* and *during* the negotiation. You propose *after* preparing and probing. You *continue* preparing and probing as you respond to an offer. And so on, until a deal is struck. Even then, the event isn't over because the deal made may well lead to future deals.

The 3 Ps comprise the systematic approach to negotiation. Sorry, there's no magic here; just a simple set of disciplines. Follow them and you'll make better deals. Ignore them and every deal will be left to chance. (If the other side follows them and you don't, chances are they'll get the better of you.)

As with all disciplines, these demand diligence. You know what Henny Youngman said when asked how to get to Carnegie Hall. "Practice, practice, practice." The 3 Ps are like exercise, homework, vitamins, a good night's sleep, and flossing your teeth. You may not get a big kick out of them, but the results are undeniable.

PREPARE

If negotiation is the commerce of information for ultimate gain, then you need information. Obtain all the information you can about the other side while controlling the flow of your own. The more you know *before* the dealing begins, the better your position.

Prepare. Research. Study. Stockpile knowledge. Don't go into a meeting until you know everything you can about your position, evidence for and against you, comparable situations in the past and present, what you're aiming for, what you're willing to settle for, and all you can about the other side, its position and views.

PROBE

Doing your homework isn't enough. You have to go beyond research and background. You have to go to the source. The best place to get information about the other side is the other side.

Probe. Ask questions, and an amazing thing happens: You get answers. Most people don't ask questions. They seem to think it's a sign of weakness, as if they should already know everything. And they're reluctant to go to the key source of information about the other side, *which is the other side.* Ask direct questions: What do they really want? Why have they taken that position? What are their short-term goals? What are their long-range plans? Ask indirect questions: Where the other person lives, where they went to school, what they do when they're not working. These are clues as to how the other side thinks, acts, and feels.

Everything you learn about the other side's needs and interests can affect the deal. For example, from the direct questions that you ask of the other side, you may find you can enable them to attain their long-range aims even if you can't meet their short-term price or goal. What you *don't* learn will have as much, or more, impact. If they won't reveal their bottom-line hope for the deal, maybe they haven't formulated it yet and your negotiations will shape their final desire. From the indirect questions, you'll learn what to talk about when you take a break from negotiating. You'll find things in common (hobbies, humor, religion, politics) and you'll learn what to avoid like the plague (hobbies, humor, religion, politics).

PROPOSE

When you finally propose a deal, your proposal will only be as good as your preparation and probing.

Propose. Try not to go first. But when you do make an offer, make it strong, solid, and reasonable. And be prepared to change it. You don't want to make the first offer. There are a number of ways to draw a proposal from the other party (covered in Chapter 7). But even if the other side leads, you will have to respond to their proposal, which is a proposal in itself. So remember, a proposal is a starting point. Smart. Revealing. But not final. Never forget, there's another side opposite you. Give them something to think about. Don't just give them something to accept or reject, to take it or leave it. (That would be a sure way to turn a potential tough negotiator into a real one.) A good proposal should lead to conversation. Exchange. Swapping of needs and wants. The process allows both sides to formulate and prioritize. Where do you go from here? What is most important?

Don't start by asking for the moon, and don't start by asking for the least you can live with. Always know, *before you propose,* where you're willing to go next. *Plan* to make concessions. If you know in advance where and what you can concede, they won't be losses, they will be part of your plan. You gave and it didn't hurt. But the other side has gotten something.

BROOKS ROBINSON'S FINAL CONTRACT OR ONE "P" OUT OF THREE MAY BE A .333 BATTING AVERAGE, BUT IT'S LOUSY IF YOU'RE A NEGOTIATOR

One day in 1976, not long after I had left my job as Maryland's Securities Commissioner to go into private law practice, I got a call from Jerold "Chuck" Hoffberger, owner of the Baltimore Orioles. He asked if I could help one of his ballplayers straighten out some financial troubles. While I wasn't salivating at the prospect of sifting through shoe boxes of old receipts, trying to balance hopelessly screwed-up checking accounts, and, with luck, undoing some fly-by-night deals, I had two problems with declining. First, I just like to help people. It's hard for me to say "no." Second, it was especially hard for me to say "no" to Chuck. My total hesitation got as far as, "Uh, Chu . . ." when he interrupted, "Ron, it's Brooks Robinson." I said, "When do I start?"

Brooks Robinson wasn't just a ballplayer; he was a legend with one foot already in Cooperstown. He *couldn't* be in financial trouble. He had to keep his mind on third base and the Orioles' pennant hopes. To skip to the happy ending, we managed to turn Brooks' ink from red to black.

So when Brooks called after the 1976 season and asked if I'd negotiate his final contract with the Orioles, I said the same thing, "When do I start?"

Brooks was paid $100,000 in 1976, but the Orioles were trying to impose the maximum allowable reduction of 20 percent and take him down to $80,000.

(Imagine walking into work tomorrow and being told your salary is being cut 20 percent!) They said Brooks was a *former* superstar, with declining statistics in his declining years. Legend or not, they said, Brooks' best days were behind him.

I attacked my job with a fervor that would make some of today's agents seem comatose. I was a combination pit bull-grad student-evangelist, staying up day and night to formulate a thesis that would forever change the sports world. Straining at the leash, I was hungry, unstoppable, a man on a mission and a marathon. Brooks Robinson didn't deserve a 20 percent cut. Or even 10 percent. He deserved a raise! He should get $105,000 at the very least. And I was going to get it for him!

I was a glutton for *information.* I read. I dug. I scoured. I researched. I referenced. I cross-referenced. My aim was to learn everything there was to know about the Orioles, their organization, and their financial condition. Did they make money? How much? Who called the shots? What did they pay other players? How did the Orioles compare with other clubs?

Fortunately, the Orioles were a public company so they filed their financial data with the Securities and Exchange Commission. Yes, they were profitable. Modestly. Though they were among the winningest teams in baseball, wins didn't equal dollars. They ran on a tight budget—really tight—and they had every intention of staying that way.

They made money but didn't part with it easily. How did they feel about the value of past glories?

I talked to everyone I could who was in any way connected directly or indirectly with the club or anyone in it. The Orioles did want to keep their ties with the past greats alive and well; they knew that name players brought fans and also helped the transition to the next stars. Frank Robinson, Boog Powell, Dave McNally, and Paul Blair had all recently retired. Management wanted these past greats to lead the way to the new generation of fans and players.

How much was that transition worth?

I kept digging, kept preparing. I studied the negotiating *personality* of the man I would face, Hank Peters, the Orioles General Manager. Was he a hardball player, out for an I Win–You Lose negotiation? Or was he a win–win type? Did he negotiate in confidence, behind closed doors, quietly and subtly? Or did he use the press as a tool to float offers and pre-empt counteroffers? Was he stubborn? Was his ego on the line? What effect would this negotiation have on his career? Did he and Brooks have a past and was it a plus or a minus? Did he have a sentimental bone in his body? Was he a soft touch for a legend getting ready to hang up his number, or was he a numbers cruncher who delivered budgets as if they were RBIs?

I went back to my *network*. I talked to reporters. I read sports stories. I read what the Orioles' media guide said about Peters. I talked to employees and former employees in Baltimore and in other big league cities. I listened to what people who liked Hank said and what people who didn't said. I learned that he was a tough negotiator, but a fair one. He valued marquee players, but he never forgot that he was part of an organization that ran on and believed in really tight budgets. He hadn't kept his job by throwing money around.

Hank looked like a guy who couldn't be swayed by an emotional pitch. But what if emotional value could be translated into bottom-line numbers?

Next I went looking for *precedents*. How did Brooks' numbers compare with those of other ballplayers? More research, more digging. I poured over Major League Baseball statistics. I put Brooks up against every third baseman. Everyone making $100,000. Superstars in their prime. Superstars in the twilight of their careers— Willie Mays, Joe DiMaggio, Ernie Banks, Yogi Berra, Ted Williams, Stan Musial, Mickey Mantle. Other Orioles of the past and other Orioles last season. I was searching for anything and everything that would justify $100,000 (and negate a salary reduction) for a player of the caliber and stature of Brooks Robinson.

I didn't find it.

The hard fact was that before 1975 and the beginning of free agency, lots of Hall of Famers-to-be were *underpaid* and they took *pay cuts* as their careers faded. Even players with stats comparable to Brooks' weren't earning six figures. Existing precedents weren't supporting the $100,000 goal.

Was the research wasted? Hardly. It was all the more valuable. Now I knew what Hank Peters might know. I would have to be prepared for it and be prepared to counter it.

Now it was time to determine my client's *real goals.* What was it worth to Brooks, not just to the Orioles, for him to finish his career in Baltimore? If we got another $10,000 from New York, was it worth it to move? Did it take $20,000 or $30,000 more to live there as well as he lived in Baltimore? Even if he got more from one of the expansion clubs like Toronto or Seattle, was it worth it for probably only one more season? What about life after he left the field? Would he want to be back in Baltimore anyway?

The answer was pretty clear: Brooks was tied to Baltimore. After turning his finances around, he had good business prospects here and he was part of the community. He hoped to expand on his relationship with the Orioles—maybe in the front office, maybe behind a microphone. Going to another club to finish his career might dull the luster on Mr. Oriole as it had, for a short time, when Mr. Colt, Johnny Unitas, left Baltimore for San Diego. And that might lessen Brooks' future earnings.

It was time to explore *alternatives.* True, the precedents weren't in our favor. And Brooks *wanted* to stay in Baltimore. I knew it, and probably Hank Peters knew it. But Peters didn't know if Brooks was *willing* to leave. I evaluated the option of going to other clubs. Only the expansion clubs would meet or exceed the $100,000. Established clubs didn't care about his intangible value—Mr. Oriole didn't mean anything at Fenway Park or Tiger Stadium.

He wasn't a hometown hero. (They had their own Carl Yastremskis and Al Kalines.) To them, he was an aging third baseman who might not be able to spear a scorcher up the line anymore. Our option was new clubs where an "old star" might be a draw and have an impact on developing younger players.

Time to take *inventory.* Where did all this preparation leave me? The Orioles weren't going to overpay—Peters would be persuaded with numbers, not nostalgia. The precedents of comparable players spelled a pay cut. Established teams wouldn't pay a premium for Brooks, though expansion teams might. Brooks wanted $100,000, but would take less to stay in town.

Would I have been better off not knowing all this? Absolutely not. What if Peters knew it all and I didn't? What if I pursued avenues that were blind alleys? It's as important to know your weaknesses going in as it is to know your strengths. Maybe more important.

It was going to be a tough battle, but we had one route open, the intangible called "economic impact": the money Brooks generated by *being there*. Economic impact is a commonly used term today in financing major civic projects like stadiums and convention centers. Back then it wasn't. Even now, it is never an exact calculation—more the art of fiscal conjecture. So I created my own guesstimate of Brooks' impact. I looked up newspaper and magazine articles. I gleaned every fact, trend, and anecdote that indicated how his presence in an Orioles uniform, on the field, and in the line-up might boost attendance, sell souvenirs, and line people up for beer and hot dogs. I estimated the value of Brooks at every home game. I calculated the return, in dollars and cents, of a "Thanks Brooks Day." I looked at Brooks as a one-man public relations office for the Orioles and tried to assess the positive community impact of the Orioles' keeping Brooks and the potential negative impact of not keeping him.

Tough battle or not, I was ready. I knew where the mines were planted. I knew every number, every fact, every stat, for and against us. I could make the case for $100,000 without stepping into a trap. I could make the case, in dollars and cents, and I could back it up. And because of what I had learned, we weren't stuck on getting $100,000 in straight salary. We were willing to accept creative ways to get there.

Bring on Hank Peters. Let him ask me anything, let him challenge me, let him put me on the spot. I was prepared, prepared, prepared.

I went into Hank's office. I looked over at him and I didn't see a general manager. I saw the jury. My case would win them over. I spread notebooks out. I laid newspaper articles across the tables.

I propped pictures up. I circled figures and percentages. I unfurled my spreadsheets. It was impressive, to say the least, and it took almost an hour. From fact to fact, from figure to figure, and finally to the finale. I made my closing argument to the jury. "Hank, clearly, undeniably, absolutely you can see this evidence demonstrates beyond any doubt that Brooks Robinson is worth at least $100,000."

I rested. I looked at Hank Peters, my jury. I waited. Confidently. It was time for an impressed Hank to furrow his brow, scratch his head, stick out his hand, and agree with me.

There was one problem. Hank hadn't read the script. He just looked across the table and said, "Thanks Ron, I'll get back to you."

What? *"I'll get back to you?"* He didn't say "yes." He didn't even say, "no." After my brilliant performance! *"I'll get back to you?"* Had I not made an iron-clad case? Was he just not listening? Oh, he was listening, all right. He heard everything. Because I told him everything I knew, all at once.

I was prepared, but I didn't probe. I didn't ask one question. I didn't get one insight from Hank Peters. I didn't even ask how the traffic was that morning.

I was prepared, but I didn't properly propose. I said, this is what we'll take. I didn't try to get him to go first. Or give me an idea of *where* or *how* or even *if* he'd make an offer.

I didn't negotiate. I orated, I speechified, I pontificated. But I didn't engage in "the commerce of information for ultimate gain." I revealed our entire position without getting one shred of information from him. He could take his time, mull over our position, respond to every argument, and defuse, disarm, and negate my points, one by one.

Most of all, *I didn't listen.* Listening is the critical link in preparation, probing, and proposing. I wasn't open to input that might have changed the outcome. I wasn't attuned to the cues from the other side. I heard only what I already knew, not new information that might have changed the outcome of the negotiation.

Hank said, "I'll get back to you" because he knew how to negotiate. And he did get back to us with an offer of $80,000. And he gave us his reasons, which by now were honed to perfection. Brooks accepted.

* * * * * * * *

There is a P.S. though. We never burned our bridges. And that paid off down the road. Late in the season, in anticipation of getting into the World Series, the Orioles wanted to make a roster move, that is, make room for a younger player by moving an older player off the roster. Hank Peters called and asked if Brooks would be willing to move off. I took the opportunity to remind Hank that Brooks had acted and played like a true professional throughout the season, despite never feeling quite comfortable with the outcome of our contract negotiations. Hank knew that was true and said he was going to make up the salary difference retroactively so Brooks would, in fact, make $100,000 for the year. The team even held their "Thanks Brooks Day" to recognize his career contributions to the Orioles. It was an early lesson in the value of building relationships. There's much more about that as you read on.

LISTENING

> *Nature has given men one tongue but two ears, that we may hear from others twice as much as we speak.*
>
> Epictetus
>
> *If only I had remembered Epictetus when I negotiated for Brooks Robinson.*
>
> Ron Shapiro

Shh! (That's another secret to negotiation.) People like to talk. Resist the urge. The other side is human, so they want to talk, too. Encourage them. Then listen. They're trying to tell you how to make the deal. Did you ever notice how often the party opposite you thinks what he or she has to say is more important than what you have to say? That's okay. Give them a chance and they'll tell you everything you need to know: What they hope for, what they'll settle for, what the real pressure points are, where they can move and where they can't. They may tell you directly or subtly. Ask questions. Listen more. Every moment you're *not talking* is an opportunity to learn what it takes to make the deal. *The best negotiators aren't smooth talkers; they're smooth listeners.*

NO WONDER IT'S HARD TO BE A GOOD LISTENER

The Wall Street Journal has reported that, "Overwhelmed by the incessant, intrusive babble of the modern world, the skill of listening has fallen on hard times." It has been estimated that most people speak at a rate of 120 to 150 words a minute. That sounds fast, but the human brain can process more than 500 words a minute. Because of this gap, many people engage in mental fidgeting, letting your mind drift off the subject, making you a poor listener.

Talk So Others Will Listen—Listen So Others Will Talk

The less you say, the more you can concentrate on what others are saying. Think about it. How much can you learn from what *you* say? Not much. You already know it, so by speaking, you're repeating yourself. But *everything* the other side says is potentially valuable. (Most negotiators spend too much time on what they're saying or on thinking of what they're going to say next.)

Make what you do say, count. The most effective things that come out of your mouth are those that shape and guide the conversation. When you frame the issues, when you ask a good question, when you nod in agreement or feed an encouraging word that fuels the speaker to go on, you are giving the other side a path to follow. That path should lead to the key subjects of the negotiation—timing, competition, pressures, price, terms.

Be an "active listener." Focus your energy on what the other person is saying. Make eye contact. Take notes. (It tells the other person that what they're saying is important and it lets you write down your ideas without interrupting.) If you don't understand, say so. (It's better to ask for clarification than to structure a deal or a proposal on a misassumption.) Repeat and confirm. ("What I hear you saying is . . ." Repeating makes sure you understand each other and it confirms that you're listening. And if you haven't understood, you'll get things cleared up immediately.) Pose candid questions. ("What will it take to make you happy in this deal?") Or try hypothetical questions to ease into a subject. ("Let's say that we're two countries making an economic pact . . .") Listen between the lines to what is said and what is omitted. (You hear gross sales figures instead of profits; Price is emphasized but quality is glossed over.) Listen for nuance and emotion. (The mention of delivery dates makes him or her nervous.) Listen with your eyes, not just your ears. Where is he or she looking? At you? At papers? Around the room? Respond, laugh, frown, nod. (Receiving information well begets more information.)

The less you say, the more others will remember. It's simple math. Say a lot and they're bombarded and overwhelmed. Say a little and they can retain every word. And, of course, the less you say, the more you can focus on what they say.

Listening Isn't Just Waiting to Talk

Do you think you're a good listener? Some people are, but they are the exceptions, not the rule. Most of us love to hear the sound of our own voices. We know the answers. We have the most informed opinions. We had the most interesting days. We tell the best stories. (Ask a golfer about his last round. Then prepare to hear a shot-by-shot travelogue of every hook, slice, and shank, from tee to rough to sand trap to green, hole after hole, times 18, each birdie, par, and bogie, not to mention every single coulda, mighta, and shoulda.) The fact is, most of us aren't good listeners. We're interrupters. We just can't wait until it's our turn to speak. *Conversation interruptus.*

WHAT IS YOUR INTERRUPTION QUOTIENT?

How often do you let the other person *completely finish* a thought? If you respond in midparagraph, you've lost a valuable information opportunity the other side was giving you. You'll never know what you didn't hear. When was the last time you had *nothing* to add to what someone else said? Do you mentally shut down instead of really paying attention? Think about when was the last time that you simply sat and *contemplated* what was just said. Do you want to really know if you're a good listener? Or a chronic interrupter? Don't ask people you work with: Ask your spouse or significant other. Ask your kids. (And don't interrupt when they answer you.)

In the very next conversation you have, make a deal with yourself to not interrupt at all. You'll be amazed at two things: (1) How hard it is and (2) How much you'll learn.

A LISTENING TEST

Try this test and see just how good a listener you are. DON'T read the following paragraph. Have someone read it to you, out loud. Twice. Listen as carefully as you can. Then take the test that follows on page 79.

"A long and extremely busy day had just come to an end at the Scoot-In-Scoot-Out Convenience Store. A shopkeeper had swept the floor and just before the door was locked, a man rushed in and demanded money. The safe was quickly opened and the owner removed the money. After the day's receipts were gathered up, the man drove off. Within minutes, the police arrived."

Test Questions

Do not look back at the text. Answer these questions.

Circle T if the statement is true.
Circle F if the statement is false.
Circle ? if you can't tell from the story.

1. A man appeared just before the owner locked the door.   T   F   ?

2. The man demanded money.   T   F   ?

3. The owner opened a safe.   T   F   ?

4. After the man gathered the day's receipts, he ran away.   T   F   ?

5. Not much money was taken from the safe.   T   F   ?

6. The police responded within minutes.   T   F   ?

7. The robber was a man.   T   F   ?

Answers

1. A man appeared just before the owner locked the door.   T   F   ⑦

    The story never identified who locked the door. It is stated that the shopkeeper swept the floor and the owner opened the safe, but it does not indicate whether the shopkeeper and the owner are the same person, or, if they are two different people, which one was about to lock the door.

2. The man demanded money.   Ⓣ   F   ?

    In fact, "a man rushed in and demanded money."

3. The owner opened a safe.   T   F   ⑦

    The story states the owner removed the money, but doesn't indicate who opened the safe.

4. After a man gathered the day's receipts, he ran away.   T   F   ⑦

    It is unclear who gathered the receipts. Also, the story states that the man "drove off." Did the man "run away" before he "drove off?" It is not clear.

5. Not much money was taken from the safe.   T   F   ⑦

    It says the owner removed the money. It doesn't state the amount of money that was removed.

6. The police responded within minutes.   T   F   ⑦

    It is not clear whether the police "responded" to a call or just happened to be patrolling the neighborhood.

7. The robber was a man.   T   F   ⑦

    We do not know if there was a robber or a robbery. While a man demanded money, a safe was opened, receipts were gathered, someone drove off, and police arrived, the same information could be true if the owner simply came in at the end of the day and took home the day's earnings.

How well did you listen? Did you hear "in a hurry?" How much did you hear what you *wanted* to hear, or hear what you *thought* was said? Were you influenced by a familiar scenario and did you mentally fill in the blanks? For instance, when we hear words like "a man appeared and demanded money," "safe," "the man drove off," and "police arrived," we may assume a crime of robbery. There are, in fact, twenty or more different incidents that could account for the facts you were given. (By the way, did you take notes or did you *assume/hear* that because this was a listening test, you weren't allowed to do so?)

There is no trick to this test, no special way to beat it. The problem is, we tend to hear what we listen for. There's a famous old story that illustrates the point well.

THE ZOOLOGIST

Two men were walking along a crowded sidewalk in a bustling business area. Suddenly one man exclaimed, "Listen to the lovely sound of that cricket." But the other man could not hear the sound. He asked his companion how he could detect the delicate sound of a cricket in the midst of the din of traffic and humanity. The first man, who was a zoologist, had trained himself to listen to the sounds of nature, but he did not explain this. He simply took a coin out of his pocket and dropped it on the sidewalk, whereupon a dozen people responded to that sound by looking all around for money. "We hear," he said, "what we listen for."

from *The Discipline of Transcendence*
by Bhagwan Shree Rajneesh

* * * * * * * *

The modern-day version of that story was told in our office one day. Our marketing director, Kelly Harris, takes an aerobics class at a health club. During her workout, she puts her baby in an adjoining room that serves as a nursery for club members' children. Kelly says when the exercise music is blasting, when the instructor is chanting a cadence, when the whole class is grunting and panting, she can hear the cry of her baby over all that noise. Not only that, but Kelly can tell her baby's cry from all the other babies' cries. She hears precisely what she is listening for.

Some of the most important applications of these lessons aren't in business, they're in everyday life, relationships with close friends and—especially—with family.

PAVLOV'S RESTAURANT BELL

I negotiate for a living. I ought to know how to listen. But even after practicing and teaching, I've sometimes committed the most basic mistakes, and where I'd least want to have them occur, with my wife, Cathi.

Some nights we go out to a neighborhood restaurant for dinner just to escape from life and get back in touch with each other, to communicate what we're thinking and feeling. I really want to hear what she has to say. But one restaurant we liked had one of those bells that rings every time someone walks through the door. And I usually sat facing the door.

So, like one of Pavlov's dogs, I'd developed a conditioned response. Every time I heard the bell, my eyes shifted to the door for a split second, which was just long enough to miss a key signal in the conversation. I may have gotten the drift of the conversation, but I missed a shading, an emotion, or phrase. Losing eye contact is more than a shift of visual focus; it's a loss of mental focus as well.

Worse yet, my wife sensed my lack of attention. Being the patient soul she is, she allowed me several dings before giving me my wake up call. "Ron," is all she'd say, one word that I hear loud and clear. It means, "I want to be heard. I'm more important than a door bell or who's walking into the restaurant."

Now I not only avoid restaurants with entry bells, but I purposely sit facing away from the door. I create habits that help me overcome bad ones. And since we've all been there, I remind myself of what it feels like when you're on the other side, not being heard.

* * * * * * * *

LEARNING TO LISTEN

Listening is not a God-given talent. You can train yourself, by simply practicing, to be a better listener. You can learn to tune in the important and tune out the extraneous:

- First, think how it feels when you're not being listened to. You feel ignored, unimportant. Instead of liking the other person, you think he or she is rude or self-interested. Conversely, people who feel they're being heard are easier to deal with.

- Look for signs of not listening in others and in yourself. Wandering eyes, distractions, side conversations, boredom, doing two things at once. Practice concentrating. Work at listening. Make the subject at hand the most important subject in your mind. Above all, make consistent eye contact.

- Don't talk. Just make a promise to yourself to not say a word for thirty seconds. Or a minute. It doesn't sound like long until you try it.

- Don't react, listen. As soon as the other person says something, you'll want to say something back. An answer. A comeback. A correction. Wait. Take brief notes. Resist even formulating your response until the other person is finished. Then think back. Most times, what you would have said a moment ago isn't what you will say now that you've absorbed the whole thought.

- Eliminate distractions. Close your office door. Forward your phone calls. Or, when you're on the phone, cover up the distractions on your desk such as mail and your computer screen.

- Fake it. Act interested in what the other person is saying. An amazing thing often happens. You actually become interested.

- Ask questions that lead the other person to talk more, not less. You'll do nothing but gain information.

- Let listening be an end in itself. Sometimes, simply hearing the other side's issues may not only enable you to find a solution, it may *be* the solution. People want to be heard.

"The building is noisy." "The interest rate is high." "Goods are late." "The boss is mad." "There's time pressure." A surprising number of disputes disappear once they're aired.

- Never stop listening. Everything you hear is information. All output is input.

By employing these lessons, you can create a better listening environment, one that is focused and free of distraction, much like a church confessional. There was a scene in the movie *Moonstruck* that memorably illustrates how the configuration, concentration, and quiet of a confessional enables the listener (priest), to hear through the distractions, that is, the attempts by the speaker (confessor) to gloss over the real issue (sin.) The scene went something like this:

MOONSTRUCK*

CATHOLIC CHURCH—MIDDAY

(An unassuming woman, Loretta, enters the confessional.)

CONFESSIONAL—MIDDAY

(Loretta genuflects and speaks to the elderly Priest on the other side of the partition.)

LORETTA Forgive me Father, for I have sinned. It's been two months since my last confession.

PRIEST (routinely) What sins do you have to confess?

LORETTA (as matter of fact as she can) Twice I took the name of the Lord in vain. Once I slept with the brother of my fiancé. Once I bounced a check at the liquor store. But that was an accident.

(The Priest seems unfazed.)

PRIEST Then it is not a sin. (pause) But what was that other thing you said, Loretta?

LORETTA (uh-oh) You mean the one about sleeping with the brother of my fiancé?

PRIEST   That's a pretty big sin.

(She winces. The Priest was too good for her.)

LORETTA   I know.

* * * * * * * *

Take a lesson from professional listeners—people like psychiatrists, counselors, and priests. Create your own confessional—a distraction-free environment—when you listen.

> *I'm all ears.*
>
> Anonymous (but successful)

LISTENING CHECKLIST

Here are 5 reminders to make and keep you listening better.

____ 1. **Don't talk.** The obvious but hard one to do.
____ Don't interrupt, keep listening.
____ Don't react, keep listening.

____ 2. **Act interested.** Pretty soon, you will be.
____ Take notes.
____ Ask questions.
____ Clarify and confirm.

____ 3. **Use attentive body language.** Send listening signals.
____ Make eye contact.
____ Lean in.
____ Nod (it encourages the talker to talk and tell you more).
____ Think.

____ 4. **Eliminate Distractions.** Create your own listening confessional.
____ Don't let your eyes wander.
____ Get rid of noise.
____ Reduce diversions.
____ Remember what it feels like to be ignored.

____ 5. **Let listening be a solution.** Sometimes the other side just wants to be heard.
____ Never stop listening (keep learning).

R·E·F·R·E·S·H·E·R
CHAPTER 4
THE THREE PS (AND THE BIG L)

Prepare, Probe, Propose

1. *Prepare:* Research, study, stockpile knowledge.

2. *Probe:* Ask questions, you'll get answers.

3. *Propose:* Try not to go first. When you do, make a strong, reasonable offer. Be prepared to change it.

Remember the Brooks Robinson Contract

Preparation: gathered information, studied other side's personality, went to personal network, looked for precedents, determined client's real goals, explored alternatives, took inventory.

Other side's response: "I'll get back to you." Preparation, alone, is not enough.

Prepared, but—didn't probe—didn't learn other side's real goals/ interests, didn't properly propose, went first without creative options.

Listening

> Nature has given men one tongue but two ears, that we may hear from others twice as much as we speak.
>
> Epictetus

- Talk so others will listen. Listen so others will talk.
- The less you say, the more you can concentrate on hearing.
- Make what you say, count.
- Be an active listener—focus, take notes, ask questions.
- Eliminate distractions—especially the telephone
- The less you say, the more others will remember.

- Listening isn't waiting to talk.
- What's your Interruption Quotient?

We hear what we listen for—Learn to hear through the noise.

> Listening applies to friends and family as much as it does to business.

"This, of course, adds a new element to our negotiations."

Prepare . . . or Else

PREPARATION:
THE AEROBICS OF NEGOTIATION

The first phase of any negotiation is the preparation phase. It is the most important phase and often the most neglected. Preparation is the only aspect of negotiation over which you have complete control. You can't control the other side, outside events, and often not even your own position—only preparation. If you are not prepared for a negotiation, you might as well not show up. You have given the other side an undue, unearned advantage.

Preparation is like exercise. Sure, it's good for you, but while you're stair-mastering, ab-crunching, and tread-milling, you feel tired, bored, and afterward, sore. It's only months later when you're running through an airport for a plane and you *don't* get winded that you appreciate all that sweat.

Don't expect a thrill from preparation while you're gathering background information, checking sources, networking, referencing, fact-checking, and strategizing. Do expect to be exhilarated when you sit down at the table and get no surprises from the other side. The more you know about them, their expectations, aspirations, limits (time, money, resources), their perceptions of you, the deal, and its ramifications, the better position you are in to make the deal you want. *Preparation is power.*

> *Failing to prepare is preparing to fail.*
> John Wooden, UCLA Basketball Coach

Successful negotiators are prepared negotiators. Preparation is an exercise in patience and persistence that *always* pays off. Remember, most people see negotiation as a finite incident. The opposite is true. *Negotiation is a process, not an event.* The process begins with preparation. Use it or lose it.

HOW PREPARED ARE YOU FOR YOUR NEGOTIATIONS?

In my preparation, I . . .   *Check One*

• Try to learn real interests of other side.	Always	Sometimes	Never
• Look for precedents for either side.	Always	Sometimes	Never
• Understand both side's alternatives.	Always	Sometimes	Never
• Consider impact of deadlines.	Always	Sometimes	Never
• Determine my strengths.	Always	Sometimes	Never
• Consider weaknesses of other side.	Always	Sometimes	Never
• Establish highest goal I can achieve.	Always	Sometimes	Never
• Determine my walk away point.	Always	Sometimes	Never
• Assemble a team to assist me.	Always	Sometimes	Never
• Assess other side's negotiators.	Always	Sometimes	Never
• Commit my strategy to writing.	Always	Sometimes	Never

* * * * * * * *

If 6 or more of your answers were "Always," you have good preparation habits which this chapter will hone further. (If all of your answers were "Always," c'mon!)

If 5 or more of your answers were "Sometimes" or "Never," this chapter will immediately improve your next negotiation.

If 3 or more of your answers were "Never," read this chapter as fast as possible.

The following exercise demonstrates the impact of preparation.

THE NUMBERS AND LETTERS GAME

Part 1—Numbers

Don't look at the bottom of the page yet! When you do, you'll see scattered numbers. Pick up a pencil. Ask someone to time you or time yourself. From the moment you look at the art, you have 30 seconds to connect as many numbers, in order, as you can. Okay, start now!

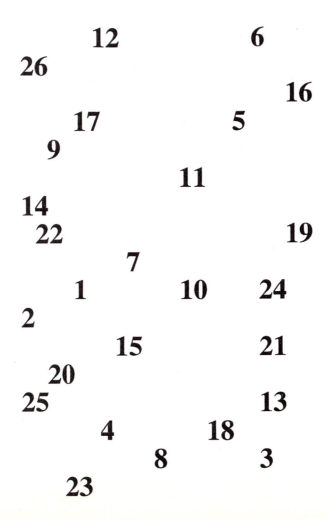

THE NUMBERS AND LETTERS GAME

Part 2—Letters

Don't look at the art on this page yet. When you do, you'll see letters of the alphabet. Do not pick up your pencil. Ask your timer to give you 60 seconds to study the placement of the letters. Then, pick up the pencil. Have the timer give you another 30 seconds to connect as many letters, in order, as you can. Ready? Go!

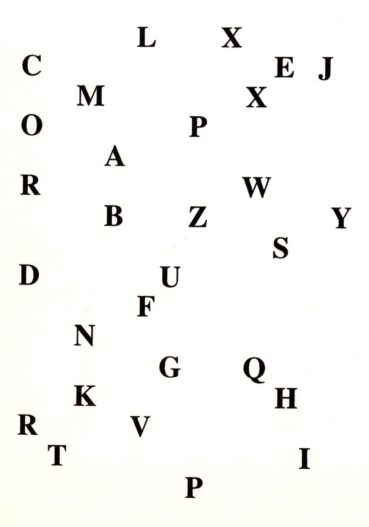

NUMBERS AND LETTERS GAME

What impact did the 60 seconds of preparation time have on your results with the letters (versus your results without prep time with the numbers)? More importantly, what impact did that 60 seconds of preparation have on your level of confidence in doing the exercise?

Most people experience a much higher confidence level after they have prepared for the letter exercise. They are able to map out where they want to go—establish a system to use and work through the exercise mentally before putting pen to paper. This preparation increases their confidence level, which, in turn, increases their performance level.

How Do the Numbers and Letters Exercises Relate to Daily Negotiation?

How do you feel when you're unprepared (or less prepared than you should be) for a negotiation? *Scared? Over-powered? Defensive? Anxious? Angry?* How do you feel when you're totally prepared? *Confident? Like a winner? Strong? Calm?* What are some possible negative results of being unprepared? *Embarrassment? A bad deal? No deal?*

The way you *feel* about your preparation is as important a factor as the actual preparation. In this exercise, some people do reasonably well in the section with no preparation time. But the vast majority do better when they've had time to prepare. That means two things: (1) Preparation helps; and (2) feeling prepared helps. Yes, you *might* do fine without preparation but why walk into a situation without giving yourself every possible advantage?

Remember, confidence is important. But it doesn't take the place of real preparation. In this next story, I had plenty of the former but not enough the latter.

MARK'S NEPHEW WHO SEES THE SCOREBOARD THROUGH ROSE-COLORED GLASSES

Never underestimate how far confidence and a positive attitude will take you. Some people are born with this outlook. My 6-year-old nephew is one of these people. I went to see him pitch in a Little League game. First, he walked the first five batters. He then struck out two kids who could barely hold their bats up. The next kid bunted the ball but ended up with a home run because of all the fielding errors. After several more walks and hits and errors and lots of runs, my nephew struck out one more kid. The inning, mercifully, was over. He had given up 12 runs. As he walked over to me, I expected tears. I said, "Nick, are you okay?" He broke into a broad smile and said "Yeah! Did you see that? I struck out the side!!!" That's looking at the positive side. That will take him far. Even into the next inning no matter how tough it may appear.

SELLING MY FIRST HOME (LEARNING THE HARD WAY)

This is what I called, "my first grownup transaction." I had a good start on my career as a lawyer; we had begun a family; we bought and were ready to sell our first home. You never forget that first house. It was the late 1960s and we bought a detached, three-bedroom, brick home on a little piece of land in a nice family neighborhood. We paid $26,000 for the house (it seemed like a lot at the time). With two children and one on the way, a dog, a station wagon, and a new swing set in the backyard, we were a living, breathing ad for American middle-class family life. And, after three years in the house, we were about to outgrow it.

The real estate market had not been great. It had been flat to moderate. But, we had made some improvements to the house—repairs, painting, decorating. I figured, the house had to be worth somewhat more simply because (1) it was three years later and (2) we had improved it.

We decided, we'd sell it for $30,000. It seemed like a fair price, not greedy, not desperate. I remember we came to our decision on Thursday evening. We were ready to put the house on the market the following week.

Then, on Friday morning, I remembered this friend, another lawyer named Gene who had always said that he and his wife, Carol, liked our house. They'd said, "If there's ever a home for sale in your neighborhood, let us know. When I got to the office, I found Gene and told him we would be selling the house the next week but we'd give them first crack at it. That way we'd both save by not having brokers' fees.

He was excited and said he and Carol would come look at the house that evening. At 5:30 Gene and Carol walked through our house, tried every light switch, opened every cupboard, and flushed every toilet. And, thankfully, everything worked, closed, and flushed. I was getting pretty excited, myself. Then, I overheard Carol in the third bedroom say, "I think we'll paint this room yellow." She didn't say, "... *if* we buy the house, we *would* paint this room yellow." She said, "we'll" as in "we will" as in *when* we buy the house, not *if* we buy it. We practically had the sale made.

Then we adjourned to the negotiation center of all good homes—the kitchen. Before anyone could say anything, Carol looked out the window and saw the swing set. She said "Would you throw the swing set in with the deal?" I thought to myself, "You mean the really heavy, cumbersome swing set that I desperately don't want to move?" I took a thoughtful pause and said, "Okay, we'll throw in the swing set." This deal was all but done. Gene asked how much we were selling the house for and I replied, "$30,000. Gene didn't flinch on the price. He said, they'd go home, talk it over, and call on Monday. I was feeling great. We'd sold the house in one day.

The weekend passed, Monday came, and Gene didn't call. Tuesday came and went, no call from Gene. Wednesday morning came and still no word. But, walking down the street that day, I saw Gene. He said the words you never want to hear in deal-making,

"Ron, I was going to call you." In other words, "I have something to say to you that I don't want to say so I've been putting it off." He said, "We bought a house." I said, trying to be calm, gracious, and all kinds of things I wasn't feeling, "Really? Where?" He said, "It's about seven houses down the street from yours." I had to know, "Gene, do you mind if I ask how much you paid for it?" "$27,500," he said, adding, "You know, we've been looking for a house in your neighborhood for a while and there have been six houses that have sold or are for sale with the highest asking price of $28,000." "Oh," I said weakly, "congratulations."

What a lesson. In that simple transaction, or missed transaction, I learned the importance of preparation. If I had walked through my neighbors' homes during their open houses, I'd have seen how much they were expecting and how their homes compared with mine. If I had examined the public records of selling prices in the area or, if I had used a professional broker, I'd have better understood market value. If I had done research and utilized the available resources, I'd have been better prepared and a better negotiator.

In the end, of course, we sold the house. The sale price was $28,000. So, it didn't cost us anything. Or did it? We had to make three more months of mortgage payments.

* * * * * * * *

HOW TO PREPARE
(AND HOW NOT TO)

> *Winning can be defined as the science of being totally prepared.*
>
> George Allen

IF PREPARATION WORKS, WHY DON'T PEOPLE DO IT?

We humans fall back on excuses (and they sound a lot like the ones we tried to get away with when we didn't do our homework in grade school).

- "I know it already. I don't need to prepare." Sure, it's your business or profession or investment so you ought to know it inside and out. You assume you're up to date, but you may not be. Give yourself a review. You're likely to find some surprises. Just because it is your business, you could be too close to it and take too much for granted. Step back and try to take an outsider's look. We guarantee, you'll learn something. And no matter how much you know about your side, you don't know enough about their side. Remember what Harry Truman said, "It's what you learn after you know it all, that counts."

- "There's not enough time." Preparation is actually a time-saver. The more you know about your side and theirs, the more shortcuts you can take in negotiation. Concepts require less explanation. Jargon is already understood. Major issues separate themselves from minor ones. When people tell us there's not enough time to prepare, we say "baloney." If a deal starts to turn into a disaster, there always seems to be enough time to postpone the deadline and hope for an eleventh-hour miracle, so surely there was enough time up front to avoid that last-minute disaster.

- "I don't know what to prepare." This one is valid. But it's not acceptable. Yes, there's a lot of background you could gather, perhaps limitless information. Yes, some information is more valuable and some less. No, you can't absorb all of it, nor do you want to. What you can do is, use a preparation plan to maximize your exposure to relevant data and minimize wasted effort and time.

THE SEVEN PREP STEPS OF
THE PREPARATION PLANNER

Following this section, we provide you with a grid to follow before every negotiation, the Preparation Planner. It's a tool that you can use to get in the preparation habit to make sure you're ready when you sit down to negotiate. The steps are:

1. *Precedents.* Knowing precedents gives you the *power of the past.* You can quote or cite, as well as learn from, those events that have already happened, thereby giving legitimacy and credence to your position. Knowing how similar transactions turned out in the past may also guide you in structuring this one. But don't just focus on a single precedent, such as the one that supports your position. Be familiar with the precedent(s) the other side might use. Case in point: Cal Ripken's 1992 contract negotiation. Our precedent was the highest paid players in the game of baseball—$6 to $7 million per year. Their precedent was the highest paid shortstops in the game—$2.5 to $3.5 million per year. We knew our precedent and we knew theirs. We were ready.

2. *Alternatives.* Employing alternatives gives you the *power of options.* Going into a negotiation without options is like going into battle with one weapon. What if the battering ram won't knock the door down? Did you bring grappling hooks to fling over the walls? If not, you're not going to get inside. Alternatives make you less dependent on one kind of deal and more open to variations. There's no take it or leave it when you have alternatives; therefore, there are far fewer impasses. Further, knowing their alternatives may guide you in assessing their leverage.

3. *Interests.* Your interests *and* theirs are the keys to getting past what seem like rock-hard positions. Interests are all about getting beyond what they *say* they want to what they might *really* want. In short, they are those things that you need most, those things that mean the most to your side and, conversely, those that mean the most to the other side. Yours are not the same as theirs. But, if you know both, you may be able to satisfy most or all of your interests and still fulfill some of theirs (e.g., You want a low price. They need cash in a hurry.). Dollars may define positions (prices, salaries, etc.) and noncash value may define interests (settling quickly, service, experience, recognition).

4. *Deadlines.* Knowing your own realistic deadline in advance will tell you how much leeway you have *before* you take an entrenched position. Similarly, understanding the other

side's deadline may give you an edge or allow you to forego a point in order to gain elsewhere. Deadlines are pressure points. Know where the pressure points are in order to push or massage them.

5. *Strengths and weaknesses.* Virtually all negotiators overestimate their own weaknesses and the other side's strengths. Try to take an honest inventory of each side's real strong points and vulnerabilities. An analysis of the other items in the Preparation Planner should be a part of that inventory. Ask yourself if your vulnerabilities appear as weaknesses to the other side or if you are more sensitive to them. The same applies to strength. Give yourself credit for your pluses. Assess the other side's strengths analytically, not emotionally. Examples of other factors include: Their company may be bigger but not as market-responsive as yours. They may have been around longer but are they as in tune with today's demands? The real strength you have is knowing your strengths and weaknesses.

6. *Highest goal/walk away position.* You will never achieve a lofty goal unless you aim for it. Where would you like to come out? What would be ideal? If you don't reach, you will surely never get it. At the very same time, know where your bottom line is. How much will you give up to make the deal? If you don't face this hard question in advance, you may find yourself repeatedly lowering your expectations as the deal progresses. Be willing to walk at a certain point. But decide where that point is before you start negotiating and write it down on the Planner.

7. *Strategy and team.* Create a team on your side. It may consist of conegotiators, experts in various aspects or good cop-bad cop, information sources, and devil's advocates with whom you can role-play. Practice before you go to the table. Assess the other side and the members of their team. Who are their decision makers? Don't get caught by a higher authority. Strategize. Do you want to control the negotiation or let the other side control the flow? Do you want to lead from strength or react to a lead from the other side? How many face-to-face meetings do you want to have? No

answer is right or wrong. That depends on your needs, your goals, the tone and style of the other side, timing, and egos. Plan your concessions. Where will you give? Where will you stand firm? How will you make a move so that it gives the least and gains the most? Write out/set forth your proposals in advance—test them, state them, and restate them until you are comfortable. Don't stop practicing until you are comfortable that your strategy works and flexes when faced with a variety of opposing strategies.

As you will see in the reminder at the bottom of the Preparation Planner, these seven steps and the responses should be added to information already gathered about the people and business with whom you are dealing.

Make the seven prep steps automatic. Get in the preparation habit. Carry a shorthand form like the one on page 102. You can follow it methodically, step by step, and create a fairly extensive document when the time allows. Or you can create an instant version, what I call my "yellow pad planner," for those negotiations that come by phone or just show up at the door unannounced. (Just remember the acronym, P.A.I.D.S. or **P**recedents, **A**lternatives, **I**nterests, **D**eadlines, and **S**trengths and weaknesses.) When someone says, *"We have a rush job and need a quote before close of business"* or *"I was driving by and saw your for lease sign,"* using the Preparation Planner, you can handle the instant negotiation. Just tell the prospect you'll call back in five minutes or an hour, or ask the client to wait in the lobby while you finish up some business. Spend that time with your shorthand version—say, four of the seven steps on a legal pad or steps 1 through 7 with key words next to each, whatever abbreviated version hits the hot spots and gives you the edge of preparation. Build your confidence by briefly spelling out, then practicing, your proposals to the other side. Once you have the Preparation Planner fixed in your mind, you always have it with you.

Make the exercise so routine that you feel undressed walking into a meeting without having done a version of it. You'll derive two benefits:

1. You will *be* better prepared.
2. You will *feel* better prepared so you'll have the added weapon of confidence.

PREPARATION PLANNER FORM

Use the Preparation Planner form on page 102 as a guide for your next negotiation. Expand space provided (sometimes a page or more per item) as requirements dictate and time allows.

> IMPORTANT NOTE: The spacing on this form is for convenience only. A truly complete Preparation Planner grows with each interaction of the involved parties. In addition to this planner information, data should also be gathered with respect to business of, and the person(s) negotiating for, the other side.

SAMPLE PREPARATION PLANNER FORM

To see how practical and helpful the Preparation Planner can be, on pages 104 and 105 is a brief composite filled in by a group of participants in one of our seminars. For another example of following the seven steps of the Preparation Planner, see The Major League Umpires story on page 257.

PREPARATION PLANNER

Client: _____

PRECEDENTS (Something that has happened before . . . a similar, prior situation . . . a persuader or learning point.)

In Your Favor   In Their Favor

ALTERNATIVES (Options . . . possibilities, however remote . . . what would you do if you are not able to make the deal.)

Yours   Theirs

INTERESTS (Beyond stated positions; what you/they want . . . focus on personal . . . emotional . . . professional needs.)

Yours   Theirs

DEADLINES (When must you be finished, when must they be finished . . . deadlines that can be created if none exist.)

Yours   Theirs

STRENGTHS/WEAKNESSES (Inventory of each side's pluses and minuses, you're not as weak as you think.)

Your strengths/your weaknesses   Their strengths/their weaknesses

HIGHEST GOAL/WALK AWAY (What is your ideal outcome? When will you walk away? What about them?)

Yours   Theirs

STRATEGY AND TEAM (What steps will you take, when and who else is involved? . . . roles? . . . probes . . . proposals?)

Yours   Theirs

The Situation

Our client, a large Continuing Care Retirement Center (CCRC), has been a loyal customer of our Pharmacy Division for many years. The client retains firms such as ours to provide medical supplies and services that meet the CCRC's fiscal and quality care standards. The client's business is composed of four distinct units of care, and they house a large population of residential living. In addition, the client is part of a Group Purchasing Organization (GPO) composed of 65 similar facilities.

Our company has been providing the client with medical supplies, but we have been one of several vendors. The client has used our company for pharmacy, intravenous equipment, and consulting pharmacy services but different vendors for other medical coverage programs. We are an approved vendor of their GPO.

On the table now is the opportunity to become their sole-source provider for medical supplies and related services. The potential increase in revenues to our company would be approximately $300,000 annually.

The client has just hired a vice president of development whose focus is efficiency/cost-control: to reduce supply costs, maximize reimbursements, and drive down resident's per-day costs. He is also looking for a provider with an inventory management software program to help manage the process.

PREPARATION PLANNER

Client: *Medical Supplier to Continuing Care Center Bidding to Become Sole-Source Provider to Center*

PRECEDENTS (Something that has happened before . . . a similar, prior situation . . . a persuader or learning point.)

In **Your** Favor *Successful medical supply program implementations with other campuses of similar size—Approved vendor of their GPO—Proven ability to move large campuses from one of several to sole-source supplier— (May want to spell out references to specific transactions. Precedent information may not only persuade, but create a model for this transaction based on past successes.)*

In **Their** Favor *Large volume of business to leverage pricing—Strong referral relationships.*

ALTERNATIVES (Options . . . possibilities, however remote . . . what would you do if you are not able to make the deal.)

Yours *Provide all medical supplies except those under certain coverages, or vice versa—Offer better pricing than current GPO by joining our GPO with over 1,400 members.*

Theirs *Use multiple vendors (i.e., bulk, Medicare B, software management)— Join competitors or other large GPOs—Stay with current vendors and expand services—Other vendors in market that provide same service and are approved vendors of GPO.*

INTERESTS (Beyond stated positions; what you/they want . . . focus on personal . . . emotional . . . professional needs.)

Yours *Securing relationship and ownership of all business—Provide sound service and product selection at acceptable margin—Provide customer with faster positive financial impact through development of facility-specific formulary.*

Theirs *Reduce expenses by lowering product cost through proper inventory management (cash in hand vs. cash on shelf)—Increase revenues, maximize reimbursement through automation—Reduce resident cost per day by monitoring product utilization.*

DEADLINES (When must you be finished, when must they be finished . . . deadlines that can be created if none exist.)

Yours *Should be completed within two to three months to allow for effective implementation.*

Theirs *Looking to have decision made, implementation complete prior to opening of new unit, five months from now.*

PREPARATION PLANNER (CONTINUED)

STRENGTHS/WEAKNESSES (Inventory of each side's pluses and minuses, you're not as weak as you think.)

Your strengths *Expertise in large campus programs—Success with facility-specific formulary to reduce expense, increase revenue—Good client relationship through other services—Large supply operation within 20 miles—Provide inventory management software program and training—Quality care resources for staff—National network of distribution centers—Supplied products evaluated for quality, service, selection, price, and past sole-source successes.*

Your weaknesses *Not always lowest cost provider—Do not provide next day routine delivery.*

Their strengths *Hired individual to manage process familiar with business—Successful, influential CCCR, can generate multiple positive referrals—Focused on controlling expenses, VP good at getting it done.*

Their weaknesses *Lack personnel to manage on-going process—Pressure to make decision before new unit is completed.*

HIGHEST GOAL/WALK AWAY (What is your ideal outcome? When will you walk away? What about them?)

Your goal *Contract for all of their medical supplies and services at reasonable margin.*

Your walk away *If unable to agree on price for reasonable margin, then walk. Lowest acceptable margin for combined business is 20 percent.*

Their goal *To receive products, services, and quality at reduced price to meet revenue, expense goals.*

Their walk away *If they perceive they're not being offered lowest price plus best service and quality.*

STRATEGY AND TEAM (What steps will you take, when and who else is involved? . . . roles? . . . probes . . . proposals?)

Your team *Acct Mgr, Supply Sale Rep, Supply Coord, Billing Mgr, Operations Mgr. (Designate roles)*

Your strategy *Offer most competitive pricing for services, differentiate by being true one-source provider, support their facility with timely delivery and management of supplies. Initially submit proposal for meeting goals rather than for bottom line. (It would be useful to spell out the proposal in writing and practice it in advance.) Plus, aim to solidify current business. Create additional proposals after responses to probing.*

Their team *VP of Development plus Exec Dir, Dir of Nursing, Billing Office Rep, Purchasing Mgr, Housekeeping Mgr to evaluate costs, product selection, quality, also delivery capabilities, inventory management and match up with current systems.*

Their strategy *Ultimate decision will be VP of Development's, listening to feedback from team.*

SOURCES OF INFORMATION

You know what information you need in order to be prepared, but *where* do you go to find it? There are three basic routes to information.

1. *Reference sources.* This is the first path to take, published source material. Start with generic information and work your way to the transaction-specific. Depending on the category of your negotiation—buying, selling, or leasing, bidding and awarding contracts, royalties and residuals, personal services, dispute resolution, business succession, divorce, or family decision making—you want to hone in on the data most relevant to your deal. Begin with government records, SEC reports, data available through the Freedom of Information Act, then go to the syndicated research services such as LEXIS-NEXIS. From there, further tighten your focus. Go to trade and professional organizations and their publications. Search the internet for appropriate web sites. Use the commercial on-line services. Keep narrowing, getting more specific in your input in order to get the most relevant output.

2. *Networking.* You're surrounded by experts. First, there are experts from inside, that is, those on your team—business partners and investors, any and all coworkers from your own company. Then, there are experts from outside—corporate lawyers, real estate lawyers, tax accountants, stock brokers, financial advisors, insurance and investment advisors, advertising and marketing practitioners, lobbyists, any of the myriad professionals whose advice you heed. Think about all they know about you and your business. Then multiply that by all the clients and businesses they serve. These, and other experts, comprise your personal knowledge network, a human library. Use it. Your accountant may have direct experience in the industry in which you're negotiating. Your stockbroker may have heard about shakeups in the boardroom of the company across the table from you. Someone knows who's cash-rich and buying; someone else knows who's under a profit squeeze and has to sell cheap.

And even someone who doesn't know anyone directly involved in your deal, knows someone who knows someone.

3. *Your client.* There's another expert in your network, one so obvious that they are often overlooked. Don't forget the one for whom you are negotiating, your client, your boss, your investors, whomever. Who knows more about the business, the category, the ups and downs, the other side, than your client? Don't ignore the most obvious source of knowledge. That source may assume he or she has nothing to add. That's why you were brought in. But if you purposely take a naive approach, ask questions that start from the basics, you'll get an instant education. Some negotiators fear that this makes them look weak in the eyes of the party they represent. On the contrary, it acknowledges that the client is an expert in his or her business. Your expertise is in negotiating.

Before every negotiation, make a list of likely sources. Consider references, from public records to industry bibles to web sites and home pages. Then run through your own network, asking yourself which experts to tap for this particular deal. Finally, sit down with the party you represent (or, if you're the party, recruit a partner or colleague) and get educated. With each source of information, turn back to the 7 prep steps of the Preparation Planner for the questions to answer.

EVERYBODY HAS AN ARNIE IN SAN DIEGO: A REAL ESTATE STORY

I was involved in a property negotiation that turned almost 180 degrees as a result of tapping into one source of information. One day, out of the blue, I got a call from a real estate client from my days practicing law. He opened with, "Ron, I got a problem." He reminded me of a piece of property between Baltimore and Washington which he'd bought for $3 million some six or seven years earlier. I had assumed he'd sold it long ago. Well, he would have but, unfortunately, a real estate slump had set in shortly after he bought. On top of that, he'd sunk $600,000 to $700,000 in taxes, insurance, and other expenses. In all that time, the land never moved. He got no offers, no inquiries, not even a lukewarm feeler.

But the day before, he had gotten a call. Somebody was interested. He said, "I'm so excited, I just don't want to blow it. Will you help me make the deal?" I said, "You know, I'm not the one to do the legal paperwork anymore, but I'd be happy to negotiate the deal." "Great," he said, "What do we do now?" I said, "We talk," meaning, we get prepared.

I asked what we knew about comparable land prices in the area. Since only a few parcels had been sold in recent times, we got a thorough history, none of it indicating an upturn in prices. We knew that my client had his parcel on the market for $4.4 million. But he'd held it a long time which was, in effect, his negotiation weakness.

I asked him everything I could about the prospective buyer. To protect everyone's privacy, we'll just call them the San Diego Electronics Distribution Company. I asked him what he knew about them. "Not much." I said, "Okay, let's find out what we can."

The San Diego Electronics Distribution Company was a public company which was good news. It meant we had immediate access to information—annual reports, earnings statements, press releases, the works. They had only gone public a few months earlier so they had a lot of cash on hand from the stock sale. We looked at their locations. They not only had a distribution center in San Diego but they also had them near Chicago, in Texas, Mississippi, and Florida. They had expanded across the country and their literature said they planned to expand further, into the Mid-Atlantic region, which is basically the corridor from Philadelphia south to Northern Virginia. That was more good news. Baltimore/Washington sits squarely in the middle of that territory.

Little by little, we were gaining information and therefore, strength. I said to myself, what else can we learn? And how else can we learn? That's when I thought of my friend, Arnie, who had moved to San Diego to run a network affiliate television station. TV general managers have a way of knowing lots of people in a town, whether it's by selling to, buying from, or serving the community with, the important players. So, I called Arnie—one call to one person. I'm not advocating shortcuts. But I do want to emphasize the power of using your network. In this case, all it took was one call.

I asked him what he knew about San Diego Electronic Goods Distribution Company. He said that since they were a wholesaler, they didn't buy advertising time, so he didn't know them as a customer. "But," he said, "it's amazing that you'd ask me about them right now." "Why," I asked. Arnie said, "The executive vice president of the company sits on the board of the Chamber of Commerce with me. At the last meeting, he leaned over to me and said, 'since you're from Baltimore, can you give me the names of some residential real estate brokers in the area?'"

I couldn't believe what I was hearing. The executive vice president of our prospective buyer wanted the names of realtors in our area. Somebody from his firm was contemplating a move, maybe several somebodies. In a very short time, we'd gone from knowing nothing to knowing a lot.

My friend added, "Oh yeah, Ron, the exec VP also asked me for the name of a good lawyer in Baltimore. I told him I didn't know any but I gave him your name instead." (I don't have to add that Arnie is a bit of a wise guy.)

My client and I went to the meeting. Instead of being desperate, we're prepared. (Well, my client is still a little on the anxious-to-sell side.) The other side walks in and starts by telling us our asking price is ridiculous (which it isn't, based on comparables). I remind them that our property already has railroad sidings leading in and easy access to highway truck routes. They reiterate that our price is out of line and add that their company may just concentrate on expansion in the Deep South, rather than our geography. That statement doesn't leave us feeling good about them from the standpoint of integrity. Their own literature and our information indicated otherwise.

But, do I call them liars? Never. We set our defensive strategy but we don't poke holes in their story because, to do so would just make communication all but impossible. This is, evidently, their idea of shrewd negotiation. Instead of challenging them on it, I simply said that we respected their following business needs. In fact, we too were considering alternatives such as subdividing the property (which, in our case, was true). So, they should do whatever they have to do. Just let us know, in case we haven't already sold our property, if they should decide to move into our area.

At that point, I was losing circulation in my leg due to my client squeezing it so hard he cut off the blood supply. Obviously, he doesn't feel quite as cool about this as I do. But he did keep quiet.

I should say, he kept quiet until we walked out of the room. "Ron, Ron, Ron, why are you taking such as risk? They were my one and only buyer!" I said, "They still are. Yes, we took a risk. But given what we know, it's a low to medium risk, not a high one." You always take a risk when you negotiate. But the more prepared you are, the lower the risk. In this case, we knew there wasn't any deeper to go in the Deep South. They were already there. They needed to expand north, to the Mid-Atlantic. And we knew they were house shopping for their people in our area.

We waited. And we waited. To my client, every day of silence was proof of his worst nightmare, a blown deal. He'd heard nothing on this property for years and now he was hearing it again. On the eighth day, the San Diego Electronics Distribution Company called back. They wanted to talk. No, they wouldn't pay $4.4 million but they did make an offer. We countered and eventually settled on $3.9 million. It was only a little more than what my client had sunk into the property. But it was at fair market value. And it was more than he had expected.

The deal was done. My client was ecstatic. All because of one phone call to one source of information in our network. Sometimes the key source will leap to mind; sometimes you have to dig for it. But before you sit down to negotiate, when you're preparing, ask yourself, "Who's my Arnie in San Diego?"

* * * * * * * *

CONFIDENCE

If you're prepared, you can go into the most challenging negotiation with confidence. You can accomplish anything. Nothing is impossible! Witness Albert Brooks, in the movie *Defending Your Life,* as an advertising executive who is dead sure he deserves a raise. He's done his homework, has his argument ready, knows just how he'll take on his boss, and even rehearses by role-playing with his wife.

INFORMATION SOURCE CHECKLIST

Reference Sources

Company Specific:

____ Web Site
____ Annual Report
____ Company Newsletters
____ Marketing Materials
____ Dun and Bradstreet Reports
____ On-Site Inspection

Industry Specific:

____ Trade Journals
____ Association Information
____ Newspaper/Magazine Articles

Government Sources:

____ SEC Reports
____ Real Estate Records

Networking

Personal Network:

____ Friends/Family
____ Coworkers
____ Current Clients
____ Suppliers
____ Competitors

Professional Network:

____ Accountants/Lawyers
____ Investment Advisors/
      Brookers
____ Governmant Officials

Extended Network:

____ "Coaches" (other
____ Organizations)
____ "Cold Call" Info Sources

DEFENDING YOUR LIFE*

IMPOSING JUDGMENT CHAMBER OF THE "AFTERLIFE"

Daniel Miller (Albert Brooks), the defendant, sits opposite two robed, "Heaven or Hell" Judges, who will decide his eternal fate. A smart, tough woman, the Prosecuting Attorney, addresses the Judges, making the case that Miller is too weak of conviction to deserve to go to Heaven.

PROSECUTING ATTORNEY   Your Honors, I would like to go to 2945 (evidence number). This is the evening before Mr. Miller took the job in advertising he was to hold until his passing. He asked his wife to help him by playing a little game.

*Excerpt from *Defending Your Life* granted courtesy of Warner Bros.

(The Prosecuting Attorney turns to challenge Miller.)

PROSECUTING ATTORNEY   Do you remember, Mr. Miller?

(Miller shakes his head.)

PROSECUTING ATTORNEY   You asked her to act the boss so you could sharpen your tools in order to get what you wanted.

(Miller nods sheepishly. Everyone turns to a large movie screen at one end of the chamber. The film rolls and there is a flashback from Miller's life. He sits across from his wife, Mrs. Miller, as they have dinner.)

FLASHBACK ON SCREEN

MR. MILLER   Do this for me, it helps.

(She takes another bite.)

MRS. MILLER   Not now, I'm eating.

(Miller puts his fork down, insistent.)

MR. MILLER   Come on, do it.

MRS. MILLER   (annoyed) What do you want me to do?

MR. MILLER   Be him.

MRS. MILLER   It's silly.

MR. MILLER   (imploring her) It's not silly. It helps me. Offer me 55,000, no more.

(She looks at him, then gets into role-play mode as the potential employer.)

MRS. MILLER   How much do you want?

MR. MILLER   (coy) How much are you offering me?

MRS. MILLER $55,000.

MR. MILLER   (assured) I can't work for a penny under 65. I'm sorry.

MRS. MILLER   Well, I can't pay you 65.

MR. MILLER   (unruffled) Then I can't work here.

MRS. MILLER   (bending) 58,000.

MR. MILLER   (firm) 65.

MRS. MILLER   (edging up) 59.

Mr. Miller   65.

Mrs. Miller   60.

Mr. Miller   (immovable) 65.

Mrs. Miller   (one more try) 61.

Mr. Miller   (confident) Let me make it plain. I cannot take the job for under 65, under no conditions.

(Miller looks smug, the self-assured executive.)

Flashback Ends on Screen.

(In judgment chamber the Prosecutor continues her case to the Judges.)

Prosecuting Attorney   Your Honors, I would like to go directly to the next afternoon and show you the real encounter.

(Again, everyone turns to the screen as flashback clip appears. This time Miller sits in ad agency office, opposite the real potential employer, a serious business-type.)

Flashback on Screen

Employer   Daniel, I am prepared to offer you $49,000.

Miller   I'll take it.

(Employer looks stunned that Miller bit so easily. Miller grabs the employer's hand and pumps it vigorously. The employer stands, realizing he just put one over on his new employee.)

Employer   (almost guiltily) I'll get you a parking space.

(Closeup of Miller in his chair, looking pathetic. He shrugs.)

Flashback Ends.

(In the chamber, Miller has the same pathetic look.)

* * * * * * * *

What happened? Miller was ready. He was sure. He was even cocky. If he was prepared, why things didn't go the way he expected? Remember the Brooks Robinson contract? There are three Ps, not one. Miller might have been prepared but he hadn't completed the other two Ps: Probe and Propose. We'll cover them next.

R·E·F·R·E·S·H·E·R
CHAPTER 5
PREPARE . . . OR ELSE

> *Failing to prepare is preparing to fail.*
>
> John Wooden, UCLA Basketball Coach

How do you feel when you're unprepared?
Scared, out-matched, over-powered, anxious, angry

How do you feel when you're well prepared?
Confident, like a winner, strong, calm

What are negative results of being unprepared?
Embarrassment, a bad deal, no deal.

Why People Don't Prepare

- *I know it already. I don't need to prepare.* Beware of surprises. Everyone needs to prepare.

- *Not enough time.* Preparation is a time-saver. More you know, less time it takes to explain or understand.

- *Don't know how to prepare.* Valid but unacceptable. Use prep time to maximize exposure to relevant data.

> *It's what you learn after you know it all, that counts.*
>
> Harry S. Truman

What to Prepare—Seven Prep Steps

1. Precedents.
2. Alternatives.
3. Interests.
4. Deadlines.
5. Strengths and Weaknesses.
6. Highest Goal/Walkaway Position.
7. Strategy and Team.

Sources of Information

1. *Reference Sources:* industry publications, libraries, online, public data.

2. *Networking:* who you know, lawyers, CPAs, brokers, marketers.

3. *Your Client.*

> **Confidence—The Secret Weapon**
>
> The more prepared you are, the more confident you feel, the better you negotiate.

"See? I told you the negotiations would be a lot more fun without a battery of lawyers."

Probe, Probe, Probe

THE OTHER SIDE IS TRYING TO TELL YOU HOW TO MAKE THE DEAL

In addition to the knowledge gathered so that you are prepared, you need to dig for information behind the other side's position. Determine their real interests or needs. That's what probing is all about. Too many people succumb to the temptation to jump to their bottom line stance—to make proposals—immediately, without taking full advantage of what they could learn about what drives the other side. The more you know about the other side's position—their motivations and expectations, their wish-list and must-list, soft spots and desperate needs, personal aspirations and psychic rewards, stated goals as well as real interests—the better equipped you are to negotiate.

If you ask the right questions and listen intently, the other side will give you the input you need to make the deal you want.

Is that really so? Then how come more negotiators don't know how to make the WIN–win deal they want? Because they don't ask questions (fearing it shows weakness or stupidity) and even when they do, they don't really listen (thinking they know the answers already).

HOW WELL DO YOU PROBE WHEN YOU NEGOTIATE?

When I negotiate, I . . .   *Circle One*

- Spend more time listening than
  talking.   Always   Sometimes   Never
- Check assumptions made in
  preparation.   Always   Sometimes   Never
- Ask "why" to learn the other
  side's interests.   Always   Sometimes   Never
- Use hypotheticals to gain
  information.   Always   Sometimes   Never
- Answer questions with questions.   Always   Sometimes   Never
- Ask the other side to restate a point
  if it is not clear.   Always   Sometimes   Never
- Take notes, review at end of
  conversation.   Always   Sometimes   Never
- Tally up issues before going on.   Always   Sometimes   Never

* * * * * * * *

If 5 or more of your answers were "Always," you have good probing habits which this chapter will hone further. (If all of your answers were "Always," c'mon!)

If 4 or more of your answers were "Sometimes" or "Never," this chapter will immediately improve your next negotiation.

If 3 or more of your answers were "Never," read this chapter as fast as possible.

Here is one of the great historic examples proving the value of probing, of getting beyond stated positions, of listening and discovering the real interests of each side.

THE MIDDLE EAST PEACE TALKS
(IT WASN'T THE TALKS, IT WAS THE LISTENING)

In 1979, I attended a dinner under a tent on the back lawn of the White House, celebrating the signing of the Camp David Peace Accords. I was filled with awe as I watched Anwar Sadat, the President of Egypt, and Menachim Begin, the Prime Minister of Israel, follow Jimmy Carter to the head table. That evening, I saw these two coura- geous leaders shake hands, engage in warm, friendly discussion, and express their sincere hopes for a peaceful Middle East. I sat next to my friend, Jim Rouse, the renowned visionary of urban development, who, with tears in his eyes, said to me, "Our President is a quiet man, but he's a man who knows how to get to the heart of the problem."

It was an indelible moment. The following is my condensed telling of a long historical process that demonstrates how President Carter used the second P—probe (though I doubt he called it that) to unlock an apparently irresolvable situation.

The peace process started in 1977 when Anwar Sadat made one of the bravest gestures of the twentieth century. He called Menachim Begin and suggested they talk peace. After literally thousands of years of anger and war, this was momentous. Even the unflappable *New York Times,* ran headlines slightly larger than usual. Amazed commentators noted that if Egypt and Israel could talk peace in the 1970s, by the 1980s or 1990s maybe the Amer- icans and Russians could be at peace.

The talks began with Sadat bravely taking his life in his hands and traveling to Israel to meet with Begin and address the Israeli Knesset. The evening news was riveting as we watched scenes we could never have imagined: Anwar Sadat and Menachim Begin being hosted by former Israeli Prime Minister, Golda Meir, for tea and cookies. Talk of their grandchildren living in peace, visiting one another's countries. To anyone who had lived through the post- World War II years of the fierce resistance to the formation of the State of Israel, the vows of its demise by neighboring nations, this was emotional stuff.

The talks went well, at first. The two leaders seemed to like each other. After initial success, Sadat told Begin that they must talk about the Sinai. Menachim Begin was stopped cold. To him, these were peace talks, not discussions of giving away key territo- ries. In effect, he said, "You provoked us in 1967 and we pushed you and rest of the Arab world back and we took the Sinai. Then, on our holiest day, Yom Kippur, you attacked us again, to take the Sinai. Again, we pushed you back. We have established settle- ments in the Sinai and we are not giving them up.

It was push and pull. Sadat said, "We want the Sinai." Begin said, "No, we want the Sinai." Suddenly the optimistic headlines turned negative. "Israeli-Egyptian Peace Talks Break Down." The worldwide hopes were in jeopardy. Would all the promise go unfulfilled?

That's when Jimmy Carter stepped in. He felt too much progress had been made to abandon the process. In August 1978, he invited both parties to neutral ground, Camp David, Maryland. They could each have a cabin (not your average cabin) and perhaps resume the talks. They agreed.

But what was Carter going to do? Was he going to try to play Solomon and divide the Sinai in half? Was he going to simply talk one side or the other out of its adamence? After 2000 years, it was clear, there was no simple solution.

Although, he certainly didn't call his process "The 3 Ps," Jimmy Carter did a great deal of Preparing, Probing, and Proposing. Of course, when you're President of the United States, you get plenty of high-powered help, particularly in the first P—preparation. Carter didn't spend the weekend at the Library of Congress cramming for the talks. He had a book under his arm that summarized the background. He had notes. He had advisors.

So, he was prepared. But he didn't just leap to the third P—propose—and suggest, "You fellows ought to do this or that with the Sinai." He went to the second P—probe. He got behind the information, behind the facts, behind the rhetoric of positions. He asked *why*.

In essence, he went to Sadat and asked, "*Why* do you want the Sinai?" Sadat might have offered many reasons from, "Israel took it from us" to "It is part of our heritage." But many countries had lost territory in war and its heritage belonged to the "holy land" more than to one nation or another. Carter knew these were not the real reasons. He asked more questions. He listened and listened. Finally, Sadat revealed Egypt's real reason for wanting the Sinai. He told Jimmy Carter, "I have risked my life for this mission." (Which turned out to be tragically prophetic.) "I have made the gesture of offering peace, which many in my country, and the Arab world, see as a sign of weakness, not diplomacy. I must gain something back, a symbol of fair exchange, for the Egyptians—the return to sovereignty of the Sinai. They have to feel they're not just giving, but getting as well." Carter heard Sadat. This was Egypt's real interest that had to be addressed at the negotiating table.

Then Carter went to Begin and, in effect, asked, "Menachim, *why* do you want the Sinai?" Begin may have offered reasons ranging from, "We need the Sinai's oil" to "We won it" to "It's part of our heritage." But Carter knew Israel had agreements to assure their oil supply, that other countries had given up land won in war, and that the Sinai didn't historically belong to one country. These weren't the real reasons.

Carter kept questioning and kept listening. Finally, Begin identified the real reason Israel wanted the Sinai: Security. Begin explained to Carter, "You've been to the Middle East. You can see that we are surrounded on all sides by enemies. The Sinai gives us early warning time. With troop movements, we gain hours to mobilize. With air strikes, we gain critical minutes to defend ourselves. We can't give up that security." That was Israel's real interest and Carter heard it.

In this excerpt from Jimmy Carter's memoirs, *Keeping Faith* (New York: Bantam Books, 1982), is the retelling of the moment at Camp David when President Carter's keen listening skills found the opening for pursuing the Sinai issue:

> [Begin] stated emphatically, "I will never personally recommend that the settlements in the Sinai be dismantled!" He added, "Please, Mr. President, do not make this a United States demand." I [Carter] noted with great interest, but without comment, the changes in his words and was heartened by it. "Never personally recommend" did not mean that he would never permit the settlements to be removed. The change was subtle but extremely significant. If others in Israel could be made to assume the onus for the decision, then finally there was at least a possibility for resolving this vital issue.

Carter could now offer a proposal that met the parties needs. He convinced Begin to give up the "land" of the Sinai but not the security. He promised to provide Israel with an early warning system as good or better than the buffer of the territory. If Arab troops so much as marched a step or one Arab airplane took off, Israel would know instantly. Then Carter told Sadat, Egypt could have the Sinai but only with conditions. The Sinai would have to be demilitarized; buffer zones and monitoring stations would have to be established in order to give Israel the security it needed.

The night of the White House celebration, I saw a sight I thought I would never see, both Israeli and Egyptian troops marching in together, instead of against each other. I saw history as a result of successful negotiation. Begin wanted security. Sadat wanted a symbol. The world wanted peace. All the interests were met because Jimmy Carter knew how to probe.

* * * * * * * *

But that's international relations. We know that political leaders have to contend with war and peace and the weight of history. But what about regular people who just want a pay raise to compensate for high quality labor? Like welders, teachers, or tuba players. Their needs and drives aren't mysterious or unknown; they're obvious. Nobody has to probe deeply to find out what their real interests are, right? Well, let's take those tuba players, for instance.

HARMONY: CONDUCTING A SYMPHONY ORCHESTRA MEDIATION

In the summer of 1982, The Baltimore Symphony Orchestra was on strike. Strikes always come at the wrong time but it would have been hard to find a worse time for this one. The city, the state, and a benefactor family were just completing a state of the art concert hall at a cost of $35 million (about $70 million today). The building was dramatic inside and out. The acoustics were superb. The sight lines were flawless. The season was sold out. They had everything but an orchestra.

The strike was over a variety of issues but eventually came down to salary. The symphony board, a nonprofit civic group, offered the players a base pay of $580 a week. The players wanted $620 a week. That makes the difference $40 a week, significant but not a world of difference, even in 1982.

The board and orchestra representatives talked and talked and got nowhere. Relations deteriorated. Federal mediators were brought in, they tried to split the difference, and made no meaningful progress. The strike stretched to the Fall of the year. First the rumors and then the newspaper articles appeared, talking about members of the orchestra being courted by other orchestras. The Baltimore Symphony had recently risen from the ranks of a good regional orchestra to a true national orchestra. They were drawing high praise, signing recording contracts, and being invited on prestigious tours. But our nationally ranked orchestra could be cherry-picked by competitors, thereby losing their "national sound," before ever moving into their new home.

I had been part of a volunteer group organized to look for ways to raise money for the future. It seemed all we did in our meetings was lament the never-ending strike. Wasn't there some way to bring the parties together? Somewhere along the way, I'm not even sure how or when, I found myself as a go-between. I was able to talk to both sides, the orchestra committee and the orchestra board. My first official act was to send the parties home for a Christmas break. We agreed to meet on January 4.

I had worked through the holiday period trying to get myself prepared. While I loved symphony music, I knew very little about it. I didn't know how many members there were in a full orchestra, what instruments made up the horn section, that cellists get carpal tunnel syndrome like ballplayers and stenographers, or the difference between a concert and a concerto. I read everything I could. I called on a member of our citizens' committee, Leon Fleisher, who had become a phenomenon as a left-handed pianist due to a medical impairment to his right hand. I did research through another friend connected with the Pittsburgh Symphony. I prepared right up through the New Year's weekend.

Unfortunately, by January 4, nothing miraculous had occurred. The board was still at $580 and the orchestra was still at $620. I put one group in my office and the other in my conference room and lots of snacks in both. I went to our law library and finished the last of my preparation.

Then I went from one group in the conference room to the other group in my office, back and forth, for hours. I had to find out the real needs of each side. I went to the symphony board representatives and asked the critical question, why. "Why is $580 as high as you will go?" Is it because the board voted on the figure? Is it because the board has to show the players who's the boss? Is it because the board has funds ear-marked for other purposes? The symphony board opened its books to me and showed me why: $580 was truly all they could afford. They were at their financial limit. They had exhausted their corporate contributors. They had committed all of their subscription money.

Then I asked the orchestra representatives, "Why must you be paid $620?" Is it because you can't live on what you're making? Is it because of inflation? Is it because you have to show the board that they need you more than you need them? It took a while and a lot more probing, but the answer came out. Sure, they'd like more money to live on but most supplemented their incomes with teaching. In fact, they respected the board. But the Baltimore Symphony was now an orchestra of national rank and the minimum pay for a national orchestra was $620 a week. It was status.

Hank Aaron once said that he could have hit 60 home runs, 150 RBIs, and batted .350 but none of it would have been as important as the day he earned $150,000 a year. Why? Because that's how much Mickey Mantle and Don Drysdale were making. It was a recognition of his level of accomplishment, his status in the game.

The orchestra wanted $620 a week. It signaled their status in the game. The board had $580. After that, they were broke. I had identified the needs of each side. But how could they be met? We had to find a way to allow each side to realize its real interest, not just its stated position.

On Day Four of our negotiations, before I left home, one of my kids asked me, "Daddy, when will we see you?" I said, "5 A.M. tomorrow." (Actually, it turned out to be 5:30 A.M.) That day, as predicted, we worked nonstop. We kept at it into the night. It got to be the early morning hours. But we were making progress so we kept going. I asked the board representatives hypothetically, "If we found new sources of money, would you agree to pay $620?" They responded "yes" but made it clear that they felt no such sources existed.

At 1:00 A.M., I had a thought. I called a colleague who was the general manager of the leading TV station in the city. He had a constant problem holding onto his number one-rated news anchor who was continually wooed by bigger market stations. (His news anchor happened to be my client.) It so happened that the news anchor had a weakness for, of all things, orchestras. The anchor had a fantasy of conducting a real symphony orchestra. I said to the station manager, "I can make you a hero with Jerry (the anchor)." The manager said, "It's one o'clock in the morning." I was undeterred. "Here's how it works. Your station donates the air time for a telethon for the Baltimore Symphony. Jerry gets to conduct the orchestra and host the telethon." The manager is now fully awake. "I don't even have to call New York. You've got five hours on the air and here's the date. Done."

Well, not quite done. Now I go to my secretary who is also there at 1:00 A.M. (and not too happy with me) and I have her prepare a contract which I am going to read to both the board and orchestra reps gathered in one room. In essence, the contract says, the players will be paid $620 a week (at which point the board members look like they want to kill me but the players look like they've won), *provided,* however, that the difference between the $580 and the $620 is made up by the funds raised through the telethon. Now both sides look at each other and realize it worked for both of them. The two sides bought in because we had brought Jerry, the anchorman, into it, and had introduced an idea that met the interests of both parties.

Throughout the process, we had been dogged by the press, but we'd managed to keep most of the negotiations confidential. At this point, though, I purposely let the story out to the newspapers and TV stations. They brought their reporters and cameras and we were all over the morning news and the next day's paper. That created an added pressure on all parties to make the deal work.

The players got $620 a week. Or did they? They achieved national orchestra status with a contract that says they're paid $620 with the proviso that the money is generated through fund-raising. The board lived up to its fiscal responsibility by not exceeding their budget of $580 a week and only paying more *if* additional money is generated *from new sources.*

As it turned out, the telethon raised all but $30,000 of the money and the anchor, who conducted the orchestra, spent the rest of his career at the station.

* * * * * * * *

The need to be understood is universal. If you take the time and make the effort to understand the person you're facing in negotiation—if you really probe—you'll be able to shape a deal that addresses their interests and yours. That's how you build relationships. (By the way, probing works in personal relationships as much or more than business.) Relationships lead to good deals. Good deals echo—they lead to more deals. It's not conjecture, it's history, proven over and over.

Probing to understand the other party is your goal. But how do you do it? How do you get to the answers you want? The best way to get answers is with a question.

W.H.A.T? THE PROBING TECHNIQUE

W.H.A.T. is a question to *remind* you to probe and it's an acronym for *how* to probe.

- **W** represents a collection of key **Ws**: **What, What else, Which,** and **Why.** First statements in negotiations tend to be positions. The other side says, *"We must own 50 percent of the new company."* That's a position. What you want to discover are their interests. But positions are easier to state. When the other person makes a statement contrary to your interests, your tendency is probably to defend and argue. *"No way. No deal. We're the majority or there's no deal."*

  Their demand to *"own 50 percent of the new company"* may be their position, but what interests does it camouflage? **What** is really important to them? Dig to find out. Is it that they feel entitled to half of the profits? That may be easier to live with than having them own half the stock in the event of a possible sale.

Keep going. Find out **What else** is important. Maybe they aren't comfortable unless they have an equal say in all decision making. Again, that may be easier to swallow than splitting profits, or equal stock ownership, particularly if your investment, industry performance, or both are stronger. Get behind the position to the substance.

Then, determine **Which** is the most important interest to them. Not all of their wishes will be of the same value to them. Nor will they be to you. Perhaps, to them, sharing decision making is more important than sharing profits. That may or may not be acceptable to you, but first you want to know where they stand. If you don't uncover priorities, you may do battle over secondary issues.

And always, always probe to find out **Why** an interest is important to them. Why do they feel that way? Is it because of a past deal gone bad? Is it a worry that doesn't apply in this deal? Is it an issue that can be satisfied another way? Must all decision making be equal or just major events such as a merger or sale?

We preach using a systematic approach in all aspects of your negotiations. The following four-question sequence is a simple systematic way to get the information you need:

—What is important?
—What else is important?
—Which is most important?
—Why is that so important?

It is important, however, that you not ask the same questions in the same way every time. You can use slight variations to obtain the same information throughout a negotiation. For instance, when you find out they are interested in a low price, keep asking questions. *"Is there anything besides price you think is important?"* (**What else** is important?) Now you might find out that the quality of goods and services after the sale are important. Or you may find they want fast delivery. Then, follow up with a summary. *"Just so I can make sure I have it straight, of the factors you've mentioned: Price, quality, service, or delivery date—*

what is your order of priority?" (**Which** is most important?) You may discover that fast delivery is equally important to price, and you can then ask, *"What makes that such a high priority?"* (**Why** is that important?) Although you should be systematic, you should not become robotic. You goal is to gain information. By using this four-question sequence or variations of it, you will be on your way to gaining the information you need in all of your negotiations.

- **H** stands for **Hypothesize.** Good negotiators are cautious about disclosing information. You ask a direct question. But they decline or sidestep. A nonthreatening method to encourage the flow of information or to break a deadlock is to get hypothetical. *Let's pretend . . . Just suppose . . . What if? . . .* Now you can discuss topics that were previously off-limits. This conversation doesn't create an absolute condition or obligation from either party, but rather, advances a hypothetical solution—one that might or might not work—strictly for consideration.

  For instance, we conducted a mediation for a statewide association of CPAs. One chapter had become so alienated from the parent organization, because of what they called "philosophical differences," the chapter threatened to pull out and form an independent body. That would have weakened the statewide association, created a vocal splinter group, and fomented bad feelings within the profession. After exploring the nature of the philosophical dispute, it became apparent that the greatest offense to the chapter had been in style rather than substance. The president of the state body had expressed his opinion in a manner deemed offensive by the chapter. So, hypothetically, we asked the head of the chapter, *what if* the president of the state body apologized for the way he had expressed himself? We had no authority to promise he'd apologize; we could only offer up the possibility. The chapter members were skeptical of the president's willingness to do so, but said, *"If he would, we would agree to sit down and talk out our philosophical differences."* We took the same *what if* to the statewide president. *"What if, rather than retract your stance on business philosophy, you revised the way you stated your disagreement and apologized for any unintended offense?* "Hmm," he considered the possibility and said, *"If the chapter would agree, he would agree."* The hypothetical led to the real. The chapter and the state body met, talked out their differences, and remained a united body.

In very sensitive situations, you may even substitute the names of players in other fields rather than refer to the parties at the table. *Microsoft and IBM. Jay Leno and NBC. The landlord of this building and the lobby newsstand.* Then you can advance ideas in even greater safety, distancing the hypothetical even further from the reality at hand. Interestingly, ideas—whether they're for those at the table or for substituted players—lead to modifications.

What if Party A offered X to Party B?
No, but it might work if . . .

Modifications lead to conversations. And when you're talking, you're not in a deadlock; you're negotiating.

- **A** stands for **Answer.** (Answer questions with questions.) The other side asks you a question to gain facts, to get background, to compare with what they know of the market, to test the water. If you just respond, you have no idea what other information they have, how your new input may compare, favorably or not, with industry data, whether you will look smart, gullible, cheap, expensive, or reasonable.

  But since they asked a question, they have demonstrated interest. Mine the interest by asking another question that probes further into the same subject. They ask, *"If your company agrees to be merged into ours, how many of your employees can be laid off to achieve economies of scale?"* You'd like to protect as many jobs as possible so, instead of responding directly, you dig deeper, asking, *"Which of our branch offices would you be keeping and which would you close?"* You now have the beginning of real information gain. You can start to learn whether your company will be merged or submerged. You can learn what the other side perceives are your assets and liabilities and even overall value.

In our seminars, we often reference a scene from the television show, *News Radio*, which demonstrates how to answer questions with questions, but carries the point to absurdity. The scene goes something like this:

NEWS RADIO*

THE QUESTIONER SCENE

An employee has just been clued-in that shrewd negotiators never actually answer a question with a direct answer, but always with another question. The shrewd employee then walks into the Boss's office to try out the new technique but gets a little carried away.

BOSS   What are you doing in here?

SHREWD EMPLOYEE   What does it look like we're doing in here?

BOSS   (baffled) What?

SHREWD EMPLOYEE   (on guard) What—what?

(The Boss, is suspicious of this weird behavior, looks for a reason.)

BOSS   Is this about the raise?

SHREWD EMPLOYEE   (not about to be fooled) Is what about the raise?

(The Boss is totally confused by all these questions.)

BOSS   Why are you answering every question with a question?

SHREWD EMPLOYEE   Why not?

BOSS   (shaking his head) I don't know. Congratulations. Now you've got me stumped.

*Courtesy of Brillstein Grey Entertainment.

SHREWD EMPLOYEE   (victorious) Thanks!

(The Shrewd Employee is totally delighted, but isn't sure over what.)

As this scenario demonstrates, you can go too far even with a good tactic.

- **T** is for **Tell Me More.** Sometimes people feel uncomfortable probing. They feel that they are being nosy or that the other side will feel as if they are being interrogated. One way to make the probing process seem more like a conversation is to use the phrase "tell me more." Most people like to hear themselves talk and by inviting them to "tell me more" you will discover additional information they may have originally omitted. Additionally, "tell me more" can be used to guide the conversation in areas of your interest. For instance, if a potential employer says that they are interested in people who are willing to work hard, at a low salary, but bring prior experience to the job, you might respond by saying: "Tell me more about your desire for industry experience . . ." As they tell you the problems they have had in the past with people coming into the organization without the necessary skills, you can begin to gather information to justify your higher salary based on your higher level of industry experience. The beauty of using "tell me more" is that it is an unobtrusive way to gather additional information and extend the probing process. By pushing one step more, following **W.H.** and **A.** with a reprise of **Tell Me More,** you may learn the other side's key interest at the very end of your probing. The real lesson is, never stop probing.

OVERCOMING PROBE-RESISTANCE

What happens when you deal with someone who enjoys being probed by your questions as much as being poked with a stick? You ask "Why?" and they say, "Because." You hypothesize and they say, "Get real." What do you do then? Don't give up. Try these tools when dealing with the probe-resistant negotiator:

- Try the *Restatement* technique. "Can you restate that?" It's amazing how often the restatement is different than the original. People tend to explain more each time they state their position, to give more detail, to soften, and even offer options to what seemed like a hard line. Now you can pose questions, ask for clarification and details. You're probing again.

- Use the *Show-Me-How* technique. The other side may make what seems like an unreasonable or unfair demand: *You must pay on delivery, not 30 days after?* Instead of reverting to a reflex rejection, ask the other side, *"Can you show me how that would work?"* As soon as the other side walks through the process in your shoes, they have to think about the challenge. *"Simple. You order merchandise and as soon as we receive your payment, we ship. You order as much as your cash-on-hand allows . . . which will be less than it would be if you had another 30 days to resell the merchandise to your customers . . . so then we'll be getting smaller orders from you than we used to . . . hmm, maybe there is another solution we could try."* Now you can begin exploring alternatives. Why do they have to have cash up front? How much do they have to receive before shipping? Is there a compromise between order date and ship date? Does the size of the order change the terms? You're probing again.

- Employ the *Says Who?* technique. If the other side simply makes an arbitrary demand—*it has to be done this way!*—thereby seemingly shutting the door on further probing, try asking them *"Who requires that it be done that way?"* You may discover the individual behind the demand is not the one sitting opposite you at the negotiation table. It may be someone higher up, a boss or an owner. It could be a lawyer or accountant. The person at the table is merely the messenger. All the persuasion in the world can't sway the unempowered representative. See if you can get the real demander to the table. At least then, you'll be talking to and perhaps probing, the right party.

By now, you should have a good sense of the other side's interests. You know what means a lot to them, what means less, which issues are emotional and which are rational, which are deal-sweeteners and which are deal-breakers. You know how they view your side, what they perceive as your strengths and weaknesses, values and liabilities. Utilizing the W.H.A.T. method, you have probably probed more effectively than they have, enabling you to initiate and control the interest satisfaction process. By also honestly assessing your own real interests, you should be able to see how you can give to get. You should begin to see how you can satisfy some of their interests while satisfying most of your own interests.

THE DON'TS—HOW NOT TO PROBE

Here are three warnings—don'ts—to keep in mind when you go digging for information:

1. *Don't mind read.* Don't assume you know what the other side is thinking and simply proceed on that premise. If you base your thoughts and proposals on your assumptions, you run a high risk of being wrong. You may assume your position is stronger than it is and make an aggressive but naive offer. You may assume your position is weaker than it is and back yourself into a bad deal.

   Let's say, you're negotiating a merger between a manufacturing facility based in LaCrosse, Wisconsin and a distribution center in Atlanta, Georgia, and a key issue is which city will be the new headquarters. You say to the third generation owner of the manufacturing plant, "Since you want to live in a cold climate . . . " Who says? Do you know that or just assume it? Maybe she's been dying for an excuse to move south or maybe she'd like to get away from her smothering family or perhaps her husband is from the south. Don't assume; ask. "Do you want to remain in Wisconsin?" "Where do you see the future of the company?" "Should we consider a different location altogether?"

It is natural to make assumptions. It's even acceptable, *if* you don't act on those assumptions. Test them first during the probe phase. Ask questions, explore, find out if your assumption is valid, close or off the mark.

2. *Don't offend the other side—Interrogation versus Interview.* You are not a prosecuting attorney. The other side is not compelled to cooperate and answer you. If you interrogate, that is go after them with an aggressive attack, expect them to shut down. When they do answer you, let them. Don't interrupt before they finish. Always ask yourself how you feel when you're being interrogated or interrupted or worse, both.

On the other hand, if you approach the probing process as an interview, there's almost no limit to what you can learn. Show an interest in their side. Soften your inquiries with lead-ins such as "So I can understand where you're coming from . . . " or "Let me see if I have this right . . . " or "Tell me more about . . . " When you want to answer one of their questions with one of your own, be careful not to come off as one-upping them or transparently ducking their question. Don't evade the question; embrace and explore it. "I'm glad you asked me that because it makes me think about . . . "

3. *Don't get off track.* The other side may try to rush you through the process. They may try to skip steps. After all, they're not following the same agenda as you. Make sure you get the answers you need before you move on. Don't hesitate to slow the process down by saying, "Let's hold off on that for a moment . . . " or "Can we go back to something you just said?" And don't let your side (you) rush you through the process. Sometimes we get impatient with the pace and try to short cut before we

have answers. Impose the same slow-down techniques on yourself.

You're prepared. You've probed. You're ready to propose and negotiate. Not quite. Actually, you're ready to get ready to propose. Then, you'll be ready to negotiate.

R·E·F·R·E·S·H·E·R
CHAPTER 6
PROBE, PROBE, PROBE

> *Ignorance is not bliss—it is oblivion.*
>
> Philip Wylie, *Generation of Vipers*

WHAT: *The Probing Technique*

W. *What is important? What else is important? Which is most important? Why?* When other side takes a position, don't counter, ask "why?"

H. *Hypothesize.* Nonthreatening approach is to pose "what if . . . ?" ideas.

A. *Answers.* The best answers are questions. They lead to more answers.

T. *Tell me more.* Take inventory on what you know. If you need more, go back and probe.

Overcome Probe Resistance

- *Restatement.* "Could you give me that again?"
- *Show Me How.* "How do you see that working?"
- *Says Who?* "Who requires that it be done that way?"

> The other side is trying to tell you how to make the deal.

If you ask the right questions and listen intently, they will give you the input you need to make the deal you want.

The Don'ts—How Not to Probe

Don't mind read. Don't assume you know the other party's position or response.

Don't offend. Don't interrogate; interview.

Don't get off track. Focus and slow down.

"Swallow us up and you'll have to swallow me up—
and I'm a poison pill."

Propose—But Not Too Fast

Getting the Other Side to Go First

ROLE-PLAYING

THE PUBLISHER-AGENT GAME

It's the year 2025. Gray-haired, former politicos, Al Gore and George W. Bush have retired from public life and are looking for a project to fill their days and make a few bucks. Bush has been spending time at his ranch, while Gore has been teaching stand-up comedy.

In an effort to supplement their government pensions, Al and George W. have decided to join forces and pursue an activity in which each has past experience. Not politics, but book writing. Earlier, Gore had authored, *It Was All Bill Clinton's Fault*, for which he got a $1 million advance. Bush had received a hefty $2 million advance for his post-presidency autobiography, *Wow, Did My Life Turn Out Cool!* Both books had big publicity but rather disappointing sales, although each publisher was able to earn back the advance.

Now the two have agreed to collaborate on a self-help book for retirees titled, *Learning to Drive—And Other Stuff You Have to Do for Yourself Now That You're Not a World Leader Anymore.*

It's up to you (aka Swifty McGuire), as the literary agent representing both Gore and Bush, to negotiate the largest advance you can get from the preferred publisher, Pretentious Press. If you and the publisher cannot reach an agreement, a deadlock will occur and the public "buzz" on the book will fade, which is bad for the authors, the agent, as well as the publisher.

AGENT OR PUBLISHER

In our seminars, we pair up members of the audience, one as agent, one as publisher, give each guidelines, and let them play out the negotiation. You can do the same, taking the part of the agent and recruiting a friend or colleague to play the publisher. As the agent, read the section on page 141, but not the one on page 142. Your colleague will read only the instructions on page 142.

Instructions to You, the Agent, aka Swifty

You realize that while a bipartisan book collaboration is news, you have a short window in which it will remain a big story. (There are already daily rumors that Chelsea Clinton is about to announce her intention to seek the presidency.) You have to make a deal fast. Your clients have told you that they don't expect to make the kind of huge killing they did with their first books, but really want to share their wisdom with the world . . . and wouldn't mind making a few bucks while they're at it. Gore and Bush have said they will accept an advance as low as $250,000 each for a total advance of $500,000.

Being a canny negotiator, you've reached an agreement with your clients that you will not receive one penny of commission for an advance of $500,000 or less. However, you will split any amounts over $500,000 on a 50–50 basis with your clients. Your entire fee will come out of the advance monies so you will receive nothing from royalties earned by book sales.

Additionally, there is the issue of your professional reputation. If you don't close this deal, your career will be in jeopardy. To ratchet the pressure up a little further, you've just learned that your twin daughters have been admitted to the prestigious Harvard-Yale combined Med School-Law School Program with a total annual tuition of $100,000, due shortly.

Before you begin, you write down on a piece of paper (for your eyes only) the least you would accept: $_____.

Good luck.

Now have your colleague read the instructions on the next page.

Instructions to the Publisher's Rep
from Pretentious Press

You have been chosen by your employer, the publisher, to negotiate the advance on the Gore-Bush book. This is your chance to redeem yourself since you lost out on the last three coauthored blockbusters, the Jay Leno-David Letterman book, the Mark McGuire-Sammy Sosa book, and the Madonna-Brittany Spears book. Each book went on to be a runaway success, each one you had in your grasp but weren't authorized to spend big money, and you watched each get away. If you do not get this book, you think that you will be looking at a pink slip.

This time, your publisher has determined, they're not about to be beaten. They will pay top dollar for the Gore-Bush collaboration. They have given you free rein to spend up to $3 million on the advance, but not a single cent more than is absolutely necessary. To inspire you to make the best possible deal, the publisher is offering you an incentive bonus of 50 percent of every dollar below a $3 million advance.

You have your personal pressures, as well. Your twin sons have just been admitted to the combined Harvard-Yale Med School-Law School Program at a total annual tuition of $100,000, due immediately.

Before you start, write down on a piece of paper (which you will put in your pocket) the most you'd be willing to pay: $_____.

Good luck.

Okay, you're ready to play. You have 10 minutes to make this deal.

CHECK YOUR RESULTS

1. What was the final amount of the advance paid for the book?

2. Who made the first offer, agent or publisher? How much was the initial offer?

3. Was the first offer accepted quickly? If so, what impact did this quick acceptance have on the person who made the first offer?

4. Where did each party set their sights before beginning the negotiations? (See the pieces of paper in the pockets.) Why did each of you choose that particular figure? Did you each consider the precedent of the prior advances ($2 million for Bush and $1 million for Gore)?

5. Did the two of you discuss issues other than money? For example, was there any talk regarding timing of publication, publicity obligations, book signings, or other sales incentives?

6. Did you consider pressures the other side might be facing? Did you feel your side had more pressure than the other side? If so, why?

CONCLUSIONS

- *What was the final amount paid for the book?* In our programs, the final amount paid typically ranges from $550,000 to $2,950,000. That's a $2,400,000 difference between the highest and the lowest, even though every participant goes in with the same set of ground rules. (And to think, some people say that negotiation skills don't matter.)

- *Who made the first offer, agent or publisher? How much was the initial offer?* We've discovered that the person who makes the first offer does not usually do as well in the negotiation. Many people tend to aim too low in negotiations and in this exercise, if you aim low, and make the first offer, you are in trouble.

- *Was the first offer accepted quickly?* If so, what impact did this quick acceptance have on the person who made the first offer? Sometimes an agent will go through the following thought process: "I know I can accept as little as $500,000, but I am really going to go for it and make my first ask an astronomically high $600,000. I am sure we will negotiate down to $550,000 and that will be fair." When the agent makes the offer of $600,000; however, the publisher jumps across the table, shakes the agent's hand excitedly and says "Wow! I'll take it. You have a deal!!" How does the agent feel at that very moment? Not very good. While the agent got $600,000 when prepared to accept $550,000, the agent has a feeling of aiming too low. The next thought the agent has is "How do I get out of this deal?"

- *Did each party set their sights "high" before beginning the negotiation?* (Look back at the pieces of paper in the pocket.) Why did each party choose that particular figure? Did each party aim high? Did each consider the precedent of the prior advances—$2 million for Bush and $1 million for Gore? Precedents are powerful. Agents who do best are those who "aim high" by using the prior book advances as precedents in the negotiation. "I want to be fair," says that kind of agent. "I do not want to ask for too much, because we want to work with you. We will just take the same amount that the authors were each paid for their last book—a total of $3 million." With that starting point, the agent usually settles well north of $2.5 million. Publishers do well by looking at the precedents in another way in order to "aim high" (or low as is the case with the publisher). "I want to be fair," says this type of publisher. "Gore's book only earned $1 million this time, and I do not see how this book can out-earn that last one, so I would be willing to go as high as $1 million for this book." People often ask us, how high should we go? We tell them to aim *reasonably high*. What is reasonable? Any offer that is supported by a past precedent. Find the precedent that best supports your goals and use that to justify your aiming high.

- *Did the two parties discuss issues other than money?* For example, was there any talk regarding timing of publication, publicity obligations, book signing, or other sales incentives? Although the agent and the publisher are only compensated on the advance, other issues such as royalty payments, timing of the book's release, and marketing budget are often brought into the negotiations. These may not be the main deal points, but effective negotiators know how to get what they want at the table, it is often good to put many more things on the table.

- *Did you consider pressures the other side might be facing?* Did you feel your side had more pressure than the other side? If so, why? Sometimes after the exercise, the agent will say, "It is not fair. All of the pressure was on me!" The publisher typically responds, "What do you mean the pressure was on you? The pressure was on me!" What they then realize is that both of them had the same amount of pressure: Both would lose their job. Both had kids in college. Both tended to think the weight of the world was on their shoulders and never thought about what pressures that might exist on the other side.

Remember, in negotiations, we tend to overestimate our own weaknesses, and we fail to think about the difficulties faced by the other side. In your preparation, you should think about what weaknesses the other side might face, and then during your probe, you should seek to clarify what these weaknesses are.

PROPOSING FOR REAL

DEAN JERNIGAN, CHAIRMAN OF STORAGE USA, THE NATIONAL SELF-STORAGE COMPANY, TELLS THIS, "LET THE OTHER SIDE GO FIRST" STORY

A piece of property was for sale on the Mississippi River. Its original purchase price was $3 million. The property had sat, unused and undeveloped, for years. One day, a potential buyer from a Los Angeles entertainment company asked for a meeting. The property owner's lawyer was sent to negotiate the deal with explicit instructions. "Let them make the first offer but take nothing less than $4 million." The prospective buyer started the meeting with a simple statement. "We are not going to negotiate. Our offer is $20 million and if you are not willing to accept it, we are prepared to walk." It turned out, the entertainment company was betting on a future legalized gambling boom to increase land values and, therefore, thought $20 million was a "fair" price. Of course, so did the property owner's lawyer who only had one regret. He hadn't handled the case on a contingency basis.

Here's a true-to-life book negotiation in which I was the real agent making a deal with real world publishers.

THE CAL RIPKEN, JR., BOOK DEAL

As the possibility of Cal Ripken's consecutive game streak started to edge toward reality, after he passed 1200 games, then 1500, and 1700, people would approach Cal, through me, to ask if he would write a book about his career. Each time they asked me, I asked Cal. And each time, he said, "No, Ron, not yet." He didn't want anything to interrupt his full concentration on his job, detract from his ability to perform on the field, game after game.

After he passed the 1800 game mark, I asked him about a book again. Again, he said, "No, Ron, not yet." The last thing he wanted to do was write about a consecutive game streak because he didn't play for a streak. He played every game because, in Cal's own words, it's "the only way I know." Even after he played in 2000 games, and people came to me to ask about the book, and I, in turn went to Cal, he still said, "No, Ron, not yet."

Then, on September 5, 1995, Cal Ripken, Jr., played in his 2,131st consecutive baseball game, breaking Iron Man Lou Gehrig's record. When the streak was formally announced, in the fifth inning, the sell-out crowd at Camden Yards rose spontaneously and erupted into a 50,000 fan cheer. (The notables and celebrities in attendance are too numerous to list, but among those standing and cheering was the President of the United States.) After ten solid minutes of ovation, Cal's teammates literally pushed him out of the dugout and onto the field to fulfill the fans' need to see their hero. Still, they wouldn't quiet down. Finally, in an effort to satisfy the roaring, clapping, stomping crowd, Cal lapped the field, waving and smiling to the fans. When he came around the third base side of the field, just above the Orioles dugout, he leaned over to my box, hugged me, and whispered in my ear, "Okay, Ron, now."

Okay, maybe I embellished a little when it came to the whispered statement. Just the same, it was after Cal's record-breaking feat that we began to pursue the book in earnest. First, we narrowed the field of publishers down to the two we thought best.

We had a favorite but we wanted a solid alternate candidate to strengthen our position and increase our bargaining power. I made appointments in New York with both, scheduling the favorite first thing in the morning and the other for a lunch meeting. I wanted to be able to honestly say to the first publisher, "We have to leave for a meeting with another publisher."

Before the meetings, I prepared, researching precedents of the advances paid to sports figures and other superstars for this type of mega-book. I found that for sports stars, the up-front money for such a book was in the $500,000 range. We knew, in Cal, we had someone who was a star even among stars so we set our sights high and decided to ask for $700,000.

But rather than walk in and say, "We want $700,000," we went to the meeting, asked questions, listened, and waited for the publisher to put a figure on the table. We followed the first rule we'll deal with in this chapter: *Don't make the first offer.* We said to them, "You're the experts; you know the market. We just know baseball. You tell us." *Their first offer was $750,000.*

Imagine if we had gone first. What if we had crossed our fingers and said, "Gee, we want $700,000." We'd have already left $50,000 on the table and this was only their opening offer. So, when they said $750,000, did I leap across the table, shake their hands, grin from ear to ear and say, "Deal!" No. We followed the second rule we'll talk about in this chapter. *Don't (immediately) accept the first offer.* If I had jumped at that first offer, what do you think the publisher would have thought? Buyer's remorse. "Uh-oh, I paid too much." And if I had jumped at the offer, I also might never have learned what our potential was. I took a lesson from Hank Peters when he sat across from me in the Brooks Robinson deal. I said to the publisher, "I'll get back to you."

We went to the second meeting, with the second publisher, and learned that it too, had a high interest. It appeared they would be willing to pay as much or more than the first publishing house. But, since we maintained our leaning toward the first, we didn't even push for a detailed offer from the second. Instead, we used our time to think and plan our next step.

When we got back to Baltimore from New York to take stock of our situation, we discovered that Cal's endorsement and licensing value was simply skyrocketing daily. Hundreds of inquiries and offers were pouring in. Realizing that Cal Ripken's market value was reaching extraordinary levels, we revised our goal to a $1 million book advance, double what the precedents had indicated.

It so happened that the editor from the publishing house was an old friend. I suppose I could have said to her, *"We know each other. Let's not play games. Let's not beat around the bush. We want $1 million."* But I recognized human nature, even among old friends. (And I didn't succumb to the temptation to go right to the bottom line which we too often do out of fear of rejection.) Instead, we formulated our counteroffer to their opener of $750,000 and asked for $1,250,000. And we never forgot the proverb that says, "many things are lost for want of asking," and followed the third rule of this chapter: *Aim high.*

Eventually we signed a deal with the $1 million advance we wanted (plus some assistance to the Ripken Foundation). The negotiation for Cal's book was a textbook example of the third P: Propose. We didn't make the first offer. We didn't grab their first offer. We aimed high.

* * * * * * * *

THE THREE RULES BEHIND PROPOSE

TRY NOT TO MAKE THE FIRST OFFER

You can only learn from the other side going first. You have a goal in mind. You expect to have to work your way up to it. But, the other side may meet or exceed it with their first offer. You might even be able to revise your expectations further upward as the negotiations continue. If you had gone first, you might have set your sights too low.

If you get a low offer, even if it's far less than you hoped for, now you have a floor, a minimum from which to build. In fact, a low offer may suggest you try to achieve your goals creatively. Let's say you wanted to sell a business for a given price but the other side's initial offer is so low it's apparent, no matter how much you can inch it up, the purchase price alone won't be enough.

Maybe you should pursue different or faster payment terms, retaining ownership, noncash remuneration such as in-kind services or other goods, or other imaginative ways to reach your goals. The knowledge you gain by the other side opening the bidding is invaluable in determining the course of the negotiation.

Never (Immediately) Accept Their First Offer

If you grab the first offer, the other side's first thought is likely to be that they offered too much, too good a deal, too high a price, too something. Since you are in the process of negotiating, they'll start finding ways to "un-offer" what they offered, to add conditions,

---

HOW WELL DO YOU PROPOSE WHEN YOU NEGOTIATE?

When I negotiate, I . . .   *Circle One*

- Encourage other side to make first
  offer.   Always   Sometimes   Never
- Resist jumping at first offer in
  acceptable range.   Always   Sometimes   Never
- Aim high (doesn't hurt to ask).   Always   Sometimes   Never
- Try to increase the pie so everyone
  gains.   Always   Sometimes   Never
- Try not to make concessions just to
  get deal done.   Always   Sometimes   Never
- Avoid reflex reactions to rejected
  offers.   Always   Sometimes   Never
- Negotiate points totally, not
  individually.   Always   Sometimes   Never

* * * * * * * *

If 4 or more of your answers were "Always," you have good propose habits which this chapter will hone further. (If all of your answers were "Always," c'mon!)

If 4 or more of your answers were "Sometimes" or "Never," this chapter will immediately improve your next negotiation.

If 3 or more of your answers were "Never," read this chapter as fast as possible.

subtract payment, to work their way down to where they're more comfortable.

And chances are, their first offer is not their best offer. Wait a little. Let the negotiations play out. Ask questions. Suggest alternatives. Counter. You'll soon see how far they are able to go. You'll learn which parts of their offer are flexible and which are immovable. The very worst you can do is end up where they started. You can accept their first offer later, not immediately, after you know it's the best you can do.

SET YOUR ASPIRATIONS HIGH

If you expect little, you are liable to reach your goals. *I'm losing money on this building. If I could just get what I paid and get out, I'd be relieved.* Fine. But what if the building is worth more to someone else than it is to you?

If you set your expectations higher, you'll often reach them. Say you're selling ad space in a program and the deadline is approaching, but you still have one page unsold. Aim low and you're just looking for anyone who's willing to buy that last page at any reasonable price. Aim high and you have a virtually sold-out program with only one page left. Who will pay enough to get it? Negotiators who ask for more, get more.

One caution: It's not enough to aim high; you must ask high. Have you ever set a high goal in your mind, only to reduce that goal the moment you got to the negotiation table because you were afraid of rejection? We all have. When faced with this situation, write down on your Preparation Planner, "Much is lost for want of asking." When the time comes to make your offer or "ask," reread that statement and bolster your confidence. There's no reason to fear that rejection. At worst, you'll be where you are now. At best, who knows?

ENCOURAGING THE OTHER SIDE TO MAKE THE FIRST OFFER

How do you get them to go first, especially when they want you to go first? And how do you do it without ending up in a verbal standoff?

"You go first!"

"No, you go first!"

"No way. I asked you to go first, first!"

- *Defer to the other side's expertise.* They may have more experience in the category than you do. Instead of being intimidated, use that to your advantage to gain knowledge. *"You're in the real estate business. I'm a manufacturer who happens to own one piece of property that my business no longer needs. You tell me what an industrial park site of this size is worth."* Use their experience as a basis for fairness or objectivity. *"You've done more deals of this type than we have. What are going terms in similar deals? What's fair?"*

- *Turn discussions into offers.* Once you start talking, the other side is likely to give enough information to suggest an offer even if they don't make one formally. Probe their thoughts, fleshing out more and more details. Then paraphrase what they've said as an offer. *"What I hear you saying is that you would be willing to pay in the neighborhood of $2 million if all the conditions were acceptable. Is that about right?"* Or ask them to restate what they've said in terms that constitute a proposal. *"You've mentioned a lot of interesting possibilities and options. Can you summarize them for me?"* By requesting help and putting it in the form of a question, you've created a nonthreatening "offer." The other side has a way out if they're uncomfortable but a way in to start negotiations in earnest.

- *Force a counteroffer bid.* If it appears there's no where to go in the negotiations, ask the other side where they *want* to go. *"You say the list price is too steep. What price could you afford?"* If you have had to make the first offer, don't bid against yourself. Try to extract a counteroffer from the other side. *"I hear you saying you're not prepared to meet our terms. Is the problem in the area of overall price, payment schedule, or delivery?"*

- *Make a tangential first offer.* Offer something important the other side wants in exchange for something more important to you. *"We know your company wants to ship fast while the produce is fresh. We can take delivery immediately, if the price per pound is right."* As response to your tangential offer to accept delivery, you're now in a position to hear from the other side what amounts to the first real offer, price.

- *Set a range without making a first offer.* Use exploratory conversation to learn what the other side expects. *"Say, I've heard houses in this neighborhood sell for as little as $200,000."* No risk. It's just what you've "heard." See what kind of response you get. *"Yes, but we put a $25,000 kitchen in ours."* Suddenly, your nonoffer, conversation-starter has resulted in the other side making an opening offer in the "range" of $225,000.

Now that you've gotten the other side to either make the first offer, or communicate the elements of that offer, how do you respond? How do you counter?

T.R.I.: MAKING COUNTERPROPOSALS

Once the other side states their position, it's frequently difficult to get them to move. Abandoning a position looks like weakness. It feels like losing. If you have determined their real interests during the probe phase, you can focus on those interests and demonstrate why it's in their best interests to modify their position. That may sound like sleight-of-hand but it's not a matter of fast-talking or putting one over on the other side. If it is not in their interests to change their position, they won't change. If it is in their best interests but they don't know it is, they won't change. Only if it is in their best interests and they come to believe that it is will they change. That's not easy to accomplish, but you can T.R.I.:

- **Trade.** Look for an interest to trade with the other side. There are two basic types of trades you can make:

  (1) *Horse trading* is when you exchange items, terms, or deal-points of similar worth.

  (2) *Value swapping* is trading something you value less for something you value more.

Your perception of value will not always be the same as the other side's perception. You may place great importance on something that is insignificant to them and vice versa. What's important when you trade is that you have something they want which you give up for something you want. You both gain.

Let's say, you sell Szechwan Drive-Thru franchises. The prospective franchisee wants an exclusive territory for its units. You don't want to give exclusivity; you want as many franchisees with as many units in an area as possible. But this particular dealer is well capitalized and requires no financing. She'll either buy ten of your units or, if she can't get the terms she wants, five of yours and five of your competitor, Hunan Drive-Thru. You offer her territory exclusivity in trade for her promise of franchise exclusivity to Szechwan Drive-Thrus only.

- **Remove.** Try to identify barriers you can remove to help the other side. Again, there are two forms this may take:

(1) *Remove pain.* If the other side is currently being harmed, seek ways to ease or stop the pain.

You represent a limited partnership trying to buy a breathtakingly beautiful mountain resort from a visionary architect-developer teetering on bankruptcy. Your group has the assets to make the deal but needs time simply because of the number of members in the partnership who have to agree. The visionary is under pressure from his lenders and is paying exorbitant interest on a short-term loan. He has to make a deal yesterday. Your group can't act that fast. But they can put up the cash to pay off his short-term loan, thereby taking the time pressure off the deal.

You've removed the pain, allowing the deal to go forward.

(2) *Reduce a risk.* You may obtain a more favorable deal by removing a risk from the other side.

A grand old civic theater wants your professional stage management company to take over the booking and running of the house. They're willing to give you a share of the profits when you bring in touring shows. But, as a civic organization, they can't gamble on shows that can lose money. In exchange for a higher share of the profits, when and if they occur, you offer the theater a no-risk, no-loss management contract.

- **Increase.** If you can increase the rewards of a transaction for the other side, you can increase the chances of making the deal. Two routes to greater rewards are:

(1) *Provide potential.* Increasing potential rewards of a transaction may help close the deal. Instead of just making a deal for today, you may consider a deal in which both parties stand to make more tomorrow. You can agree to become partners and share the future payoff when it comes.

For instance, you're interested in a high-priced piece of speculative property—supposedly due to triple in value when the new highway goes through and retail zoning passes. You offer to pay 75 percent of today's asking price but agree to give the seller 25 percent of any profit you realize from greatly increased selling price of the property after the highway and rezoning. The seller gets less than they wanted now but the possibility of much more later.

(2) *Increase pie.* Finding ways to make the entire pie bigger may entice the other side.

You own a minor league baseball team. Across the table is the owner of an empty stadium. Together, you two can do business. But the city, whose land the stadium leases, has a restriction against night games. Without night games, you can't draw as many fans so the stadium owner can't get as much rent. Instead of the two of you driving a harder and harder bargain with each other, bring the city in as a third partner and perhaps you can all make out better.

A STORY, EXERCISE, AND REVIEW

PIG HEARTS AND PIG HEADS

This is a composite of two true stories. Only the anatomical parts of pig bodies and certain university officials have been changed to protect both pigs and officials.

A respected faculty member of a major university developed a biotech invention that facilitated the transplantation of pig hearts and other vital organs into human bodies without the normal complications of rejection. The faculty member, who we'll call Dr. Bacon, came up with this breakthrough in the basement laboratory of his home on his own weekend time. He realized he was onto something astounding, but needed to do further research work in order to perfect it into a viable product.

With visions of altering the course of human science, he approached the university dean, Dr. Rule, asking for free lab space in which to work on what he now considered his own invention. Rule, who goes by the book, in turn, consulted the university's law firm, Absolutely & Knott. Much to Bacon's disappointment, Rule responded by saying that university policy clearly states that any invention or creation developed by a faculty member while at the university is owned by the university.

In fact, in accordance with this policy, Dr. Bacon must immediately sign the invention over to the university who will then hand it to their Office of Technology, Licensing, Endorsement, Usage, Marketing, and Total Profit who will see if there are companies who might want to take over development of the project.

Bacon is burning up. Not only did he come up with this discovery on his own time, but when he first approached the school for funding of his research, they rejected the idea completely, saying it had no future. Now they want to cash in unfairly. He refuses to sign the invention over to the university. He feels they are about to steal his "baby." The university's position is inflexible. There are no exceptions.

Bacon says, *"I invented it! I own it!"*

Rule says, *"Policy is policy. The university owns it!"*

What can the two parities do? In our seminars, the solutions we find, much like the solution that the real inventor and I finally found, are derived from employing the principles of the 3 Ps.

PREPARE

We begin with *information gathering*.

- *Precedents.* Both sides, the faculty member and the dean, search for other deals with this university. If they can't find a similar situation that was resolved to their satisfaction, they will go looking for deals at other universities. They're likely to come across solutions that favored the inventor (when their was no strict policy in force) and/or solutions that favored the college (when rigid policies existed). Digging further, they have to look for the specific terms within each deal, trying to uncover compromise or mutual benefit. Each side looks for precedents it can use to justify it's demands.

- *Alternatives.* What alternatives do Bacon and Rule have? Bacon could take the invention elsewhere, but the university could sue for ownership. Bacon could simply stop the invention development until his contract expires, but this delay would be costly to the project. Rule could amend the policy, but it would take months of legal work. Rule could ignore the policy, but to do so would be in contradiction of the duties of his office. He could fire Bacon and disclaim all rights to the invention, but he would prefer that Bacon remain at the university. Taking a hard look at the alternatives, each has incentives to reach a mutually satisfactory agreement.

- *Interests.* What does Rule really want? What are the university's real interests? Obviously, the university wants to avoid setting new precedents that it might have to follow with another faculty member. The university, however, would like the prestige of the new invention. The potential financial rewards would also help in a time of decreasing federal funding. Presumably, Bacon wants to control the invention. He does not want the bureaucracy of the university deciding which test tubes he can use for his invention. Bacon, however, also wants to stay at the university. The facilities are first-rate and the faculty could assist in additional research that will be needed.

- *Deadlines.* The same deadline faces both Rule and Bacon. If they can't determine a way to work out the problem, there are others working on similar inventions who could beat them to the patent office. If the patent is issued to someone else, Bacon and Rule both lose.

Additional preparation should include strengths/weaknesses and highest goals/walkaways, as well as strategy and team. The university's home city and state are pressuring the school to develop a biotech industry to help the local economy. Also, other universities with less restrictive policies on ownership of inventions, have stolen several prominent faculty members from the university. Although the university must maintain its policy, it wants to find a solution. Bacon needs a solution because his personal finances are limited and he has children headed toward college. Bacon may want to save the world, but he also needs to support his family.

Probe

What kind of questions does each side ask the other? Remember, you each want to discover the other party's real interests, not just their stated goals. *That means the faculty member, Bacon, has to ask more than the obvious of the university, for example:*

- What would happen if you gave me the rights to my invention? Let's walk through the likely outcome.
- Who would be the loudest critic? Who would be the most powerful?
- Have you ever done such a thing and had negative results?
- Has any other school, which had a policy to the contrary, made an exception? Why did they make the exception?

- Why was the policy created?

- Is the precedent the major issue? Explain not just the literal meaning of, but the rationale behind, the precedent.

- Why, other than precedent, does the university need to keep the policy in effect?

- Do you want me to stay at the university? How do you see my future here?

Similarly, Rule and the university have to get beyond the obvious when probing the inventor, for example:

- Do you think the policy is fair? What would you do if you ran the school and such a situation arose? What would you tell other faculty members in like circumstances?

- Why do you want to own the invention?

- Hypothetically speaking, if the university had been more responsive to your initial requests, would you have been willing to comply with policy?

- How much is the money a factor? You have already chosen an academic career over the commercial world where you could make much more.

- Do you like your faculty position or do you see your future in research? Do you want to stay at the university? Have other universities wooed you? What could we do to make your situation here more appealing?

- Is the potential fame and prestige important to you? Or do you look at this simply as a way to fund your research.

- Is "ownership" the key issue or is it credit for the invention?

PROPOSE

What proposal or proposals meet some needs of the parties? Who should make the first offer? Is money the key or are there intangibles to be included? Can a proposal be fashioned that addresses the concerns of both parties? If the rules are the rules, is there no deal to be made?

The law and the leverage are on the side of the university. But they run the risk of losing a key talent. Unfortunately, that potential loss is the inventor's only clout. What he must do is find an alternative that meets his needs and the university's. Remember:

The best way to get what you want is to help them get what they want.

Here are some possible solutions:

1. The faculty member sells his invention to a third party. He profits and it's the university's burden to pursue an individual or company who may have deeper pockets to fight and can claim to have been unaware of the school policy.

2. The faculty member simply stalls on his research work until such time as he leaves the university for another job, one at which he has prenegotiated his rights to his inventions. The onus will be on the university to prove that he did not develop the idea or the critical phases of the idea at his new employer. The faculty member, however, will be faced with possibility of a competitor overtaking him.

3. The faculty member assigns the invention to the university and then the university licenses it back to him for a nominal fee. The university, in effect, complies with the letter of their policy, but essentially gives the invention back to its inventor. The university will have set a new precedent when the next similar situation arises.

4. The faculty member assigns the invention to the university who sells it to a third party who has agreed to share profits (and possibly, publication rights) with the inventor. The Office of Technology is able to deliver funding to the school, the inventor sees profits, and the policy is loosely intact.

WHAT REALLY HAPPENED?

The result we worked out was combination of elements of each of these proposals. Recognizing the interests of the parties, we applied creativity to fashion a proposal that met the needs of both sides.

The faculty member agreed to assign ownership (literally) to the university but simultaneously a licensing agreement gave the development of the invention back to the inventor. He joined forces with a pharmaceutical company (approved by the university) who would help him develop the invention and market it. In addition to approval of the pharmaceutical company, the university kept the right to decisions on issues of patent law and the choice of independent investigator for the conduct of human testing. Both parties would share in the revenues (the university via royalties) if the project succeeded.

The faculty member was able to meet his interests:

- A financial stake.
- Development control.
- Credit as the inventor while remaining at the university.

The university was able to meet its interests:

- A financial interest through a licensing royalty fee.
- Maintenance of the policy precedent.
- Participation in the choice of patent firm and pharmaceutical company.
- The retention of the faculty member.

It was a true WIN–win. Despite the fact that the faculty member, Dr. Bacon, did not have the obvious leverage, by utilizing the 3 Ps, we were able to get him a big WIN while giving the other side a smaller win. The professor, as a practical matter, kept control of his invention. The university retained its policy.

R·E·F·R·E·S·H·E·R
CHAPTER 7
PROPOSE—BUT NOT TOO FAST

Three Rules of Propose

1. Try not to make the first offer.
2. Never (immediately) accept the first offer.
3. Set your aspirations high.

> **Remember: Much is lost for want of asking.**

Encourage the Other Side to Make the First Offer

- *Defer to their expertise.* "You've been in this business much longer than we have . . ."
- *Turn discussions into offers.* The other side often gives enough information to constitute an offer. Listen, then paraphrase what they've said as an offer.
- *Force a counteroffer.* If they think the terms are too steep, ask what they'd like.

> **Don't bid against yourself.**

- *Make a tangential offer first.* Offer something important to other side, but not so important to yours.
- *Set a range without making an offer.* Explore highs and lows and look for a response.

Making Counterproposals

T.R.I.

Trade: Look for an interest to trade with other side.

Remove: Try to take barriers away. Remove pain and reduce risk.

Increase: Find ways to increase the rewards of the deal. Provide potential (upside). Increase the pie (more for everyone).

"So now we deal mano a mano, as it were."

Difficult Negotiators

We've all dealt with difficult negotiators. In the movie, *Swimming with Sharks*, Kevin Spacey plays a classic, arrogant Hollywood mogul. In one scene, his aspiring assistant simply requests he be treated with more civility. That's the extent of the negotiation—civility. But Spacey's character, the macho-aggressive, difficult negotiator, verbally dismembers his junior associate. The gist of the scene goes like this.

SWIMMING WITH SHARKS*

HOLLYWOOD MOVIE MOGUL'S OFFICE—DAY

Buddy Ackerman, driven, deal-maestro movie producer, sits behind the cockpit of his desk, wearing a phone headset, flipping through papers, deal memos, and so on. His sycophant assistant, Guy, waits at the side of the desk, ignored by the Ackerman.

GUY   (tentative) Well, I wanted to talk to you about the phone calls.

*Clip from *Swimming with Sharks*, Courtesy of Trimark Pictures, Inc.

163

(Ackerman doesn't acknowledge the underling with even a glance.)

ACKERMAN No apology necessary. Everyone's allowed at least one mistake. You've used up yours. Let's not dwell on it.

GUY (all nerves, half-stuttering) Well, that's just it. I don't feel that I made a mistake.

(Ackerman stops reading but doesn't look up. Ominous pause.)

GUY (oblivious to danger) And, well, I would appreciate it if you didn't yell at me in front of the entire office.

(Ackerman looks up, eyes icy.)

ACKERMAN Excuse me. What?

GUY Uh, the yelling. I . . .

(Ackerman leans back, carefully puts his papers down, pulls off his headset.)

ACKERMAN (patronizing) Oh, you disapprove. I'm sorry, did I . . . did I hurt your feelings?

GUY No, no, no. I just don't feel it's necessary and it certainly doesn't help me. And I think that . . .

ACKERMAN (stands up) Well, I'm glad you brought this up.

GUY Great. Great.

(Ackerman begins to walk around the office.)

ACKERMAN Because I've found that an office can't run properly unless the lines of communication are open.

GUY (eager to agree) Right, right, yes.

(Ackerman closes the office door, then the cabinet door behind his desk.)

ACKERMAN So, in that case, let's make a few things clear.

(Ackerman sits back down. Guy sits down, apprehensive.)

GUY (lamb being led to slaughter) Okay, great, great. This is helpful.

ACKERMAN Let's review. What did I tell you the first day?

(Guy is blank, afraid to answer.)

ACKERMAN (total disdain) Your thoughts mean nothing. You are nothing.

(It hits Guy where this is headed and it's bad.)

GUY   I, I . . .

ACKERMAN   (irritated) Please shut up. At least allow me the courtesy of finishing what I have to say. That's the very least you can do after I've had to endure your insults.

GUY   This is a bad time.

(Guy tries to get up to leave but Ackerman leans over him.)

ACKERMAN   (yelling) Who do you think you are, you snot-faced little punk? Let me make this clear for you. Okay? And now try to follow me because I'm going to be moving in a circular kind of motion.

(Ackerman makes a little circle with his finger, then begins to circle the room, carving Guy up, little by little, as he walks in tighter and tighter circles.)

ACKERMAN   So, if you pay attention, there will be a point. (going for the kill) You are nothing. If you were in my toilet bowl, I wouldn't bother flushing it. My bath mat means more to me than you. (picks up a notebook) See this? This means more to this office than you. And yet you do not hear any complaints when I do this.

(He flings the notebook across the room. He picks up a fistful of pencils.)

ACKERMAN   These pencils. More important.

(He throws them at Guy who holds his hand up. Ackerman grabs pens off his desk.)

ACKERMAN   These pens. More important!

(He throws the pens at Guy who ducks. Ackerman flings paper clips at Guy.)

ACKERMAN   These clips. More important!

(Guy gets up, backs out of the office door.)

ACKERMAN   (total disdain) You miserable little cry-baby. You don't like it here? Leave. There are a thousand people who would kill for your spot. Who would kill for the opportunity to be here. I could spit and hit somebody who can do this job better than you. (on a roll) This is the fast track to the top and

I don't see you breaking any speed records! Why can't you show a little backbone? Huh? Huh?

(Guy peeks through the slightly opened door.)

ACKERMAN   (whining, imitating Guy) I don't think the yelling necessary. (crescendo) You've got to be a little more thick-skinned, you turd. You've got to be a man to do this job!

(Ackerman fires a book at the door. Guy recoils, pulls the door shut as the book hits. Ackerman smugly chuckles to himself, adjusts his clothes, and goes back to work.)

* * * * * * * *

What a despicable guy! He's so smug, so crude, so cruel. Aren't you glad you don't have to deal with him? But you do. That scene may be from the entertainment business, but difficult negotiators are everywhere. They just have different names, wear different clothes, make different demands, and have different styles. If only they didn't exist, negotiating would be so much more pleasant. But they do exist. You can either ignore that reality or learn who they are, what makes them tick, and how to deal with them effectively.

. . . AND THE AWARD FOR MOST DIFFICULT NEGOTIATOR GOES TO . . .

In the course of a career, you'll deal with so many kinds of difficult negotiators, you'll be hard pressed to name the single most difficult. But to tell you the truth, in my case, it wasn't a sports team owner or a corporate titan or a political power broker. It was an elderly man who owned a farm.

THE OLD MAN AND THE FARM

A real estate client called me a few years ago with a real challenge. He and his partners were well on their way toward developing a new community by buying up large tracts of farm land.

They had acquired 172 farms that would comprise the tract. They had made good progress with the local county as far as zoning and planning ingress and egress from the highway. The only problem was the 173rd farm, which they had not acquired, and just happened to be situated on a stretch of highway that would be the link to the entire community.

I asked the obvious question, "How could you get so far along without the key piece of property?" His response will strike a familiar chord with any of us who've been down the road with a deal and suddenly faced an obstacle we should have seen earlier. "I thought it wouldn't be a problem." I asked, "Can you change the pattern of the roads leading in and out?" He said, "Maybe, but it could take another six months or more." Projects like this have momentum. When they take too long, the momentum slows and the project dies. He needed to act now. He asked if I could try to intercede and negotiate to acquire the farm right away.

I started with preparation. I asked him all the questions I could to give me background. Is it an active farm? What's the owner like? Is he well off? How long has the farm been in his family? Is he married? Does he have children? My real estate client told me everything he knew. The farmer was 83 and a widower. The farm had been in his family four or five generations. The farmer had three children but they didn't live on the farm. It was an active farm and it was the farmer's most valuable asset. As far as my client could tell, the farmer did not have a lot of cash assets.

I said, "Okay, I'll try to negotiate for you. But if you turn this over to me, I need leeway. I need to have control over what the farmer is paid and the terms of the deal." My client said, "If you can make a deal, do it whatever way you can." It was clear, they needed a deal badly.

Did I go right over to see the man and make him an offer? No. I did more preparation. I wanted to be ready with a strategy. I found out that not only was the farmer an old man who lived alone, but he wasn't the nicest man in the world, either. In fact, he was a very nasty fellow. He didn't like to talk to people. He was known to throw sticks at people who set foot on his land. The word was, nobody could even get near him, let alone sit down and negotiate. I started to get a picture of him and I let it sink in.

I wrote a note to myself on my pad: "Four or five visits. Do little of nothing on first couple of visits." Why did I write that down? Because I could tell this negotiation was going to be like a marathon. I would have to pace myself. My client might be in a hurry, but I'd have to proceed at just the right tempo if we had any chance of making this deal.

Was it worth that kind of time and effort commitment on my part? Yes. My client would lose millions of dollars invested, as well as the enthusiasm and trust of his co-investors for future deals. On the other hand, if, somehow, this deal could be pulled off, everyone stood to gain.

I'll never forget the day I finally drove out to see the old farmer. It was thirteen miles north of where I live, many miles north of where most people live, truly the heart of farm country. I came to a long gravelly driveway and made my way down, looking around the whole time for flying sticks. I walked up to this old farmhouse, onto the porch, and there, next to the front door is— yes, I swear—a shotgun. My client told me all kinds of things about this guy but he never mentioned a shotgun. Well, I figured, at least it's where I can see it. (I'm an incurable optimist.) I reached for the bell, which was one of those old ones you turn. I turned, it rang but there was no answer. I turned it again. More rings, no answer. I was in about my third mid-turn when the door flies open and this grizzled old character yells, "What the hell is going on? Who the hell are you? What do you want? Get off my damn porch." And that's the printable version. He tore me apart for a good five minutes, using every four-letter word I'd ever heard.

What did I do? Did I give it right back to him? I counted. Just like Thomas Jefferson said, when you're upset, count to 10 and when you're really upset count to 100. I got into four digits. I followed the number one rule in dealing with difficult negotiators. *Don't get emotional.* Let them get emotional, but don't let their emotion get you emotional. *Don't take it personally and don't get personal.* I just kept counting. (By the way, the same applies at home. When your spouse or significant other is upset, it's rarely a personal attack. It may feel personal and it's tempting to get personal back when it feels that way. But usually, your partner is dealing with something or someone other than you and it's carrying over into your life together. He or she may have a legitimate issue with you that has just gotten out of hand.)

Back to the farmer. He finally ran out of breath and four-letter words. When he did, I didn't say anything about buying or selling or making deals. I said, "You've got a nice farm here." He laid into me all over again, unloading another barrage of salty language. At his next pause, I said, "I live on a farm, too." I handed him my card and said, "I'll see you again," turned my back, prayed he didn't pick up the shotgun, walked to my car, and drove home.

Four days later, I came back. There was the shotgun next to the door. I rang. He came out. He let me have it again. But he stopped a little sooner this time, unless it was my optimism again. I said, "I live on a 170 acre farm. Yours is over 500 acres. How do you handle it?" He just looked at me and didn't speak. I repeated my question, "How do you handle it?" He stared at me for a while. Then he told me about this cooperative that existed in the north part of the county that helped him.

What I was doing was "sailing" with the old man, not literally, but figuratively. If you sail, you know if you want to move forward, you can't sail directly into the wind. You have to sail at angles to the wind, from side to side, working your way forward. You're tacking. That's what I was doing with the farmer, not going directly at him with my demands, but moving from side to side, asking apparently unrelated questions. It takes patience and though tacking is not the shortest distance between two points, it's often a far more effective way to make progress than a direct assault.

Well, the farmer and I talked a little bit about his concerns with farming, the pressures, where he needed help, and how difficult it is to run a farm. I could understand his problems and he could tell I did. After a while, I said, "I'll see you again." That was the whole conversation on my second visit.

I came back a third time and I acknowledged some more of his concerns. I said, "I understand this farm has been in your family for four or five generations. I suppose you really would like to give it to your children." He looked at me, wondering where this was leading. I went on, "You've got three kids and I have seven. My older ones are spread all over the country. Yours are too, right?" I could tell by looking at him, I was touching on something that he felt. We were bonding, only a little, but still bonding. I asked if he thought his kids would come back and live on the farm. He said he doubted it but he still wanted to leave it to them. He said, "It belongs in our family."

That's when I started negotiations. I said, "I know you own this land, but unless you have a lot of money, you're not going to give this place to your children." He got hot. Who was I to tell him he couldn't leave his farm to his own children? I said, "I'm not your lawyer. Do you have a lawyer?" He said he did. I asked if he had talked to his lawyer about his estate. He said, "I haven't talked to him about anything for years!" I suggested he talk to his lawyer about the difficulty of giving the farm to his children. Then I changed the subject to cattle. I asked him about raising and slaughtering cattle. Shortly after, I left.

On my fourth visit, by the time I got up to the house, he was asking me questions. First, he told me the lawyer said I was right. He didn't have the cash it would take to cover the taxes. I told him I wasn't an estate lawyer and he should consult one. The lawyer, in turn, told him that since his wife was deceased, he couldn't get a marital deduction and if he gave it to his kids he'd be taxed brutally.

That's when he asked me what I'd give him for the farm. Four visits later, after being hollered at, after counting, after talking about farms and children and estate taxes, we were finally talking about a deal. Tacking was paying off.

I told him he'd be paid more than any other neighboring farmer had been paid, "You will get what's called 'most favored nations' treatment." I told him it was because he'd been through tough times and had good reason to hold back in selling. He would get paid a dollar more than the highest amount paid anyone else. His eyes lit up.

Was it enough to just give him more than anyone else? Is that the secret to winning over the difficult negotiator? Just give them a little more? No. You have to give them something else, something that acknowledges their particular concerns or needs. They want to win and the best way to get what you want is to help them get what they want. We needed to enable the old man to save face—give him a small win—so we could accomplish our big WIN.

What could we do here? He wanted to keep the farm and stay in his house. We let him. We paid him handsomely for 570 acres of his 581 acre farm. We gave him the 11 acres surrounding the house and worked around it. My client could develop and build access roads and still leave him alone. Of course, we might need to use his parcel some day but the reality was, he was 83. We leased it to him for five years with a five-year option at $1.00 a year. It was WIN—win. We liked the deal. He liked the deal. He must have because he never once picked up the shotgun.

* * * * * * * *

DEALING WITH THE DIFFICULT NEGOTIATOR (WITHOUT BECOMING ONE)

Let's take a recreation break. If you play golf or tennis and you get angry and then hit the ball, where does it go? Into the net? Into the trees? It tends to go everywhere except where you want it to go. It may feel good, for a moment, to let your frustrations out on the tennis or golf ball, but the results are usually terrible. The same holds for negotiation. It may feel good to lash out (or lash back) at the difficult negotiator, but if you do, the negotiation will likely escalate, possibly to a full-scale war. Remember, in golf, tennis, and negotiation, when you let your frustrations out, the results are usually terrible.

> *When I'm angry, I count to ten before I speak. When I'm very angry, I count to one hundred.*
>
> Thomas Jefferson

DON'T TAKE IT PERSONALLY—DON'T GET PERSONAL

Difficult negotiators' conduct may seem unfair, inflammatory, provocative, even mean. They use these emotional approaches to put you in an emotional—less rational, less measured, more

> ## A FULL COURT EMOTIONAL
> ## AND PSYCHOLOGICAL PRESS
>
> Former Chicago Bulls' coach, Phil Jackson, in a story in *INC. Magazine*, discussed teaching his players to deal with emotional and psychological attacks. Rather than succumb to the temptation to strike back emotionally or physically, he drilled them in the art of re-focusing on the game every time they were attacked. When the Bulls played the Pistons in the late 1980s—a team notorious for their outrageous tactics—Detroit often won because they could incite the Bulls into fighting back, thereby losing concentration. When Bulls learned to control their desire to strike back and turn it into focus, they changed the outcome of the games. Jackson stated, "Everybody on our team was slammed around . . . players were tackled, tripped, elbowed, and smacked in the face. But they all laughed it off. The Pistons didn't know how to respond. We completely disarmed them by not striking back. At that moment, our players became true champions."

volatile and vulnerable—state. They want you to lose focus on your game plan. If you do, you're prone to make mistakes.

BE PREPARED

The more difficult the negotiator, the more prepared you should be. Before I met with the old farmer, I used my research about him to formulate a strategy for dealing with him—multiple meetings, tacking, finding common ground. Know what to do before the situations occur and you will overcome the most difficult negotiators without reverting to becoming one of them.

TAKE A TIME-OUT

People are reaction machines. We are a mass of nerve endings, not computerized responses. Be conscious of your human tendencies and you've taken the first step toward staying calm in the face of provocation.

Don't respond to emotion with emotion. That's easy to say, not so easy to do. After all, you've just been bombarded, even if only verbally. The best way to assure you won't have an emotional response to an emotional prod, is to have no response.

SLOW DOWN

Take your time. Again, start counting. Stop the process altogether and *call a time-out.* Ask for a break. Go to the bathroom. Get coffee. Do anything that interrupts the emotional momentum. Emotion tends to build on itself. Break the chain and the emotion recedes. It's amazing how the expression, demand, or challenge that causes a visceral reflex loses its bite even 30 seconds later. It's even less upsetting after a few minutes. Write it down. That will make it even less emotional. Look at the words and the meaning. Ask yourself what the other side was *trying* to get you to do. As soon as you start to analyze it, you begin to defuse your emotions and move toward rational action.

LEARN TO TACK

As demonstrated in the story of *The Old Man and the Farm,* tacking is an invaluable negotiation tool. When sailors meet strong head winds, they tack, turning the ship at an angle to the wind, moving forward in zigs and zags, rather than confronting the force and being rebuffed. Sailors are patient. They don't have engines, only nature. But they inevitably get where they're going. To get where you want to go in negotiation, use the tools of tacking.

Tacking

1. *Understand their pressures.* Why is the difficult negotiator being difficult? Maybe the person is just plain unpleasant, one of those social misfits who doesn't like anyone and lets it show. Maybe, but chances are, there are other forces at work. Someone or something is applying pressure on them: There's an unreasonable but unseen boss in the background. They just hate this kind of task. They had a deal like this once

before and it went bad. There's a deadline looming. There are financial pressures at home.

Start tacking, by asking questions that may reveal the real reason for their behavior. Instead of attacking the deal or the deal-maker, probe into the surrounding issues. The moment you get an answer, you begin to mute the emotional fervor. You'll find yourselves discussing unpleasant bosses, the negotiation process, other deals, deadlines, and your personal lives.

2. *Acknowledge their concerns.* Once you know some of the issues or pressure points affecting the other side, continue tacking by letting them know that you have some as well. Joke about those bosses of yours. Share stories about your past deals. Commiserate on the ticking clock of deadlines. Tell them you've got bills to pay, too; who doesn't? Simply acknowledging their concerns may turn the heat down. Then you can return to the issues of the deal as people who share the same or similar concerns.

3. *Let them save face.* (This is how tacking often concludes.) Just as I did in the situation with the old man, craft solutions that the other side can justify to themselves or those they answer to. Satisfy their need to win by conceding a less significant point. Address the issues behind their issues and they can walk away with a victory or the appearance of a victory. You don't need the trappings of a win as long as you get what you came for.

Here's a tacking case in point: Fresh feelings, strong wills, and conflicting goals—a challenging negotiation. If ever there was a call for tacking, this was it.

CAL RIPKEN WANTED THREE MORE YEARS— THE OWNER WANTED TWO

Just before we were about to enter into negotiations for Cal Ripken's new contract, I had come out of a tense negotiation representing Orioles broadcaster, Jon Miller. In a short time, Jon had risen to national stature as one of the best baseball commentator's in the game, not only as the Orioles announcer but doing play-by-play for ESPN. Jon is one of those rare guys who has a feel for the game that comes through his voice and style. You hear Jon and you're at the game. At a very young age, he has joined the class of a Vin Scully, Ernie Harwell, or Harry Carray.

In a classic case of two sides seeing a situation very differently, Jon and I were simply never able to get together with the Orioles management on a new contract. While Jon wanted to stay in Baltimore, eventually he began to look outside the market. Finally, Jon accepted a very lucrative five-year contract from the San Francisco Giants and an extension on his contract as ESPN's primary play-by-play announcer. Unfortunately, what had been very cordial relations between the Orioles ownership and me, were now somewhat strained.

I hoped that, over time, relations with management would again be friendly, but we were facing an immediate challenge—the extension of Cal's five-year contract due to expire in 1997. Cal wanted a three year extension. The club stated, due to Cal's age, it only wanted to give him a two-year extension. The Orioles feared that at age 40, Cal might no longer be a premier player. We felt, due to Cal's intensive training programs, he would be a very young 40-year old. I had had some preliminary discussions with the club's general manager, Pat Gillick. Shortly thereafter, the club owner, Peter Angelos, decided to personally negotiate the Cal contract.

I met with Cal and we assessed our strategy. I told him, it may not be in his best interests for me to be front and center in these negotiations. (Sometimes the best tactic is to replace yourself.) As professional as both Mr. Angelos and I may be, if either of us, even unintentionally, let feelings from the Jon Miller incident affect Cal's negotiations, Cal could suffer for it. Peter and Cal had a good relationship and it made sense for them to discuss the contract directly.

From that point on, Cal attended a series of lunches and dinners with Peter. (Interestingly, that became a model for future negotiations such as those with Brady Anderson.) Cal and I would meet to discuss the negotiations, but when it came time for the face-to-face sessions, I remained in the background. Although we did the preparation together, it was Cal who attended the meetings, did the probing, and eventually, the proposing. Cal used his "power of nice" to achieve what might not have occurred through me.

What happened? Cal got his three-year contract. Peter Angelos got his two-year contract. It sounds impossible but creative solutions often seem that way at first. In essence, the Orioles signed Cal to a two-year contract plus a third option year. If the Orioles chose not to exercise the option for year three, then the club would make a substantial buy-out payment to Cal—$2.5 million—and therefore, only be obligated to two of the three years. Nevertheless, we felt confident that Cal's performance would remain at levels that would make it unlikely the Orioles would pay $2.5 million to *not* have him on their team.

* * * * * * * *

Some commentators thought Peter Angelos and I might allow the Miller dealings to fester and affect the Ripken contract. Instead, both us were sensible, savvy negotiators who put emotions aside. I learned long ago to compartmentalize negotiations. (It seems, so did Peter Angelos.) That was then. This is now. I asked myself one question: "What approach would get the best results for my client?" I recognized that Cal would be better served by my taking a secondary role. I didn't let my ego get in the way. Staying in the background was the best way to get the deal done.

FAST FORWARD TO 2000
THE ORIOLES GOT THREE YEARS,
CAL WANTED ONE MORE

How many years did the "Orioles' two-year/Cal's three-year" contract deal end up lasting? Three. When the end of the second year came, instead of paying Cal $2.5 million *not* to play, the Orioles' management realized he had more good playing days ahead.

The team exercised their option to pay him his full salary for a third year.

But then the inevitable question of, what about next season, arose. Despite a recurring back injury that had plagued Cal during the 2000 season, he wanted to play at least one more year. Once again, it was time to negotiate. Peter Angelos continued to link me as a cause of Jon Miller's earlier departure. Though that perception was mistaken, and though we had tried to dispel it, there was no diffusing Peter's lingering anger. Cal and I decided the best course was to remove whatever obstacle my presence might create as the link between the Angelos and Ripken camps.

Of course I was tempted to respond to critical comments by Peter Angelos that had filtered back to me, but I knew neutralizing my emotions and not taking things personally was vital to helping shape a productive negotiation strategy for Cal. After all, with Cal having turned 40 in August of 2000 and with the reality of overcoming the issue of back problems, we had enough challenges to Cal's goal of repeating his prior season's $6.3 million salary.

Unlike the last contract discussions, this time around, Cal did not want to negotiate specifics, one-on-one, with the team owner. Cal and Peter had informal talks, but we felt someone else should hammer out the details. (It seems Peter was comfortable with that approach, as well.) We shaped a strategy that utilized another agent in our group—Ira Rainess—who had worked with Cal on an array of business matters, to negotiate with the Orioles' General Manager. Our team brainstormed and charted a course behind the scenes, but minimized any friction that might have arisen from my speaking on Cal's behalf.

Ira carried out the intended strategy perfectly, employing the 3Ps, including the presentation of an initial proposal to the Orioles that left room for compromise. In the end, Cal and the Orioles agreed on an additional year, the 2001 season, at a $6.3 million salary. And by not taking negotiating tactics personally, by removing emotions, by sticking to the 3Ps, by utilizing team strategy, the door to future deals remained open.

EMOTIONAL TACTICS—
NON-EMOTIONAL RESPONSES

When the other side gets emotional, see their use of emotion for what it may well be: a negotiation ploy or tactic. It is simply a device to elicit a particular reaction from you, just as an opening low bid is meant to get you to drop your high asking price and eventually meet somewhere near the middle.

DON'T GET EMOTIONAL BACK

Emotional attacks are negotiation tactics, not personal condemnation. Don't counter emotion with emotion. Don't counter personal attacks with personal attacks. Just as the non-emotional response will neutralize the emotional ones, the impersonal approach will neutralize the personal. It takes discipline and a reminder of your purpose. Remember, the best retaliation against being called nasty names is to make the deal you want, not calling them even worse names.

> The way to avoid emotional responses is to be ready for emotional tactics.

Tactic: Anger

You've made certain proposals that cause the other side to take offense. You asked for too much. They're furious. Your proposal is unreasonable. They're outraged. They get loud and volatile. You better give in on something or they'll stay angry. They insist you make a concession in exchange for them lowering their rage.

Response: Find Out Why

Do you ignore their anger? No. You respond to it, but *not* to the emotional blackmail. What is it about your request that made them angry? Did they fully understand it? Can you put it another way or explain your reasoning better? Perhaps you can learn information from them as to *why* they're angry and what it takes to put the negotiation back on track. Respond to the anger, not the demand.

Tactic: Insulted

The other side claims to be insulted by your offer. In fact, they're so insulted, they insist you make another, more realistic offer. They're trying to get you to bid against yourself. Don't. Remember, it should be difficult, if not impossible to insult a negotiator with an offer. By definition, an offer demonstrates you are engaging in business conversation. It may be a low number; it may have tough terms; it may have out clauses, but it is no more insulting than the other side coming back with a high number, better terms, and no out clauses. This is the process of negotiation, back and forth.

Response: Learn What Wouldn't Be Insulting

If the other side says they've been insulted, ask them to tell you what kind of offer they would consider "not insulting." By doing so, they're showing what aspects of your offer were unacceptable and are, in fact, countering rather having you bid against yourself.

Tactic: Guilt

Guilt can be a powerful and effective emotion when employed by a skilled deal-maker. You should feel bad for asking for so much? Just because you have the upper hand, you've put us in a corner. How can you do this to us?

Response: Focus on the Issues

Remember, guilt is a negotiation device, just like anger. It's used to make you feel bad and soften your requests. Isolate the emotion from the issues. Focus on the issues. What would they propose back? How would they proceed with the deal? What do they see as fair? Don't feel guilt (unless you're negotiating against your mother).

Tactic: Exasperation

The other side is overwhelmed, too busy, inundated with problems. They want you to solve this one. They're under immense pressure, their world is chaos. You handle this and get back to them. This is just another negotiating ploy. They're taking themselves out of the give-and-take process necessary to making a deal. This forces you to be both sides, making concessions in anticipation of what they might want. It also allows them to come in at the last minute and reject everything you've done (since you did it without them).

Response: Understand

Tell them you understand the pressures they face. Ask if there is anything you can do to help with their immediate problems or if they'd rather wait to do this deal when things have calmed down. Sympathize with their exasperation but keep them in the process.

Tactic: False Flattery

Watch out for anyone who keeps telling you how brilliant you're doing in the negotiation. We all like to have our egos stroked. Deft negotiators will use this foible to praise us into concessions. After all, if we've gained every point all day, why not give up a minor one here and there? Some compliments are real, but beware of a flood.

Response: Re-Focus

Smile. Say thanks. And re-focus. Don't be surprised if the compliments ebb as the deal comes to a close.

> ## WHEN YOU FACE EMOTIONAL TACTICS, GET R.I.D. OF THEM
>
> - **R**ecognize the emotion as a tactic.
> - **I**dentify exactly what kind of emotion is being employed.
> - **D**eflect the emotion in order to re-focus on the issues.

CHALLENGING PERSONALITIES

Negotiators don't come in just two flavors, difficult and easy. They possess an infinite array of characteristics, in an infinite number of combinations. The one with the laid-back, easy-going style may be the most infuriating to get to commit to final terms. The one who's most boisterous may end up equally far-sighted and visionary. The impatient one may be the smartest.

Challenging personalities make challenging negotiators. The first step in getting them to make the deal your way, is recognizing the characteristics you're up against.

The Extrovert

Personality Traits. Think of Rodney Dangerfield in *Caddyshack*. Extroverts are outgoing, impulsive, and full of energy. The plus is enthusiasm. The minus is lack of focus.

Identifiers. Extroverts tend to be fashionable and stylish. They want you to notice them. They're emotional and stimulating, catalysts of conversation. Their work space is often cluttered with work and memorabilia. They enjoy spectator sports where they can let out who they're rooting for, loud and clear.

Negotiation Style. The Extrovert can't resist saying, "That reminds me of a story . . ." It might be a story that illustrates a key point in the deal and enlightens both of you. Or it could be an un-related anecdote that wanders and wastes time. The Extrovert be-lieves in bonding but can mistakenly make bonding an end in itself which makes friendships, not deals.

How Extroverts Become Challenging. They don't prepare because preparing isn't "doing." They'd rather "do." They talk instead of listen. Action is mistaken for progress. Extroverts can be infuriat-ing because you can never pin them down on details. They agree with you one day and then change their story the next. Eventu-ally, you may have trouble separating fact from fiction.

How Not to Negotiate with an Extrovert. The tendency is to just keep chasing and changing with the Extrovert. They keep telling new stories; you keep trying to adapt. Eventually, frustrated by the ever-changing deal landscape, giving in seems to be the only option.

How to Negotiate with an Extrovert. Don't attack. Don't revert to sarcasm. The worst signal you can give them is a rebuke. Let them do what they do best—extend themselves. Their surroundings are often cluttered with trophies, celebrity photos, and momen-tos. Each one is a story. Listen. Extroverts seek recognition. Give it to them. Let them know how much this deal will enhance their reputation. Then, when it comes time to deal, document. Get promises in writing. Keep the Extrovert focused by using agen-das. Also, look for the Analytic who supports the Extrovert. Often, there will be a numbers-cruncher who is part of the Extro-vert's team. Find that person and get them to focus on the details.

THE PRAGMATIC

Personality Traits. The quintessential difficult negotiator. Think of Gordon Gekko in *Wall Street,* saying "Greed is good." The Prag-matic always wants to take charge of the negotiation. Pragmatists have lists of deal points or key issues they want to tick off so they can get to the bottom-line fast. They're impatient and consider time almost as valuable as money. Time is used to make deals. The faster the deal is done, the more deals can be made. Not surprisingly, Pragmatics tend to be loners.

Identifiers. Pragmatics generally wear the uniform of business. It's simple, it's functional, most people dress similarly. Their offices are efficient, neat, organized. Their surroundings are design-neutral. Pragmatics like participatory sports. They play; they compete; they win or lose; exercise. Why cheer for a team of strangers?

Negotiation Style. They play hardball (and they throw fastballs, often at your head.) They want to win and they want you to lose. The latter is almost as important as the former. They set high goals and are intimidating, purposely.

How Pragmatics Become Challenging. They lack patience. They get bored with the process. After all, there are other deals to be made. Consequently, they may miss opportunities within the deal at hand. They abhor loss of control and sometimes revert to dictates and threats. As a result, they cause deadlocks and are rarely willing to expend the effort or time (why not go out and make another deal, instead?) to work it out.

How Not to Negotiate with a Pragmatic. Don't give in right away. Pragmatics love to watch you squirm. If you give in too easily and don't put up a fight, their appetite for confrontation won't be satisfied. They'll want more. Appeasement is not a solution.

How to Negotiate with a Pragmatic. Know what you want and be prepared to stand your ground. They want to win and they want you to lose. Let them think you've lost. Start off by aiming high. Put additional items in your proposal that you'll eventually give away. After a struggle, (perhaps just before a deadlock), give in. Let the Pragmatic declare victory while you go home with the deal you wanted.

THE ANALYTIC

Personality Traits. Think of Mr. Spock in *Star Trek*. Everything must be based on logic. Analytic negotiators are very cautious, obsessed with process more than outcome, gathering information, not skipping steps, eliminating emotion, determined that things be done "right" regardless of results. They try to take the human element out of a human process.

Identifiers. Analytics look the part, formal and conservative. Life is structure. Their desk is organized. Their files are stacked in order. Phone calls are returned. Records are kept. When it comes to free time, their hobbies are technical rather than physical. They build models, tinker with computers, collect stamps, pursuits that are finite, neat, and measurable.

Negotiation Style. They are accurate and correct, always prepared. They're slow and deliberate at the table, never moving to the next point until the one at hand is settled. They're not interested in bonding and are, therefore, not attuned to the needs of the other side. They believe that if they're methodical enough, the deal will be made.

How Analytics Become Challenging. Analytics slow the negotiation process down to give themselves time to study all available information and alternatives. You have a deadline and need approval from Corporate, but the Analytic says, "the company's regulators need just a little more time and some additional documentation." You don't have time. You don't need more documentation. You want to get the deal done. The Analytic becomes a nit-picker who stops the deal dead in its tracks. Because of their inability to things any other way, you end up in deal gridlock.

How Not to Negotiate with an Analytic. Do not try to jam the deal down the Analytic's throat. The more you push, the more they resist. Avoid "selling" your idea to the Analytic. If you talk about "dynamic opportunities" or "ground-breaking ideas" and the Analytic will just wave a yellow flag and slow you down.

How to Negotiate with an Analytic. Slow down to their pace. Do nothing unpredictable. If you're an Extrovert, you're going to put the Analytic on the defensive. Since preparation is so important to them, do your homework. Find past precedents to support your position. Use historical, time-tested, and therefore, comfortable data. Instead of trying to convert them to your principles, embrace theirs—find precedents for your position within their principles.

THE AMIABLE

Personality Traits. Think of former President Clinton when he "feels your pain." Amiables are relationship-driven. People are more important than facts. They avoid confrontation at all costs, moving slowly, eschewing quick decisions. They take a team approach, building consensus, preferring to make a deal no one hates but isn't the best over one that's better but makes some people uncomfortable.

Identifiers. Amiables look like you'd like them—casual, open, conforming. Their actions are tentative and reserved, do nothing to upset others who they wish to like them. Their work environments are personal, even homey. They invite visitors to relax, roll up their sleeves, loosen ties, and work without formality.

Negotiation Style. They believe in win–win and practice it. They're the best listeners, with built-in empathy, aiming to leave the deal with all parties feeling their needs have been met. Amiables live up to their name, wanting to come away from every negotiation with both a deal and a relationship.

How Amiables Become Challenging. Amiables are difficult to pin down in their decision-making process. Amiables want so much to be liked that they will tell you whatever you want to hear at the moment, only to change their tune when the next person expresses a different position. Eventually, negotiations break down because the Amiable is unable to make a commitment or decision.

How Not to Negotiate with an Amiable. The worst thing you can do with an Amiable is to immediately be on the attack. The Amiable may capitulate to satisfy you, but then reverse their decision as soon as the pressure is off. Do not rush the Amiable to make hasty decisions because they will not be long-lasting decisions.

How to Negotiate with an Amiable. Focus on people issues. Let the Amiable play host; be the guest. They may be reluctant, at first, to accept new ideas. Avoid impatience. Let time pass so the Amiable can build a relationship. From there, the deal will unfold.

COMBINATIONS AND PERMUTATIONS

Challenging negotiators come in all shapes, sizes, and variations. So do the means to handle them. Realize that your next difficult negotiator isn't likely to be a textbook Analytic or a classic Amiable, as we described. You're more likely to run up against a Pragmatic-Extrovert who sets an unrealistic deadline,

---

NEGOTIATING AGAINST GOD

Charlie Casserly, the general manager of the Washington Redskins was trying to sign Sean Gilbert, an extremely talented defensive lineman. Each side had put its best-and-final offer on the table. The Redskins offered $3.6 million per year. Gilbert said, he would not take less than $5 million. Neither side would give an inch. Negotiations broke down. No matter what the Redskins tried, they could not get Sean Gilbert's agent, Gus Sunseri, to even discuss reducing his demand of $5 million per year. Charlie Casserly could not understand why this figure was totally nonnegotiable. That is, until he read an AP report in the sport section. Sunseri said, "It's over money, but it's not about money. It's a spiritual thing. Sean feels he's had a revelation from God that this should be the figure" (in his contract). Now that's a challenging negotiator. Charlie ultimately decided that "no deal" was the best deal.

tries to get you to make concessions out of guilt, rejects your first proposal out of hand, and is skeptical of your deal projections. And sometimes, you'll encounter a truly unique negotiator.

Realize that in order to negotiate successfully, you'll have to employ a combination of the tools provided, customized to the particular challenging negotiator-mutants who appear opposite you. Listen to their stories, flex with their timetable, recognize guilt as a ploy and get to what's behind it, let them save face, brainstorm a menu of alternatives, offer an outside standard of projections, and be prepared to revisit and revise throughout.

R·E·F·R·E·S·H·E·R
CHAPTER 8
DIFFICULT NEGOTIATORS

Dealing with the Difficult Negotiator
Without Becoming One

- Don't take it personally. Don't get personal.
- Be prepared (for difficult negotiator); have a strategy.
- Take a time-out. Slow down, cool off.
- Learn to tack. Don't sail into the wind.
    1. *Understand their pressures.*
    2. *Acknowledge their concerns.*
    3. *Let them save face.*

Emotional Tactics	*Non-Emotional Responses*
Anger	Find out *why* they're angry
Insulted	What *wouldn't* be insulting
Guilt	Focus on issues
Exasperation	Understand
False flattery	Refocus

WHEN YOU FACE EMOTIONAL TACTICS,
GET R.I.D. OF THEM

- Recognize emotion as a tactic.
- Identify what kind of emotion is being employed.
- Deflect the emotion, refocus on issues.

Challenging Personalities

Type	Characteristics	Challenge
Extrovert	Likes to talk, tell stories	Doesn't focus on details
Pragmatic	Takes charge, in a hurry	Lacks patience, gets deadlocked
Analytic	Logical, methodical	Slow, misses deadlines
Amiable	Listener, wants to be liked	Difficult to pin down, changeable

"My people will get back to your people."

Negotiating from Weakness

You don't know what pressure is until you play for five bucks with only two bucks in your pocket.

Lee Trevino, pro golfer

What if you're negotiating with someone who has the upper hand, that is, more clout at the table? Let's say, their side has property you "must" have. Or their company is the "only" customer for your goods. Or, maybe, they know that you're "under pressure" to make a deal. How can you still be a formidable negotiator? How can you achieve your interests? How do you negotiate effectively when you're in a weak position?

PERCEIVED WEAKNESS VERSUS REAL WEAKNESS

Are you really negotiating from a weak position or is it just your perception? That's the first question you have to answer. Too often, we exaggerate our own weaknesses, assuming them to be greater than those of the other side. Don't assume the other side holds all the cards. You may have a good sense of what their strengths are, but you don't know what *they* perceive as their own weaknesses or your strengths.

ASK QUESTIONS

The best way to determine the other side's state of mind is with thoughtful inquiry. You don't have to ask, "Do you think you have me where you want me?" But you can dig into the subject by getting surrounding or ancillary information by asking:

- What other deals of a similar nature have they made?
- What brought them to you for this deal?
- What can they tell you about the background of their company or their players?
- Who are some of their references?
- What do they know about your company and/or players and what can you tell them?
- How do they see the negotiations going? Timing? Goals?

The content of their answers will tell you how they perceive their side and yours, as will their *style* of answers. For example:

- Are they arrogant? This may be an over-compensation for their own fears.
- Are they confident? Perhaps they are realistic about their own strengths. This will be helpful to you in determining your strategy.
- Are they hesitant? Maybe they are worried about your strengths or their own deficiencies.
- Are they open and friendly or closed and guarded? Again, this will tell you about their self-perception.

CONSIDER THE REAL POSSIBILITY
THAT THEY ARE AFRAID OF YOU

Both sides go into negotiations with trepidation. It's natural. You probably don't know each other. You may not trust each other. You have different, perhaps opposing interests.

Take a step back and assess your own strengths. Try to put yourself in the other party's shoes. *How would you like to deal with you?* What would be most intimidating about your position, most influential, least assailable? What do you have that would be most enviable? That's what the other side is seeing.

Now ask yourself, who has the stronger position? Or, more pointedly, does one side even have the stronger position? You may well find yourself better armed than you thought. You may be able to enter the negotiations on an even footing, or maybe with the scales tilted in your favor.

But what if, after honest evaluation, you conclude, you really are in a weaker, more vulnerable position? Then what do you do?

EXPAND THE GOALS

If you are in a weaker position, it's on the basis of the apparent goals of your negotiation: *You want to win a contract, but you have to protect your profit margin. You're a seller and you want to get a favorable price. You're a potential merger partner and you don't want to get swallowed.* You've discovered that you lack strength when these are the goals. Don't sacrifice your goals; change or expand them.

Money isn't your only goal nor is it the other side's, though it may seem so. Turn hard dollar deals into percentage of profit deals where you make more if they make more. Consider joint ventures instead of buyouts. Change the terms or timing of a purchase to make a higher (or lower) price more palatable.

Look for intangibles which may be important to the other side. If you're joining forces, whose corporate name will prevail? Who will control the press spin on the deal? Do you have other resources valuable to the other side such as customer leads or referrals?

Make the deal bigger than it is. If you're looking at a one-time deal, perhaps there are other pieces to add. Bid on multiple contracts, not just the one at hand. Sell several parcels of land. Consider joint venturing with the other side. Put renewal or option clauses in the deal, raising the potential upside for both parties. Bring in more partners for an even bigger deal.

LOCATE ALLIES

Even if you can't strengthen your position, there are several ways to strengthen your negotiating team and, in turn, bolster your position.

1. *Add to your team.* Bring in another entity, company, co-investor, buyer, or partner. You will immediately change the equation. The new player's strength could be in your area of weakness. Let's say, you're a high-quality manufacturer selling to a distribution company. They're skeptical of your ability to deliver goods to their various warehouse locations on a timely basis. So they're forcing your price down to compensate for possible late delivery. Bring in an established shipper to partner with you. Suddenly, you've changed the balance.

2. *Find an expert.* Bring in other experts to help. They will look at the deal through the eyes of their respective specialty. You'll get an accountant's view; a stock-trader's view; or a marketer's view. They may assess your vulnerabilities differently. They may bring creative solutions to the table that you have overlooked or taken for granted.

3. *Locate others similarly situated.* Rosa Parks was arrested for refusing to give up her seat to a white passenger and move to the back of the bus. There was little she, or any other individual, could do to end segregation in the South. But Martin Luther King, Jr., knew the power of numbers. Where one individual was powerless, one hundred, one thousand, or one hundred thousand individuals working together took African Americans from the status of individual weakness to a position of group strength.

When you feel weak or alone in your position, find others in a similar situation, join forces, and gain negotiation clout.

IMPROBABLE ALLIES—UNEXPECTED IMPACT

Because of my love for the game of baseball, during the Major League's labor dispute, I found myself in the role of informal mediator. It started with frequent conversations with Randy Levine, the chief negotiator for the team owners, and Don Fehr, the head of the Players Association. Both Randy and Don have extensive backgrounds in labor law. In order to decipher some of the issues raised in our conversations, I turned to law school classmates who were also experts in labor law. While it was not enough to put me on an even playing field with Randy and Don, at least the expertise of my law school friends gave me a comfortable position on the bench.

As the labor dispute continued, I was spending as much as 20 hours a week talking to various parties. The Players Association and the club owners had teams of negotiators and substantial resources. Being an informal mediator, without official designation, title, staff, or budget, I often felt weak, by comparison, as I reached out to the two sides.

In an earlier story, I told about the ill-fated meeting at the Mayflower Hotel in Washington D.C.—one of the low points of the baseball dispute. While the principals were not making settlement progress, during my time at the Mayflower, I was able to forge an alliance with Tom Reich, one of the game's most respected player agents. Following those meetings, we, in turn, connected with Randy Hendricks, Jim Bronner, Bob Gilhooley, and Tony Attanasio, other highly regarded agents who shared my strong desire for a solution to the player-owner battle. By creating this network of similarly situated parties, by working together, the six of us were able to influence the process to a greater extent than any one of us could have, working alone.

Our ad hoc confederation of allies strengthened our position but we knew, as agents, we would still be perceived as primarily representing the players' interests. To broaden and bolster our influence and credibility, we needed a partner whose interests were parallel to those of the owners. Propitiously, Aramark, one of baseball's biggest business partners, providing food, concessions, and other services to a number of teams, approached me about working on the problem. Joe Neubauer, Aramark's Chairman, not only offered profound insights and strategies, but had great respect from Don Fehr, creating another link between the players and the owners. It's no coincidence that Aramark's motto is "Unlimited partnerships." I believe it was the unlimited partnerships that we, collectively, were able to build during the labor dispute that helped us turn our negotiation weaknesses into strengths.

While the official representatives of each side continued their protracted, publicized, and frustrating negotiations, we worked quietly, cooperatively, in the background. The public didn't know of our involvement. It wasn't until the settlement was reached that our influence even came to light.

It took a federal judge's order to bring about the resumption of baseball. And then it was eight months after that order that a real settlement was finally negotiated between the players and the owners. While management's chief negotiator, Randy Levine, and players' head, Don Fehr, were the principal architects of the peace, *The New York Times* recognized the impact of our unofficial alliance: "The new labor agreement would not have been possible without the behind-the-scenes initiatives of a group of player agents."

* * * * * * * *

We each played different roles in baseball. As agents, we could be rivals, vying to sign the same player. Representing a player, we could be out to get the most money from a club for one client, which would leave less for the next agent's client. When it came to Aramark, we were even on the opposite sides of the age old labor—management spectrum. We were competitors; we were adversaries, but in this case, we had one common interest—the game. In fact, we were similarly situated. Unlikely allies can forge a strong negotiation force. When you look for allies, look beyond the obvious, to those who share the overall goal—the business or endeavor that feeds all of you. If you're successful, afterward, you can always go back to being rivals.

NEVER LET THEM SEE YOU SWEAT

You may evaluate the situation and determine, in all objectivity, that the other side possesses all the leverage. But they may not know it. They may not be as smart as you are. They may not have gone through an objective evaluation. They may assume you have strengths that don't show. There's no reason to give away your insecurity. The way you act telegraphs how you view your pluses and minuses.

> *Play the role of the sheep and you will get slaughtered.*

If you act weak, you will be treated as if you're weak. Let them know you're not as liquid as you'd like to be and they will demand more collateral. Send signals that you have pressure to close a deal regardless of cost and you certainly will pay a premium.

- *Keep talking.* A dead giveaway that you feel less than secure in your stance is cutting off or limiting communication. You're withdrawing. Withdrawal says fear, regrouping, or retreating. It's as loud a signal as yelling, "I surrender."

  Continue talking; continue negotiating. Keep finding common ground. Keep looking for common interests. Keep getting to know the other side. The other side is much less likely to extract a pound of flesh from a party they've come to know, than from a stranger.

- *Act confident.* Whether you are confident or not, act that way. That doesn't mean, act cocky. Conduct yourself with sureness, steadiness, and a sense of control. Two things will happen. You'll communicate that confidence to the other side and they will not sense vulnerability. You'll get more confident by acting confident. It's self-perpetuating. Many deals are won more on confidence than on pure merit.

THE INVENTOR AND THE INVESTOR

I represented a young man with a great imagination. He had watched athletes in competition—tennis players, ballplayers, bowlers, golfers—constantly wiping the perspiration off of their hands to better grip the racquet, bat, ball, or club. Most of us barely notice such a thing. An inventive mind sees opportunity: *People who play sports need something to keep their hands dry.* He came up with an invention to do just that, a compound that absorbed perspiration on contact. The compound was so effective, the inventor convinced a major, superstar athlete to give it his endorsement and become an investor in the company.

The problem came when the superstar's advisors grew impatient with the way business was being run. Unless they were given control of the company, they threatened to revoke the superstar's endorsement, thereby deflating the value of the company and sending it into bankruptcy, leaving the inventor with nothing.

The inventor didn't have the financial resources to fight or buy out the superstar-investor. Sure that his position was weak, the inventor panicked. I sat with him and we worked through the process of negotiating from weakness. First, we *tested the basic assumption:* Was his position really weak? Yes, on most objective measures. The success of the company was predicated on the superstar's endorsement. No endorsement—no company. It was that simple. Was the superstar-investor's position truly strong? Yes, because of the investor's deep pockets, he could buy the company out of bankruptcy and jettison of the inventor. But, did the investor and his advisors really want bankruptcy? Placing the company in bankruptcy might taint the superstar-investor's well-manicured image. That was a big risk just to take control of such a small company. Therefore, it was unlikely they'd take the fateful steps that might impair the superstar's reputation. That was, in effect, our strength and his weakness.

Next, we *searched for allies,* someone to act as a fail-safe. What if the investor's people did put the company in bankruptcy? Who might be willing to replace the investor with fresh funds? We found some interested candidates but, frankly, no one who was willing to commit. No strength here.

So, the inventor and I set out to *expand his goals.* The primary issue was control. Who would run the company, the inventor or the investor? I asked my client, "Why do you want control of the company?" He said that he saw the company as the platform from which to launch new inventions. It became apparent that my client's goal was to develop more and more inventions. To do so, he would need capital. Therefore, we expanded our goal from complete control to some control and, more importantly, additional capital.

We were determined to *never let them see us sweat.* (We sweated plenty, over our relative strengths and weaknesses, over locating other investors, and over finding ways to expand the goals. But we did it in private.) In front of the investor's people, we appeared calm. Why? Because we had thought through the process and had a plan. We never stopped talking and negotiating. We kept the lines of communication open. We didn't allow animosity to creep in because, if we were able to work out our difficulties, the inventor and superstar-investor would still be in business together, albeit in a different relationship and configuration.

By focusing on the expanded goal of financial reward, we moved *past* the issue of control. Maybe the investor's advisors could run the business better. What the inventor wanted was to be sure that if the product succeeded, he reaped the fruits of his genius. We offered them what they wanted—to run the company—in exchange for a favorable royalty deal—a financial return on each product sold. The needs of both parties were met. The weaker position of the inventor was negated.

* * * * * * * *

BRAINSTORMING

> *There's nothing more dangerous than an idea if it's the only one you have.*

Another ramification of feeling like the weaker party is that you can't see other alternatives that may be available. If you sense your vision has been clouded in that way, you can use the tool of brainstorming to help come up with creative approaches to seemingly insoluble dilemmas.

Few situations can make people feel as weak as facing a government agency. Imagine you walk into a Zoning Board meeting with a proposal to build a shopping center in a booming residential area. You unroll your plans and make your case: It's a state-of-the-art mall offering 200 stores to a community that is drastically underserved for its retail needs. You sit down. One board member says, 200 stores seems like too many. Another says, as far as he's concerned, they don't have any underserved retail needs. Another says, malls are ugly. The last member adds, shopping centers cause traffic jams. Unless you have something else to say, they're going to put it to a vote. And you're going to lose.

Talk about being in a weak position. The government officials across the table have ultimate power. They can reject your proposal dictatorially, irrationally, close-mindedly or just plain unfairly, but no matter, it's their door to slam. What do you say? How do you counter? If you're like most negotiators, you don't know. You came with your best argument. Period. And that was your first mistake.

When you're David, squaring off with Goliath, it's not a bad idea to bring more than one stone. How? In negotiation terms—brainstorm. Get a partner or two, lay out the problem, and purposely generate a vast array of solutions. Pre-empt complaints. Offer alternatives. Overcome likely objections. Demonstrate flexibility. Approach the problem differently.

After conducting a brainstorming session, you might come up with the following ideas:

- Prepare a study of the number of households in the residential area, members per household, typical shopping needs, distance currently traveled to shop, cost of travel, time away from home, and other statistics to illustrate the service the mall would provide to families.

- Present an environmental impact plan to show how the center will be sensitive to natural surroundings.

- Answer concerns about parking and traffic patterns before questions are raised.

- Offer to have a community panel for input into the structure and placement of the mall.

- Create a tie-in with local schools to display students' outstanding work in the mall courtyard.

- Show three plans, each with a different number of stores so the Board dwells on size the center should be, not whether there should be a center.

These are only examples. You could've brainstormed many more, then narrowed them down and refined the best of them. But most people don't know how to brainstorm. They think negotiation is a one-on-one contest. They think they know all the answers and the input of others would simply be distracting. In our office, we adhere to the saying, "None of us is as smart as all of us." When we face a tough situation, we follow the four rules of brainstorming:

THE FOUR RULES OF BRAINSTORMING

1. *Brainstorm in groups of four or less.* You must have two to brainstorm. Two people will have more ideas together than if they each have ideas separately and add them up. One person's ideas spark another's. However, there is a point of

diminishing ideas. Groups of more than four tend to stifle ideas. The group becomes an audience instead of participants. Judgment sets in. Status can play a part. All of these factors inhibit ideas.

2. *Don't criticize ideas. Let them flow.* A great idea can be the first words out of someone's mouth. Or the last. Let them all come out without succumbing to the temptation to evaluate, accept, or reject. Nor should anyone feel the need to apologize for an idea either before or after uttering it. Just throw it out there. If it isn't good, or even if it's awful, it could be the seed of an idea that's great. Do the sorting and sifting later.

3. *Keep at it. Creativity is more perspiration than inspiration.* Effective negotiators are creative negotiators. But many people are intimidated by the prospect of being creative. They shouldn't be. Everyone has the capacity to create ideas. It is an exercise where you force yourself to think of that which is not apparent. You impose a rule, for instance, that you must come up with 20 answers to a question that seems to have only two answers. Among those 20 are bound to be another one or two creative solutions. Volume begets creativity. Don't worry about the ideas that don't work. You only need to use those that do.

4. *Make it fun.* Like most preparation, brainstorming is not inherently fun. So, make it fun. Sometimes we brainstorm by splitting into two groups. Each side gets a packet of Post-it Notes®. The idea of the game is to write down ideas, one per note and connect all the ideas into a chain of notes. Depending on the issue, we take from five to fifteen minutes to generate ideas. People become so involved in coming up with ideas, connecting them, and trying to construct as long a chain as possible, they invariably come up with new solutions, no matter how many times we've done a problem before. Of course, some of the ideas aren't great (maybe some are even awful) but that isn't the point. Finding one or two good solutions is the goal. By making it fun, we

come up with new ideas, ideas we might never have found if we were sitting around a conference table seriously debating the merits of a problem.

Brainstorming Exercise

Try it yourself. Get a partner. Better yet, get three more people and make two teams of two each. Take five minutes to brainstorm the problem explained next.

Remember the Rules of the Game

1. One idea per note.
2. Connect the notes end-to-end to make a chain.
3. After two minutes, look over the list and put an X over what you think is the best idea you have so far.
4. Keep going, writing down more ideas, and grow the chain until your five minutes are up. The winner isn't the team with the *best* idea. It's the team with the longest chain, the *most* ideas.

The Salary Negotiation Problem

You are underpaid. (This is a fact, not just your opinion. Don't bother to prove it.) Naturally, you want a raise. You mentioned it to your boss last week. She said, "it's just not in the budget." She did say, she'd sit down and talk to you about it next week but not to get your hopes up because there is simply no money available.

> Your Brainstorming Challenge: Come up with as many alternatives to a straight dollar raise as you possibly can.

Brainstorming Results

Look over your list. Notice how you came up with good ideas and not-so-good ideas throughout the process. You didn't have all your best ideas first or last or in the middle. Some ideas grew out of others. Some took you down blind paths. Others were unexpected but creative. Many of the ideas only occurred because you had another person to play off.

Look at what you thought was your best idea in the first two minutes (the one you X'd) to see if it is still your best. Probably not. That's why we make the teams aim for quantity, not quality. Too many people decided what is their best approach and stop there. In fact, your best idea may come later and be an unexpected approach.

Here are some ideas we've seen:

Deferred income instead of salary.

Get paid the same but work fewer hours.

Get paid the same but have the company make tax deductible donation to a favorite charity.

Offer to give you child care in lieu of a raise.

Get a promotion to a higher title with the salary that accompanies that title.

Larger office.

More vacation time.

More staff support.

Enroll you in a 401(k) matching savings plan.

Provide you with an education supplement for children when they go to college.

Get a company car or other deductible benefit.

Offer profit-sharing and/or a stock option.

Incentive or performance plan for outstanding work.

Commission instead of salary.

Home office equipment to allow you to work at home.

Next time you're about to go into a negotiation session, stop. Ask yourself what's your best, strongest, most compelling idea. What will you say when and if a difficult negotiator simply dismisses your best, out of hand? Use the brainstorming exercise, in advance, to negate a weak position. During tough negotiations, when it seems that the deal will deadlock, engage the other side in a brainstorming session. Brainstorming is one of the tools you can use when trying to break a deadlock—the subject of our next chapter.

R·E·F·R·E·S·H·E·R
CHAPTER 9
NEGOTIATING FROM WEAKNESS

Perceived versus Real Weakness

- *Question*, probe, explore.
- *Learn your vulnerabilities* and theirs.

> Consider the possibility that the other side is intimidated by you.

Expand Goals

- *Money isn't the only goal*—percentage of profits, partnerships.
- *Look for intangibles*—control, influence, public relations.
- *Make the deal bigger than it is*—for both sides.

Locate Allies

- *Add to your team*—bring in partners who have strengths you lack.
- *Find an expert*—outside knowledge.
- *Locate others similarly situated*—create alliance of common interests.

Never Let Them See You Sweat

> Play the role of the sheep and you will get slaughtered.

- *Keep talking*—keep the deal going.
- *Act confident*—confidence makes more deals than clout.

Brainstorming

1. **Brainstorm in groups of four or less—small and manageable.**

2. **Don't criticize ideas. Let them flow.**

3. **Keep at it. Creativity is more perspiration than inspiration.**

4. **Make it fun—create a game of idea generation.**

*"Frankly, Dennison, this was not the merger proposal
I was expecting."*

(Mort Gerberg © 1998 from *The Cartoon Bank*. All Rights Reserved.)

Unlocking Deadlocks

IF NOTHING WORKS, CHANGE SOMETHING

Two parties have been negotiating long and hard. They've stated their respective positions, made offers, heard counteroffers, listened to each other's needs, even traded a few lesser points with each other, but finally have come down to *the* pivotal issue. It could be price or timing or terms or control. But whatever it is, neither side feels they can give any more. They're eyeball to eyeball and nobody's blinking. Now what?

Now you've reached deal gridlock. Nobody's going anywhere. How do you break it? Who moves first? Who gives without feeling like the loser? What do you do about the egos that need massaging?

As with all impasses, something has to change—almost anything—whether it's at the heart of the matter or tangential to it.

Two left-turning trucks get blocked halfway across an intersection by a crossing onslaught of bumper-to-bumper taxis. Horns blare, cabbies swear, neck veins bulge, and pedestrians can't even walk on the "walk" sign. Who's going to move? How much? When? Truckers won't; it's defeat. Cabbies won't; it's retreat. More horns, more cursing, more gridlock. Finally, a little blue subcompact, ten cars behind the cabs, inches slightly left and slightly up. The cab next to him pulls a little right and a little forward. Ten cars, one by one, angle off and creep up a little, each opening a few inches of daylight, eventually adding up to just enough of an opening at the intersection. Two truckers scowl. One turns. The other turns.

Gridlock unlocks. All because one element, not necessarily at the heart of the problem, changed. When deals deadlock, look for the little blue subcompact.

WHAT SHOULD YOU CHANGE?

Change Locations

If you've been meeting at your office, offer to go to theirs. Settings can be intimidating, stifling, stale, or negative. Being on your turf may create a sense in the other party that they've already given just by being there. In addition, either or both parties can get tired of staring at the same walls. Imaginations and energies wane. After too much time passes without progress, the negotiators may subconsciously associate the surroundings with lack of progress. *This is where we don't get anywhere each day.* Just by going to their office or a neutral site, you will change the dynamics of the negotiation. Everyone will sit in different seats. You'll each face different directions. The pictures on the walls will be new. The chairs may be more comfortable. *Moving sometimes feels like movement.* It may not be logical but attitudes shift with locales.

Change Negotiators

Maybe you're the problem. It may not be that you're negotiating poorly, but that the other party isn't hearing you anymore. (You may be guilty of the same thing in reverse.) Nerves may be on edge after too long at the table. In the heat of negotiation, things may have become personal. When emotions supersede logic, negotiators tune out the substance and let animosity set in. Progress halts.

Do what a smart basketball coach does when his team is being shut down by a man-to-man, full court press and they need one basket to change the momentum. If the players on the floor are stalled, take someone out—in this case, you—and substitute with a fresh player. Send in your partner or associate. Make sure they're briefed on the status of negotiations, but don't prejudice them as to outcome. The whole purpose of bringing in someone new is to bring in a fresh perspective.

The simple change of bodies, a new face across the table with a new style, is often enough to jump-start a stalled deal. One of the hardest moves to make is to remove yourself. But remember, it has less to do with you than with the dynamics of deal-making. It's not a failure on your part, it's a strategic move.

Call in a Mediator

This is a more dramatic version of the previous suggestion. Maybe both sides are so entrenched, so mired in the impasse, they're unable to see a way out. Then, no one from your side can bring movement to the negotiations and no one from the other side can, either. Both have become so passionate in defense of their positions they require a dispassionate participant.

Go outside of both parties to a neutral party. Mediators have to possess certain qualities beyond impartiality. They must be respected by both sides and able to maintain total confidentiality so the parties can express themselves freely. Mediators have to be expert in the negotiation process, though not necessarily in the specific business or topic. A good mediator can grasp the fundamentals of the deal well enough—mail order sales, personal services contracts, separation agreements, patent royalties—but not become so consumed by esoteric details that he or she loses sight of the broad goals of the deal, which is often what has happened to the negotiators, themselves.

The best mediators are good listeners. They assesses both positions, probe for sensitive spots, look for areas of mutual interest, and bring simple conclusions to the table. Their lack of emotional attachment to positions enables them to do what the negotiators couldn't, put the deal ahead of feelings.

We were involved in a mediation that was born of a firestorm of feelings, from name-calling to silent treatments to playing the press against each other. Two men who had to work together, professionals in their field, claimed to dislike each other with such a fervor that each called for the firing of the other. That's when we came in. (It's funny but nobody seems to call in mediators when the parties are only mildly annoyed with each other.)

STEPPING BETWEEN TWO POLICE OFFICERS— ONE WHITE, ONE BLACK, BOTH MAD

Mark and I were privileged to present a *pro bono* program to the Baltimore Police department. We worked with 30 of the leaders of the Baltimore City Police Department, up the chain of command to the very top. No matter how blasé we might have wanted to appear, we were a little intimidated. We had faced tough audiences before, from hostile NFL general managers to hard-charging Manhattan real estate barons. But when the officers walked into the seminar in full uniform, with official firearms on their hips, we realized this was not your average seminar.

At first, the officers were so conditioned by their paramilitary structure, they insisted our lessons did not apply to them. "We don't negotiate," one Colonel said, "We give orders." After a daunting start, however, they began to respond to our concept of WIN–win negotiation. They started to see how it could apply not only among their ranks but on the streets, as well. Sometimes when facing a 15-year-old, wanna-be tough-guy, talking, probing, and listening works better than a threat. By the time the session was over, the officers were thanking us profusely, telling us they were genuinely inspired to put WIN–win to work. We had really gotten through to them. Or so we thought.

A week after the seminar, the newspaper carried a big head-line declaring that two of the Police Department's top officers were locked in a very bitter, very racial, very public dispute. Both the Commissioner and the Colonel had been at the seminar. Evi-dently, they were experiencing a problem more challenging than those we'd dealt with in the seminar. Mark and I felt we had es-tablished a rapport with the two men. We called the Mayor and asked if we could be of service in trying to bring the two parties together. The Mayor took us up on our offer.

The two officers agreed to come out to my farm to discuss their differences. Their dispute had grown over time and was comprised of a collection of complex issues. Practicing what we preach, we spent a day giving ourselves a cram course in those is-sues. Naturally, we agreed to keep the specifics of those issues confidential but we can share the following matters of public record: The Colonel, when he'd been a Major, had been passed over when the Commissioner was recruited from another city to take command. However, the two men had worked together for several years, seemingly successfully. Beneath the surface, a rift had emerged between them. Small misunderstandings turned into substantial disagreements, eventually turning into major impasses. Recently, the controversy had made front page headlines such as "Racial Tension Stifles Leadership of the Police Department." The papers, looking to sensationalize and sell more papers, focused on the racial differences more than the complexity of the issues un-derlying their battle.

We completed our Preparation Planner and reviewed our in-formation just prior to the evening's negotiation. We knew both men would come with entrenched positions. We knew we would have to break a strong deadlock. By offering to mediate and by changing locations from the downtown offices of the Police De-partment to the rural setting of my farm, we were already em-ploying deadlock-breaking tools.

We waited for their arrival, wondering who would arrive first, the Commissioner or the Colonel. Much to our surprise, they came in the same car. The Commissioner was unfamiliar with the area but the Colonel knew the way. So, they'd decided to make the ride together. Two men who were at each other's throats publicly, shared a ride to the mediation session. Maybe there was hope.

We went into the house, sat down, and began to slowly approach the subject. We listened. We asked questions. Borrowing from the Middle East negotiations, I asked my wife, Cathi, to play Golda Meir and bring us cookies on a break. Like Sadat and Begin, the Commissioner and the Colonel liked cookies. (Who doesn't?) After more talk, we adjourned until the next day.

We met again. Again, we sat and talked and listened. At one point, Mark sat with one party while I sat with the other, in order to put each at ease enough to deal with the most sensitive subjects. Then we got back together. Yes, sometimes the conversation got heated. And sometimes things got too quiet. But throughout, we were impressed with the dedication that both men had to the city, the police force, and to their jobs. Slowly, we began to see a thaw. Again, without breaking any confidences, we identified areas of agreement, not just those of divergence. The tools of deadlock-breaking were working. The location had changed. The tension of one person's office, ringing phones, paperwork stacking up, watchful eyes of other officers, the rank of uniforms, were all absent. The view wasn't of teeming urban activity, but of pastoral serenity. The sounds weren't blaring car horns and sirens but quacking ducks and mooing cows. A mediator had been brought in, actually two. The pressure wasn't only on the two principles. Somebody was listening to both of them. Somebody neutral wanted a solution for the sake of the parties, not for a personal agenda.

At the end of the second day, a cautious resolution was reached. The racial aspects had been put aside and the real problems had been addressed. They had found enough common ground to find a way to try to work together. A press conference was called the following day. The deadlock was broken. As is often the case, the nitty gritty issues make almost no difference. They vary from negotiation to negotiation. It's the entrenchment that sets in after the issues that creates the impasse. And it's finding a way to change something that gets the process unstuck.

* * * * * * * *

FIND REASONS TO AGREE

This method of unlocking deadlocks is so obvious, it's the one most often overlooked. By the time you reach deadlock and get to the issue that you cannot agree on, you've undoubtedly passed by lots of issues on which you do agree. But that sticky one seems to render all the previous negotiation useless. In fact, you start to feel that the two parties don't agree on anything.

RECOUNT THE POINTS OF AGREEMENT

Was the deadline okay? Were the terms? Did both parties complete due diligence? Were your profit definitions the same or compatible? Did you concur on market value? Were the shareholding percentages acceptable? Number of offices? Employees? Benefits? Measurements of success?

In most negotiations, there are many more issues of agreement than disagreement. Unfortunately, we lose sight of them once deal paralysis sets in. All we see is the battle issue: Who gets how many board seats? Will the payment be cash or stock? Whose name goes first in the merger?

When the sticking point has you stuck, go back to the unsticky points. List every single area of agreement. This accomplishes two objectives:

1. It shows you how close you are to a deal.
2. It reminds you of why making a deal is a good idea.

GET CREATIVE

Dee Hock, the visionary leader of VISA, has said, "The problem is never how to get new, imaginative thoughts into your mind, but how to get the old ones out. Every mind is a room packed with archaic furniture. You must get the old furniture of what you know, think and believe, out before anything new can get in. Make an empty space in any corner of your mind and creativity will instantly fill it."

Deals deadlock when both sides become too attached to past positions. Six weeks ago, proposals were exchanged. They weren't set in stone then, but positions harden over time. Now, both parties are negotiating as if their original proposals were carved into holy tablets. Each side has lost the ability to use creativity to look at the situation in a new light. If you have to, clear all of the deadlocked issues off the table and start over again. Agree that without new ideas, the negotiation is over. Get creative.

WRESTLING WITH DEADLOCKS

Herb Kelleher, the unorthodox but highly successful innovator behind Southwest Airlines, lived up to his reputation when he found his company in a slogan dispute. It seems Southwest was using the phrase "Just plane smart" to describe its no-frills pricing only to discover that Stevens Aviation, an aviation sales and maintenance company was already using "Plane smart." Instead of each side's lawyers unleashing the usual barrage of letters and litigation threats, Kelleher and his counterpart, Kurt Herwald, came up with a unique solution. They'd arm-wrestle for the slogan. They created a media event around the mock-battle, charging admission, and selling souvenirs. Rather than fight over rights or compensation for use of the line, all proceeds from the publicity event went to charity. The dispute was settled. Kelleher, 61, lost to Herwald, 37, in what was obviously a set-up by the two bosses. But, in another fixed outcome, both companies got to use the line. Their companies got press and television coverage beyond their wildest dreams. Plus they saved what Kelleher estimated to be as much as $500,000 in legal costs.

As discussed earlier, the way to get new ideas is to brainstorm. But even before you start generating new ideas, follow Dee Hock's advice and get rid of that old furniture. Here are some guidelines to help you clear the attic and make room for new ideas:

1. *Start all over again.* Ronald Reagan and Mikhail Gorbachov were deadlocked in arms talks at a summit in Iceland. Both

sides had staked out their positions and neither was willing to budge. After a particularly difficult exchange, Reagan stood up, smiled, told the group they were not going to make any progress, and that they might as well start all over again. Reagan reached across the table and said, "Hello, Mikhail, my name is Ron and I think it's time we talked about the arms race." It broke the tension and got meaningful talks initiated. By "starting over," Reagan made it possible for the parties to see past their entrenched positions and be more open to new ideas.

2. *Keep a secret.* At times, negotiations deadlock because negotiators try to please third parties who aren't even at the negotiation table. The negotiator might fear reprisals if these third parties ever hear that certain taboo secrets were even discussed. Before beginning your talks, obtain an agreement that all information exchanged will be held in strict confidence. With this protection, negotiators' mental attics that are cluttered with worries over absent, third parties can be cleared out to make room for new, productive, deal-making ideas.

3. *Recount interests.* Don't talk about positions. Don't take stands. Don't mention deadlines. Focus, instead, on each side's real needs, goals to be met, hopes to be fulfilled, both short and long-term. Tell the other side, "It's my understanding that you are most interested in salon-quality hairbrushes shipped and delivered to meet your overseas customers' timetable. Am I correct in my understanding?" If the other party agrees, ask them, "What do you think are our main interests in this deal?" By focusing all parties on interests rather than positions (i.e., "We refuse to pay for shoddy hairbrushes"), you create room for new solutions to develop to whatever problems may arise.

4. *Don't stop.* When you're engaged in creative problem solving, if successful, pretty soon the hypothetical blends right into the real. You're addressing interests instead of egos; one or both of you has come up with a new approach; together, you're modifying it to work for your circumstances;

you're both finding different ways to "win." You're negotiating again. The deadlock is broken. Keep going.

I had a negotiation a several years ago that was deadlocked, dead-in-the-water, every kind of dead there is. My client was almost ready to give up. So was I. And so was the other side. Almost.

EDDIE, EDWARD, AND ONE MILLION DOLLARS

Baseball trivia quiz: Who was the fourth player in the history of Major League Baseball to sign a $1 million per year contract? *Hint:* He's one of only three players to reach both the 3000 hit and 500 home run marks. *Answer:* Eddie Clarence Murray, who is more affectionately known as "Eddie." I knew the answer because I was the agent who negotiated the contract. One million dollars may not seem like much by today's standard when players sign contracts worth $10 million per year and the average salary is approximately $1.5 million per year, but breaking the $1 million barrier was quite a feat in 1981.

Eddie Murray had already begun to demonstrate Hall of Fame abilities in the years preceding 1981. He was a Gold Glove first baseman. He could switch-hit for both average and power. He was what baseball people call, "a complete package." The year before, in 1980, Nolan Ryan, the legendary strike-out pitcher, had signed the first $1 million per year contract in baseball. Superstars Dave Winfield and Dave Parker had also joined those ranks. When it came time to negotiate Eddie's salary, we viewed their contracts as relevant precedent for Eddie Murray. We set out to achieve a five-year contract worth $1 million per year.

The new owner of the Orioles in 1980, Edward Bennett Williams, affectionately known as EBW, was a famous trial lawyer known for his courtroom savvy in defending various notorious clients. Larry Lucchino, General Counsel of the Orioles in 1980, was a law partner and protégé of EBW. It was Larry who first approached me about Eddie's contract. After a period a of negotiations with GM, Hank Peters, the Oriole offer was stuck at $600,000 per year for four years.

I told Larry we were disappointed and asked him why the Orioles were proposing only $600,000. Larry made it clear that, although the Orioles were a perennial winner on the field through the 1960s and 1970s, their attendance and television revenues lagged behind comparably performing teams. For the Orioles to remain a competitive team, stars like Eddie Murray would have to accept smaller contracts than their counterparts elsewhere in the game. The Orioles felt that they could not compete with the escalating salaries of larger market clubs and were determined to keep their payroll down. The Orioles also felt there were many players who wanted to play for a winner so much, they would accept less than they could get elsewhere.

Eddie was clearly worth $1 million per year. We knew he could get that amount from other clubs in a few years, when he became eligible for free agency. But Eddie's heart was in Baltimore. He wanted to stay, but he also wanted a contract for $1 million per year. I labored hard to demonstrate to Larry why Eddie's achievements plus the recent increase in players' incomes justified a $1 million salary. As with the Brooks Robinson contract negotiation, I had done my preparation. I had learned my lesson from dealing with Hank Peters. Rather than just spilling my guts when I negotiated with Larry, I took my time, asked questions, and listened. The negotiation went on and on, week after week. We still wanted $1 million and the Orioles refused to budge from their $600,000 offer. Larry and I had reached a deadlock.

I was frustrated that we were going nowhere and, worse, Eddie wanted to get his contract resolved so that he could focus on baseball. In order to break the deadlock, I started by using two methods previously discussed. I suggested to Larry, "It seems we have reached an impasse. Why not arrange a meeting so that we can bring EBW into the process?" I knew that Larry would want to still be involved in the process, so we could not totally *change negotiators*, but adding EBW to the other side's team served virtually the same purpose. It brought in a fresh perspective.

Next, I *changed the location* of the negotiation. While the talks, up to this point, had been conducted either at the Oriole offices in Memorial Stadium or at my law firm in Baltimore, I decided to travel to Washington, DC to meet with EBW. I wanted to put him at ease by going to him, rather than having him come to us. That way, he could still feel we were on his turf, even if we were discussing a $1 million deal.

To start the meeting, I used another deadlock-breaking technique by *summarizing all of the deal points* that Larry and I had reached agreement on previously. I did this to show good faith on our part (not attempting to revisit already agreed-to points) as well as demonstrating our willingness to work together. After my summary, EBW demonstrated his negotiating skills by probing me with the following question. "Ron," he asked, "does Eddie really need $1 million per year to survive?" It was a fair question. "No," I responded, "But remember, a ballplayer's career is much shorter than your average lawyer, doctor, or computer programmer. Eddie has relatively few years to earn his life's income. It's only fair that he try to maximize that income while he is able."

After being probed by EBW, I knew it was time to probe back. I decided to answer a question with a question. I asked EBW, "If Nolan Ryan is worth $1 million and only plays once every four or five days, do you think that Eddie, performing at an All-Star level, is worth $1 million playing every day?"

"I certainly think he is worth it," countered EBW. "It's that the Orioles just cannot afford $1 million right now." Again, practicing what we preach, I probed, "Why can't you afford $1 million right now?" EBW explained that, while he had plans to improve Orioles' attendance and television revenues by marketing the club in Washington, DC, York, Pennsylvania, as well as other cities and towns in the Mid-Atlantic region, that was an investment that wouldn't pay off overnight. "I think we'll have one of the most successful franchises in baseball, but it will take both time and money. While we're trying to transform this local team into a regional team, we need every penny we can get to bolster that marketing plan."

At that point, I knew (1) they wanted to keep Eddie and (2) they would pay him the money *if* they had it. It was time to use some creative problem solving to break the deadlock. We approached the problem from the standpoint of finding ways to increase Orioles attendance immediately, and if they could be found, exploring whether these efforts could fund Eddie's salary. Both sides agreed, it would take at least two years to see the results of this aggressive marketing effort. For Eddie to be paid $1 million per year, the Orioles had to come up with the money now.

The Orioles needed an immediate source of cash to fund the contract. Or did they? EBW's question stuck in my mind, "Does Eddie really need $1 million to live on?" As I told EBW, no, Eddie did not need the money now, but he would need it later in life, either after his performance declined or after he retired from the game. I huddled with my partners and we engaged in a *brainstorming* session. Finally, we came up with a solution often used by lawyers when negotiating a settlement to a lawsuit. Rather than paying the $1 million per year, the club could pay Eddie approximately $700,000 per year, and the remaining $300,000 would be put off, or deferred, to a later date. This was one of the earlier uses of deferred compensation in a Major League contract.

The solution was creative, as it had to be in order to fit the needs of both Eddie and EBW. Eddie now had a contract with the stated value of $1 million. He didn't need the final $300,000 immediately, so the club would owe it to him. The Orioles got what they wanted. They were obligated to pay Eddie $700,000 per year in the short term. That left money available to increase their marketing efforts.

In the end, the EBW and Larry Lucchino were visionaries. By tapping into the regional market, they were able to take Baltimore from a town that had trouble getting significantly past the one million fans in attendance, even in a playoff year, to a team that draws over 3 million a year win or lose. By the time Eddie's remaining $300,000 per year was due, there was plenty of money available.

* * * * * * * *

OBJECTIVE MECHANISMS

The single biggest roadblock to successful negotiation is people. If people weren't involved, deals would be objective. They would add up or not, deliver profits or losses, meet timetables, create cash flow or tax write-offs, result in mergers or spin-offs. Deals would be measured against absolute criteria.

But people are subjective beings, fueled by feelings, not just facts and conclusions. Humans don't have strictly objective needs in their deals; they have subjective *wants*. One negotiator *wants* to achieve the highest sale in the company's history. Another *wants* to show the other side who's stronger. Still another *wants* to make the deal that no one else could make. In fact, more deals are made because humans—with wants, drives, and other emotional motivations—are involved than if deals were determined only by cold, quantifiable measurements. But many deals are lost or stalled because of those same human factors.

When deals become too personal, negotiation runs into trouble. Logic leaves; egos enter. Once that happens, their personal success is on the line, not just the success of the deal. Ego is now bigger than the merger, the buyout, the price, the savings, the growth potential, the lease, the contract, the bid, or the bottom line. Ego is everything. The deal isn't. Which negotiator's ego will prevail?

The deal comes to a halt. Deadlock sets in. Ego vs. ego. In order to re-start the process, you need to de-personalize it. Someone has to introduce *objective mechanisms*. An objective mechanism is a standard that exists apart from one party or the other's prejudice. It is purposely nonhuman, nonemotional, unfeeling, impartial—no winners, no one to blame.

Remember, the process is negotiation, not ego-tiation.

Here are some examples of objective mechanisms to de-personalize deals:

You Cut—I Choose

This is a variation on the old parental trick to keep kids from fighting over the last piece of cake. No matter how carefully Mom tries to divide the cake evenly, when she hands one piece to Sam and the other to Samantha, one of them is sure to cry foul, "She got the bigger piece!" So, Mom hands the knife to one (Sam) to do the cutting and lets the other (Samantha) have first pick of the slices. It makes Sam try his best to cut evenly (with no one to blame) so he doesn't give Samantha (with no one to blame, either) the obvious lion's share.

Let's say, two negotiators are at a standstill. They each represent partners who must liquidate the assets of a company. Each partner wants to retain certain assets, sell others, and put the remainder up for auction. Therefore, they must first divide everything in half. But the division isn't easy. The company's assets are comprised of a variety of goods, from manufactured inventory to tooling machinery, as well as real estate, short and long-term investments, partnerships, contracts, and patents. After countless unsuccessful attempts at an equal split, one negotiator suggests that he or his partner divide the assets and the other negotiator or her partner select which half she would like. No one can complain that the other got the bigger piece of cake.

SEALED BIDS

Where "You cut–I choose" works because both parties see what's happening and nothing is hidden, the sealed bid approach works for the opposite reason. Neither party sees what the other is doing, but they both don't see equally. Each side submits a bid or a number or a date or a name, the envelopes are opened and each has agreed to accept the other's proposal.

OPEN THE ENVELOPE

I had an experience with a real estate developer and an investor where we used the sealed bid method to solve an unsolvable dilemma. The two had a falling out and the relationship simply had to come to an end. In fact, that was the last thing they agreed on. They tried to split up the total properties owned, with one taking certain parcels and the other one taking different parcels. As soon as the investor wanted a site, so did the developer. When the developer was willing to part with a piece of land, the investor was sure it was worthless.

After months of fighting over who would get which parcel, it became obvious that one had to buy the other out. But that presented its own problem. How much would one party, suspicious of the other, pay for the other's interest? Each thought the other was trying to steal the property. Neither wanted to "lose" to the other. I represented the developer who asked me to try to intercede since they were getting nowhere. My first observation was that they were right. They were getting nowhere.

I suggested they call their respective accountants, have separate meetings with them, and each determine the value of the total holdings. After that, I said, each of them should submit a sealed bid to the other with an offer to buy out the other side and own all of the properties. In other words, what would the investor pay the developer for the developer's half? What would the developer pay the investor for the investor's half?

The key rule: **The lower bidder would be bound to sell the property to the higher bidder for the latter's price.**

They agreed and each submitted a sealed offer. We opened the envelopes. My client, the developer, offered to pay $1.2 million for the investor's share. The investor offered $2 million for my client's share. The investor "won." My client was thrilled with the $2 million payment. He got more than what he thought half the property was worth so he was happy to sell. The investor ended up with all of the property for what he thought was a fair price, so he was happy to buy. Both parties benefited from taking emotion out and going to a "blind" method.

* * * * * * * *

EXTERNAL CRITERIA

When parties can't agree, maybe they shouldn't try. Sometimes they should turn to outside measures and standards.

A landlord wants to raise the tenant's rent 8 percent every year in order to cover anticipated increases in overhead, but the tenant thinks an annual increase of 4 percent is more than adequate. Maybe they should turn to external criteria such as government figures on the inflation rate. Let the rent increases follow neutral data, not the landlord's or the tenant's.

Use the Consumer Price Index, the Dow Jones Averages, Standard & Poor's, published market values, gold prices, OPEC, census data, interest rates—any information that comes from *outside* the negotiating parties and therefore stands as objective.

ARBITRATION

As the word says, it's arbitrary, meaning determined by an individual at his or her absolute discretion. Arbitration by an outside party is effective when all methods that directly involve the negotiating parties have been exhausted. An additional perspective is necessary to bring the deal to closure. Arbitrators (and mediators) are professional deal makers with no vested interest on either side. All the negotiating parties have to agree on is who the arbitrator will be. In some cases, they've decided in advance, just in case they reach a stalemate. In mediation, the opinion is a strong suggestion, not obligatory. In arbitration, the judgment generally carries more weight. In binding arbitration, the settlement is mandatory.

For instance, in sports negotiation, if an athlete and a team cannot arrive at a mutually agreeable contract, it goes to arbitration. In baseball arbitration, for instance, it's an all or nothing arbitration. The arbitrator must take either the athlete's figure or the club's figure and nothing in between.

In labor-management strikes, frequently arbitrators (lawyers, former judges, professors) are brought in because the two sides can't agree and the longer they disagree, the more damage they do to their industry.

Arbitration, particularly binding arbitration, is drastic but in true standoffs, very effective. Sometimes the mere specter of arbitration works to close deals. Both sides know that if they can't settle their deal, a third party will, and it's possible that neither of the two sides will be happy. So, they try harder to find a solution of their own.

Above all, check your ego at the door. Don't feed it. Don't indulge it. It'll be fine. Nothing is better for an ego than a successful deal.

SOMETIMES NO DEAL IS THE BEST DEAL

> *Don't let the thrill of the hunt lead you to a bad deal.*

We've all suffered from "negotiation fever" at one time or another. That's where you get so caught up in the heat of making a deal, you lose sight of the quality of the deal. If you weren't involved and you were just an observer, you'd whisper in your own ear, "Stop! It's not worth it." But it's hard to remind yourself to be objective. Some deals just aren't worth making. The trick is knowing which ones and when.

IF DEAL FEVER PERSISTS, KEEP SAYING, "NO"

How bad does a deal have to be to be worse than no deal at all? In an episode of the television show, *Ned and Stacey*, there was a scene that carried negotiation demands to absurd extremes and showed the equal absurdity of how far people will go once they're caught up in the fever of a deal.

Ned and Stacey, saddled with a money-losing muffin shop, finally find two business sharks ready to buy the property and level it for their own development. Just before the deal closes, Ned is overcome with guilt. He can't bring himself to take the shop away from the dedicated, elderly couple who lovingly run it. In order to get out of the deal, he tries to raise his demands on the buyers to their breaking point. Both sides have already settled on a price but Ned arbitrarily ups it. The buyers are so caught up in the chase, they agree. Desperate, Ned gets creative, *"I want . . . a monkey. A huge monkey."* His own partner, Stacey, looks at him in shock. But the buyers can't stop themselves. Again, they agree. Ned has to go further, *"And I want to meet Kristy McNichol."* Amazingly, the buyers acquiesce. Ned reaches for the totally absurd, *"And I want a sponge bath."* Finally, enough is enough. The buyers walk.

It may have been a sitcom, but don't think deals haven't been made with terms as ridiculous or moreso. Deal fever makes people forget they have the option of no deal.

During years of corporate law practice, I never gave a sponge bath to get a deal done, but there were a few times when I took a bath by doing a deal I simply should not have done. I'd have been better off with no deal.

Sometimes negotiators get so enthralled with the process, they lose sight of their goals. Remember, you came to the table to buy, sell, invest, sign a contract, place an order, or merge. You didn't come to buy for too high price, sell too low, invest with a lousy return, sign a punitive contract, or merge yourself into oblivion. You didn't come just to make a deal, no matter how adverse the conditions of the deal. The goal isn't the deal. The goal is the fruit of the deal. Don't pick rotten fruit.

Unfortunately, the negotiation engagement takes on a life of its own. Working out Paragraph 4 on Page 9 becomes so daunting and so challenging that, when and if it's finally agreed upon, your focus simply moves on to Paragraph 5, instead of stepping back and asking yourself if you're still heading toward the achievement of your overall objectives. That's how bad deals get done.

The best deals occur when you remain emotionally detached (much easier said, than done) from the result. If you could really not care about closing the deal, and assume another deal will always come along, you'd probably make better deals everytime. Recognizing that detachment is hard if not impossible to impose as a self-discipline, you can employ the tools we've already explained to take ego, pride, fear, anxiety, greed, revenge, and other common deal-related emotions out.

But, perhaps the best way to make a good deal, is to remind yourself throughout, that "no deal" is a viable, reasonable option.

When Is No Deal the Best Option?

- *When the other side forces you below your bottom line.* If you've prepared before sitting down, you know your starting point for a deal and you know your ending point, the level, price, timing, terms, or whatever, below which you cannot go. This is the point past which you not only don't want to go, but literally can't. That's why it's called the bottom line. Any lower and the deal no longer pays out, has a return, works, or makes sense for your side. Don't get sucked into going below that point and convincing yourself that somehow circumstances will change and maybe it will still work out. If it didn't work out in your calm calculations before you sat down, it surely won't work out when you've signed under duress. Stop.

- *When you have better alternatives than the one proposed.* Never stop evaluating the quality of the deal. Remind yourself, at given junctures (every two hours or every two days depending on the length of the negotiations) to look at the big picture. How good is the deal that's on the table? Is it good by absolute standards or merely as good as it's going to get with the other party? What else can you do? Where else can you go? If you know there's another buyer, seller, landlord, tenant, supplier, shipper, or partner with whom you can make a better deal, don't get drawn into a lesser deal just because it's the one at hand. Stop.

- *When you're confident the other side cannot abide by the terms of the deal.* Don't think you're the only one who can get seduced into making a deal just because it's the one on the table. The other side is just as susceptible to temptation. In fact, in their quest to make the deal, they may agree to specifics they can't meet. They might wish themselves into a price they cannot afford, dream themselves into an overly ambitious profit, or just plan to get lucky enough to meet an unrealistic timetable. Again, you have to step back and take a reality check. Can they really do what they say? Can they deliver? Or will you spend as much time and effort enforcing the deal as you have in making it? If the answer is "yes" or even "maybe," don't make it. Stop.

- *When long-term problems can outweigh short-term gains.* Either side may be guilty of falling for "instant gratification" instead of eventual satisfaction. It happens with deals just as it happens when you down that fudge brownie sundae because it's in front of you and hate yourself in the morning when you get on the scale. You may opt to partner with an investor you don't really trust because together, you and

Mr. Slippery, can land a contract you couldn't otherwise get. However, after the contract has come and gone, you're now the partner in Slippery & Partners. Or you agree to deliver your No-Stick Zippers to Global Trousers, Inc. on a 52 week-a-year schedule that will practically kill your drivers, just so you can beat out your arch rival, Slick-Zip. Okay. You got the deal. Slick-Zip loses. But, now you have to deliver. And deliver. And deliver. Who really got stuck? Before you make a deal right now, take a break and force yourself to look at the future. If tomorrow doesn't look as good as today, don't sign. Stop.

ANOTHER $10 GAME

Since we rarely give away $10 when we play the $10 Game, we often give our seminar participants a second chance, at the end of the day, to win the money. We tell the participants we're going to "auction off" $10 to the highest bidder. We then tell them that the only rule is, the top two bidders must pay us the full amount of their last bid.

At that point, the bidding starts. Most people are cautious at first, but pretty soon, someone says, "Okay, I'll bid one dollar," (since I can get $10 back). We look for the second bidder, asking, "Does anyone offer $2? You can make $8 with a winning bid of $2." Another person inevitably joins in and the horse race is on. We turn back to the first bidder. "You don't want to lose do you? Bid $3 and you still end up making $7." After the first bidder raises the bid to $3, the second bidder goes up to $4, and, in no time, one of the two has bid $9. This is where it gets interesting.

Now we tell the other bidder, "You can bid $10 and break even. If you don't bid $10 and you come in second, then you still have to pay us the amount of your last bid which was $8." That bidder usually ups to $10, as a defense. Then we tell the $9 bidder, "Right now you're the losing bidder and you have to pay us $9 as your last bid. Of course, if you bid $11, you will win the $10 and only end up $1 in the hole." Suddenly the bidding escalates *beyond* the value of the prize, just to avoid losing. On occasion, the bidding has escalated past $20 before we stop the auction. (No, we don't make the bidders really pay us.)

If we had asked the people, before we began the exercise, if they would bid $20 to win a $10 bill, they would have said, "Absolutely not." But once they get caught up in the competitive atmosphere—once they seek to "cut their losses" by bidding more—the participants begin acting irrationally and making bad deals.

Although not as stark an example as the exercise, the same kind of irrational behavior sometimes takes over in corporate deals.

ECONOMIES OF SCALE VERSUS DEAL FEVER

Mark and I were hired to consult with a corporation which was acquiring various medical practices, which, as a consolidated entity, would benefit from economies of scale. As a part of our preparation, we worked with an accounting firm to establish a precise formula for setting prices to pay for each practice. The formula took into account revenues, number of physicians and employees, all relevant business factors. What the formula did *not* take into account was the Founder's "acquire at all costs" state-of-mind, once the negotiation or "bidding" process began.

It was a $10 auction atmosphere except for the decimal point. The medical practice auction was in increments of millions of dollars. Time and again when the bidding got out of hand, we would tell the Founder, "Walk away from this one. No deal is the best deal." The Founder was unswayable. The carefully determined price formula was disregarded because of the Founder's irrational acquisition frenzy.

The Founder had raised $20 million, projected to acquire 10 medical practices. Because the bidding got out of hand, the money ran out after the purchase of only 5 practices. As a result, those efficiencies and economies of scale of the consolidated practice were severely diminished. Several years later, I talked to the Founder and he told me that he learned from his mistake. "I let my emotions over-rule our planning and lost sight of the big picture."

* * * * * * * *

Not only is "no deal" sometimes the best deal, but as demonstrated by the story of "The Pizza Sauce Salesman," at times it may lead to a better deal.

WHEN PIZZA HUT SLICED THE PRICE
OF TOMATO SAUCE

I was on a plane recently, woke up from my nap, and discovered I was traveling next to a tomato sauce apostle. This fellow was the director of National Accounts for Hunt Wesson, a division of Con Agra and the makers of Hunt's Tomato Sauce. You may think sauce is sauce. Wrong. He believed in his product. He lovingly and painstakingly told me about the tomatoes, the spices, the recipe, the care, jarring, the shipping, the quality control. He told me more than I really needed to know since I had no plans to compete in the business.

But, as I often do, I asked about recent deals or negotiations. He said he'd just been through one of the biggest of his career. It seems that Hunt's was one of the largest of six tomato sauce suppliers to Pizza Hut, providing the sauce for 30 percent of all their pizzas (which is a lot of pizzas). He swore that his sauce is so good, you could tell, just by tasting a Pizza Hut pizza, if it was made with Hunt's or not, which is to say, Pizza Hut was a satisfied customer.

Nonetheless, one day he got a call from the purchasing agent at the pizza chain. She informed him the company had decided to put the sauce contract out for bid to all six suppliers and select the two best bidders to divide the entire business.

I asked him how he felt given the quality of his product and his long-standing relationship with the customer. He said, he just took it as another bid on another contract, another negotiation. He followed the disciplines he always followed.

First, he called his team together. He elicited opinions from the quality control people, the production people, the sales department, and, of course, the financial people. They reanalyzed their current pricing structure at current order levels and then reanalyzed what they could offer given the possible increase in order level. They did a form of a preparation plan. Then they arrived at a bottom-line financial analysis to determine how far they could reduce their price, while maintaining a reasonable profit margin, and without any sacrifice of product quality—their lowest, best number. That was the number they had to write down on a piece of paper. They didn't think they even had the usual opportunity of making an offer, getting a counteroffer, then countering the counter. They had been told, submit your final bid first.

So, they did just that. But they also submitted a value analysis along with the price. They reminded Pizza Hut of why dealing with Hunt Wesson is worthwhile. Quality is assured and guaranteed. There's virtually an unlimited supply of product. If you suddenly need more, you can get it. Should there be a service or delivery question, Hunt Wesson has distribution centers dotted across the country. They sent in the document and the price and they waited.

Ten days later, he got a call from the purchasing agent. Since she worked on practically a daily basis with each supplier, she knew each of their bids even though the bids had not been formally opened yet. Before that happens, she told the Hunt Wesson man, "you should submit a new bid." He asked, why. She said, "We agree, your product and service are excellent, and we want to continue doing business with your company, but you're 2½ cents a barrel too high. You're going to finish third."

I said, "Boy, what a break. So, you lowered your bid and got the contract, right?" "No," he said, "we didn't change our bid at all." They re-grouped, thought about it, reviewed their analysis, and decided they'd come to the right conclusion in the first place. He called the purchasing agent and reiterated their quality story, reminded her of the long-term relationship, and explained that their bid was the lowest possible number at which they could make a reasonable profit. He even apologized to her for not being able to go lower.

A few days later, he got another call from her. As she had predicted, Hunt Wesson had finished third. She discussed a winddown period of two and a half months, after which the relationship would end.

Did he let her have it? Did he tell her what a huge mistake she'd just made? No. He shifted back into "sales-mode." He thanked her for being a good customer and wished her the best. He offered to help out as much as possible during the wind-down. Why? Because he knew something, anything, could happen down the line, and she and/or Pizza Hut might once again become a customer. Not long after that, he wrote a letter to her and her boss, the executive vice president, thanking Pizza Hut for a great relationship and wishing them well.

The best deal was no deal. The man from Hunt Wesson didn't take it personally. He took it as business. He had analyzed the situation in his preparation plan. He knew his bottom-line. He didn't go below it. He even developed alternatives. He knew it wouldn't be easy to replace a customer as large as Pizza Hut, but he saw a growing chain on the horizon called Macaroni Grill. They would be his first call should the Pizza Hut negotiation fall through. He weighed the short-term victory against the long-term burdens. He resisted today's deal for tomorrow's profit squeeze. In the end, he didn't make a deal just for the sake of making it.

Is that the end of the story? Not quite. Remember, he kept the relationship intact even as it was winding down. About six weeks after that, he got a call from his old customer, the Pizza Hut purchasing agent. She had a crisis: Runny pizza. (Evidently, one of the supplier's sauces wasn't worthy of their dough.) That may not seem like a tragedy to you, but you don't have Domino's and Little Caesars breathing pepperoni in hot pursuit of your customers. Suddenly, Pizza Hut had to turn to their best source, not their cheapest. She told the Hunt Wesson man, Pizza Hut would give his company the lion's share of their business and he could virtually name his price.

What a turn-about! I asked him how much he raised his price. He said, "It was a good price when we bid and it was still a good price." In fact, all they did was adjust slightly to cover the costs of short-term delivery demands. Hunt Wesson went from 30 percent of the sauce business to 70 percent. In this case, no deal turned into a bigger deal.

R·E·F·R·E·S·H·E·R
CHAPTER 10
UNLOCKING DEADLOCKS

If Nothing Works, Change Something—
(Moving Sometimes Feels like Movement)

- Change location.
- Change negotiators.
- Call in a mediator.

Find Reasons to Agree

Recount the points of agreement—two benefits:

1. Shows both parties how close you are.
2. Reminds both parties why the deal is a good idea.

Get Creative

1. *Start all over again.* If you're stuck, start fresh.
2. *Keep a secret.* Confidentiality minimizes worry about what third party would think, allows room for new ideas.
3. *Recount interests.* Don't talk positions, talk real interests.
4. *Don't stop.* Keep talking, go from hypothetical to real.

Objective Mechanisms

Remember, the process is ne-gotiation, not ego-tiation.

- *You cut–I choose:* the kids method.
- *Sealed bids:* fair and honest.
- *External criteria:* for example, government, industry data.
- *Arbitration:* neutral outsider.

When No Deal Is the Best Deal

When other side forces you below your bottom line.

When you have better alternatives than the one proposed.

When the other side can't abide by terms of the deal.

When long-term problems outweigh short-term gains.

"Guess who took over the company?"

Building Relationships

11

TODAY VERSUS TOMORROW: HOW LONG IS THE LONG RUN?

Who is the real deal maker: (a) The hit-and-run Hollywood producer who scores a fast profit on a script he options on Tuesday and resells to another studio on Thursday? or (b) The development executive who, instead of turning a fast buck, invests in a writer-director's idea, gathers funding, puts together a crew and stars, negotiates foreign cable, and video rights, and has an option on the writer-director's next two ideas, as well? The answer is, both. One is in it for the moment (the deal on the table) while the other is counting on the future (all the deals that may emanate from the deal on the table). Neither is right or wrong. But even if you successfully make several one-time deals, you have to start over each time.

If you pursue deals that have the potential to lead to more deals, your *return-on-effort* will pay out longer with larger rewards. Studies by Bain and Company, a Boston-based consulting firm, have suggested that a 5 percent increase in customer retention rate could double profits of a small to midsized business. Bain also found that the average Fortune 500 company could double its revenue growth rate with that same 5 percent increase in customer retention.

If you deal as if there's no tomorrow—classic win–lose—your deals won't lead to more deals. If you burn bridges, destroy the other side, squeeze the last buck out, "take no prisoners," you can't expect the other party to want to do business with you again. They'll run from the negotiating table, let alone consider returning to it. That's why so many hit-and-run negotiators have conveniently adopted the philosophy that each deal is a one-time event. Go in, score, get out.

FROM THE PENNANT IN 1979 TO THE WORLD SERIES IN 1983 (WITH HELP FROM THE POWER OF NICE)

The Orioles fell one game short of winning the World Series in 1979. It was a team that had all the makings of a World Series winner, if the players could be kept together. But keeping a team of that caliber together during the dawning of free agency was a real challenge. Hometown heroes were leaving daily for big bucks in other markets. It so happened, in the rarest of situations, I represented 15 members of that team. We had negotiated very hard for every one of them, but we and our clients, also tried to understand the other side, the team.

So, when it came time to renegotiate contracts, how many of the players opted to leave Baltimore for greener pastures? How many did the Orioles decide just weren't worth the price? None. Eddie Murray, Ken Singleton, Rich Dauer, Scott McGregor, Doug DeCinces, Rick Dempsey, Dennis Martinez, among others, all stayed. They each achieved WIN–win. They stayed with the team and in the town they wanted and got paid market or near-market value. That was and is, unprecedented in modern sports. It wasn't because one side caved into the other. It was because bonds had been made, relationships had been built and deals had been made that lead to more deals.

In 1983, the heart of the team was there and that team won the World Series. It was a long-term dividend of the Power of Nice.

On the other hand, if you follow the principles of WIN–win—if you set out to get most of what you want by helping the other side get some of what they want —you'll build relationships that can spawn additional deals, ad infinitum. That's getting the highest return on effort. That's getting the most from *The Power of Nice.*

RELATIONSHIPS START WITH BONDING

Every negotiation takes place in an environment. That doesn't just mean the physical setting, the conference room, or the office. It means the feelings, sensitivities, tensions, fears, and hopes that comprise the atmosphere of the negotiation. They make up the environment as much, or moreso, than the four walls, table, and chairs. *Bonding*—finding what you have in common with the other party, rather than where you're at odds—can create a more positive negotiating environment.

Just as negotiation is a process, not an event, so is bonding. Bonds are built. You find a link that leads to conversation, that leads to another link. Pretty soon, you have a chain that stretches from one party to the other, like a bridge. The more you travel it, the more familiar you become. After enough travel, you don't just have a bond, you have a shared set of experiences—a relationship.

When you reach an impasse with someone you don't like or simply don't know, you're more likely to let the impasse stand. When the same situation occurs with someone whom you've come to know, understand, and even like, you're going to look for ways to get past the deadlock. It's just human nature. A good negotiating environment can carry you past bad negotiating moments.

The value of relationships is immeasurable. Ask a manufacturer who's been under the gun to deliver and who called on the supplier they can always count on. Ask the giant developer who gets three bids on every set of drawings but one bid is always from the builder that took a chance on his company when it was starting up. Ask the stockbroker whose clients swear her word is the Dow Jones gospel.

Relationships can accomplish what acquaintances can't. Relationships make for not just one deal, but deals that lead to deals, repeated deals, sub-deals, off-shoot deals, renewing deals. Why make a deal when you can make several?

THE MEET-AND-BOND STYLE

The opposite of the hit-and-run style is *meet-and-bond*. When you encounter the party with whom you'll be negotiating and, instead of focusing on your differences, look for connectors, you are bonding. Purposely search for things you may have in common, shared interests. After all, you already have a pretty good idea of where the two of you will be opposed. Whatever your asking price, they're likely to want a lower one. If you want cash terms, chances are good, they'll want to stretch out the payments. The deal itself is bound to be full of push and pull. To minimize animosity and to appreciate each of your points of view, it helps to see each other as people, not just positions.

Bonding is finding links between two parties. The link may be familial, social, business, political, or recreational. It's anything you and the other person share, from the most common such as both having young children, to the most specific, such as being collectors of vintage French wines. The bonds you discover may have to do with the deal directly, indirectly, or seemingly, not at all. Both of you may have been charged by your respective CEOs to come back with deals that will impress the board of directors, not cost much, have low risk, and high return—all goals in which you can sympathize with each other's pressures. The bond may appear to have nothing to do with the deal and yet everything to do with getting it done. Perhaps you both do have young children and you've both promised your families a vacation *if* you can get the deal done by spring break. In either case, if you don't bond, you'll never know.

START THE BONDING PROCESS

Gather Information

Remember the Prepare phase of negotiation? Before you actually meet with the other side, look back at the research you did on them. Chances are, within that data are cues about the background, interests, and habits of the person or people you're facing. Chances are, you have something in common. When you do come face to face, you already have a base of bonding information on which to build.

Observe

Bonding clues will be all around you. If you meet in the other side's office, look at what's on the desk, floor, and walls: vacation pictures, inspirational quotations, those yarn-wrapped pencil holders made by a kid in arts and crafts, running shoes tucked under a credenza, a paperweight made from a sailboat pulley, college degrees, honorary certificates, fraternity mugs, celebrity photos, family pictures, a doubles team trophy. If you meet in neutral territory, study the other person: style of dress—conservative or bold, jewelry—lots, little, flashy, or antique, shoes—Italian, sensible, or beat-up boaters, college ring, diver's watch, body type—jock or couch potato.

Talk

Ask questions. Make the first gesture. Bonding is the difference between *"Hello, here are my five key issues. What are yours?"* and *"Hi. Judging by your tan line that ends where a glove would go, I'd say you're a golfer. Me, too."*

Use the cues and clues you observe to start the conversation that creates bonds:

> "I have a pencil holder like that only mine is in green and orange yarn. How old is your artist?"
>
> "What island are you on in this photo? I'm looking for a getaway this winter."
>
> "Is that President Bush in that picture with you?"
>
> "I couldn't help but notice your watch. Do you scuba dive?"

Once you make the gesture of building the bond, it's likely to build on itself. Ask about a vacation, a child, a college, or a hobby, and you'll get a response. After all, the other person put that picture on their office wall because it's a favorite. You're asking them to tell you about something they like. If you have similar interests, you two may not be arch rivals after all. You may be two people who could be friends and happen to have a job to do. You now have something negotiators need but rarely recognize, empathy. You understand the other person and their personal interests, and they, yours. Once you do, you're both bound to be more open to understanding each other's interests in the deal.

It's easier for strangers to practice win–lose negotiation. Once you've bonded, you have a better chance to achieve WIN–win results.

Here's a bond I built at the eleventh hour, just in time to turn the deal around.

SCHOOL TIES

I had been working long and hard on a deal to get multimillion dollar funding for a biotech project. We had found our investor. We had a commitment for the money. We had gotten to the last step, drafting of the contract. At that point, the chairman of the board of the investing company told me to deal directly with their lawyer. "You're a lawyer. He's a lawyer. You two get it done."

It sounded good to me. After all, the hard part was done. We had the funding committed. Then I got the first draft of the contract. It was 95 pages. I got on the phone with the lawyer. We talked about the preambles for almost three hours. That was not the first real page of substance, just the "whereas" clauses that precede the substance. He was rock-hard, immovable, mechanical, and anything but human. Three hours later, I knew his position. He knew ours. We had gotten nowhere.

I hung up and sat there thinking. I have to find a way to bond with this guy. *If there's a way.* There's bound to be a way. *Maybe not this time.* Everybody has something. *Maybe not this guy.*

We had another telephone call scheduled for the next day. Instead, I got up early and drove two hours to Philadelphia to meet with him face to face. I figured, if we're going to bond, we're going to do it in person.

I walked into his office and it was as if the connection between us jumped off his wall. There was a framed diploma from a small, Eastern college. It just so happened to be the same small, Eastern college from which I had graduated. I said, "You went to Haverford?" He said, "Yes, I did. Where did you go to school?" I said, "Haverford." There we were, two Haverford grads. We'd had nothing in common the day before and today we had four years in common.

I enjoyed my years at Haverford, but it wasn't my whole life. It was his. He lived not far away, so he could visit often, support the school, and he could volunteer. He was involved with the Alumni Association and annual giving. He asked for my donation on the spot. I gave. The hard, immovable, mechanical, anything but human lawyer was human when it came to his alma mater. He even smiled when he said, "Haverford."

We finished the negotiation in less than a week. Bonding didn't change the basic issues. It changed the tone with which we approached the issues. It enabled us to find solutions to problems.

* * * * * * * *

REBONDING

Bonds are like muscles. If you don't keep them active, they weaken. Often people do a great job of bonding right up to the time they close the deal. Once the deal is done and the check has cleared, many people forget the power of bonding. Several years later, when it's time to renew the contract, the customer can't tell the incumbent vendor from the rest of the competition. Bonding was allowed to disintegrate—relationship was not established.

Even long-term relationships need to rebond from time to time. Remember, "It's not the sale, it's the relationship that counts." We make it a practice to keep track of the people with whom we negotiate during the times when we aren't negotiating. A phone call to say, hello. A holiday card. A congratulations on a promotion. There are countless, simple and sincere ways to bond once the relationship has been established.

When negotiations break down, or appear that they might, look for opportunities to rebond. Get away from the negotiation table. Do something social. Bring in new parties, spouses, other partners, people who share personal interests, not just business interests. Of course, the best approach is to keep bonds active and they will be strong when you need them most.

Here's a situation where I literally went out of my way to rebond with the other party.

DOUBLE DELIGHT

For several years, there was a general manager of a club located in the Midwest with whom I'd had dealings from time to time. However, to say we had any kind of relationship would go beyond the bounds of exaggeration. I knew where his office was. He had my phone number in his rolodex. That was the extent of our rapport. He had a reputation as a pretty cool customer and he was living up to it.

I figured it was time to build a relationship. Did this just occur to me like a bolt out of the blue? Hardly. I had an ulterior motive. Someday, perhaps soon, I was going to have a major transaction with him. When "someday" came, and it always does, I didn't want to deal with an adversary or a stranger. I wanted to deal with someone I already knew, someone I could talk to, someone with whom I shared something other than a contract we would be shoving back and forth at each other.

So, even though, at that moment, we had absolutely nothing to negotiate, I decided to go see him. Like everyone else in business, the one thing I don't have to spare, is time. But I knew this was an investment worth making. To use my time as economically as possible, when my next trip to the West Coast came up, I booked a stop in his city.

I called the general manager and asked to see him. I flew out, got in a cab, went to the stadium and showed up for my appointment with nothing on my agenda. Why did I have to be there in person? Why didn't I do it over the phone? Because I wanted to see him, see him in his habitat, see him when he talked to me, see how he talked, when he smiled, if he smiled.

I wanted him to see me, as well. I wanted to meet face to face. You can't do that over the phone, in an e-mail, or by fax. But once you have done it in person, phone calls and faxes can be much more effective.

I walked into his office. I looked around. I was searching for links, human connectives between him, the cool general manager and me, the client advocate. I scanned the room and saw: Autographed baseballs. Baseball books. Game day programs. A team jersey. A couple of team hats. Photos of him with players, past and present. Photos of him with the team owner. Endless baseball paraphernalia. Basically, I disregarded all the baseball-related items in the room. We'd known each through baseball and so far, had never really bonded that way. It wasn't as if he grew up in my hometown of Philadelphia and we shared fond memories of watching the Phillies from the bleachers. We hadn't each played minor league baseball, collected baseball cards, or had the same baseball heroes. Baseball was business.

So, I looked further: More photos. Pictures of his family. Pictures of his wife. Pictures of his children. I stopped. I have kids. I love kids. That's a link. But, lots of people have kids. Some people are close to theirs, some aren't. Some people are proud, some aren't.

Then I noticed two more photos, one on either side of a family shot. Pretty prominent placement, I thought. Only these weren't pictures of children or even pets. These were roses. A light bulb went on in my head. This man has pictures of roses on his desk in front of him all day long. He loves roses.

I said, "That's the most beautiful Double Delight I've ever seen." He looked at me and said, "How'd you know it was a Double Delight?" I said, "Do you grow roses?" He said, "Yeah, I grow roses. Do you?" I said, "Yeah." We both grew roses! That was our link. Outside of baseball, it's his passion. And it's mine, too.

For the next hour and a half, we discussed organic fungicides, pesticides—pro and con—weather, colors, varieties, how many leaves to cut under to make them regenerate. We traded problems and we swapped secrets. We didn't talk baseball or business but the whole tenor of our relationship changed then and there.

I called him during the winter when it got unseasonably warm and asked him what he does when that happens. He did the same with me during a cold snap. We talked about special diseases that threaten roses, particularly in the East. He told me, if he was in Baltimore to see a game, he wanted to see my rose garden.

When "someday" came and it was time for us to make a deal, we knew each other. That doesn't mean he collapsed and gave in to every request I made. Or that I acquiesced to his demands. It means we listened and talked and heard each other. It means hurdles didn't turn into stonewalls.

Did we become friends? Yes. Is he my best friend in the world? No. But we've bonded. We're two parties who negotiate as people, not just positions. As a result, we make better deals, and I stress, *deals*, plural, not singular. Because just as "someday" always comes, so does the day after, and the deal that goes with it.

* * * * * * * *

NO FAUX BONDING

There's a very important point to make about bonding. It's not a ploy. It's real. You can't pretend to share something with the other person. First of all, it's likely to blow up in your face. If you don't really love Persian cats, don't know the first thing about Greek cooking, or never hiked the north face of the Rockies, you're bound to give yourself away. Secondly, the whole idea of bonding is to genuinely invest in the relationship. Find the link, don't fake it.

There's a sequence in the movie, *Used Cars,* where a salesman attempts to bond with every customer. It goes something like this: A shopper walks onto the lot and the salesman strides over, sticks his hand out and says, "What's your name?" The innocent shopper says, "Mr. Polanski. I'm looking for a Buick." The salesman breaks into a mile-wide smile and says, "Really? My name is Kowalski and I sell Buicks." Wow! They're both Polish. Who says you can't trust a used car salesman? Coincidentally, when the next customer is Swedish, Spanish, Irish, Scottish, or Jewish, the salesman will be whatever "ish" is called for.

Don't pretend to be what you aren't, like what you don't like, or play what you don't play. Look for the real link. Look for the true common interest. And, if you don't do it early in the negotiation, which is better, do it late, which is better than never.

THREE BONDING RULES TO KEEP IN MIND

1. *Meet face to face.* You can't bond with a stranger.
2. *Go to their turf.* You can learn more about someone in his or her own lair than in neutral territory. Don't be afraid to play an away game. On their own terrain, they'll be comfortable, just comfortable enough to let you see them, know them, connect with them.
3. *If negotiation breaks down, rebond.* Have another bonding session. Get away from the negotiation table. Do something social. Bring in new parties, spouses, other partners, people who share your interests, not your business.

PRACTICE MAKES BONDING

A participant in one of our seminars came up to us during a break to talk to Mark. She was in business in the United States, but wasn't American, and most of her customers were younger. She was older and she was Spanish. Therefore, she didn't know American television shows or movies, didn't follow American sports, couldn't share growing up stories, had no family here, and had no connection with any of her customers except business. She asked how she could bond with customers with virtually no links available. Mark and she engaged in a bonding exercise right then and there.

BINGO! WE BONDED!

I said to her, "You're from Spain?"

She said, "Yes."

I asked her, "What part?"

She replied, "Barcelona."

I said, "I love Barcelona."

Interested, she said, "You've been there?" Right away, she softened. I liked her hometown.

I explained, "Yes, after I graduated from law school, I traveled all around Europe. I spent three days in Barcelona. It's a beautiful city."

As soon as I said it was beautiful, she got a nostalgic look in her eyes. "Ah, yes, I grew up there. It's so beautiful." We appreciated the same things.

I asked her, "What do you remember doing there when you were growing up?"

"Well," she said, a little sheepish but willing to share this with a fellow Barcelona-lover, "One of my fondest memories is playing bingo."

I smiled knowingly.

She went on, "They had bingo parlors everywhere. You see, after the regime fell, the government allowed the bingo parlors that had been closed, to re-open. My mother used to take me to play bingo when I was a little girl." I could just see her re-living those times with her mother.

She had me thinking back at that moment, too. I said, "You know, you may not believe this but here, in Baltimore, my mother used to take me to play bingo all the time at the local Catholic schools. They all had bingo parlors to raise money for the parish. My mother took me, too."

She smiled at me. Memories of bingo in Barcelona. Memories of bingo in Baltimore. Bingo, we had bonded.

* * * * * * * *

A BONDING EXERCISE

First, pick a bonding partner.

It can be anyone you *don't* know, a stranger. *A worker in your office from another department, number 63 when you're number 62 at the deli counter, somebody else in the dentist's waiting room, the passenger next to you on a plane.*

Next, observe.

Check out your co-bonder. Look for cues. *What's she reading? How is he dressed? What's in the shopping bag? Short hair or long? Manicured nails. Serious face or ready smile? Looking at her watch. In a hurry? Carrying a briefcase. Wearing a pager. Pens in pocket. Something in his contact lens.*

Now, find a link.

The magazine article on fishing. You fish, too. Nice necktie. What time is it? I had a beeper, switched to a cellphone. What'd you get at the outlet stores? Need any contact solution?

Add links to your links.

Keep going until it's time to go back to work, the deli man asks for your order, the nurse calls your name, or the plane lands.

THE VALUE OF RELATIONSHIPS

I can't stress enough, the values, both measurable and intangible, of building relationships (instead of just making deals one at a time). Nor can I over emphasize that you never know what the long-term benefit of a relationship will be. No story drives home the importance of building relationships more poignantly than this one.

THE DEAL OF A LIFETIME: HOW KIRBY PUCKETT BONDED WITH CARL POHLAD, THE MINNESOTA TWINS, AND THE TWIN CITIES

How can building a relationship that may or may not pay off sometime in the future possibly be more important than making a

THE POCKET BONDER

A Quick Guide to Links, Connections, and Common Interests

Environment and Style

Office walls—The gallery of a person's life. Photos, awards, degrees.

Desk—The comfort zone. Everything there is important. Souvenirs, kid-stuff, photos, company mottos, mission statements.

Cars—Alter ego. Fast, plush, safe, exotic, functional.

Clothes—The style of the person. Aggressive, conservative, neat, messy, severe, natural.

Speech—Audio clues. Sports metaphors. Literature or movie references. War analogies. Name-dropping. Place-dropping.

Recreational Links

Sports/Spectator. Momentos, souvenirs, autographs.

Sports/Participatory. Trophies, framed scorecards, golf or running shoes on floor, clubs, racquets, rods in corner, bandages, limps.

Hobbies—Spare time. Collecting anything. Stamps, coins, antiques, toys, books. Hunting, fishing, diving, photography, golf, gardening, reading, movies, travel.

Pets Dogs, cats, birds, fish, horses. For fun, for show.

Human Connections

Families—The obvious connection, often the best.

Spouses—With careers. Without. First marriage, second.

Children—The big connection. Babies and late night feedings, adolescents and acne, teenagers and driving, college kids and tuitions, married and having babies.

Friends—Who knows who you might have in common.

Heroes—Mentors, influentials. bosses, (photos, quotes, books).

Culture Links

Art—Painter, sculptor, jeweler. Museum-goer.

Music—Classic, opera, swing, jazz, rock, country. Player. Listener.

Theater—Broadway, on & off.

Dance—Modern, ballet, country.

Civic Activities

Boards,charities, causes, politics—(be careful).

Miscellaneous

Ethnic Heritage—Never underestimate the power of a shamrock. Handle with diplomacy.

Ailments—Bad backs, allergies, pulled muscles.

Jokes—Some people collect them.

Alma Mater—Grade school, prep school, college, grad school, military, fraternity, sorority, Rotary, Kiwanis, Elks, Scouts.

lucrative deal right now? How can the unknown, down the road, compare with a bird in the hand, particularly a golden goose?

Passing up instant gratification isn't an easy choice to make, but it is one that's often worth it. Back in 1992, Kirby Puckett, the superstar of the Minnesota Twins, was about to become a free agent. He had built his career with the Twins and he wanted to stay with them. We knew that he might have to make some sacrifices to stay since Minnesota is what they call, in baseball, a small revenue market.

Large, medium, small, or minuscule market, we were miles apart when the negotiations began. To use the baseball cliché, we weren't in the same ballpark, or planet. We felt Kirby's value was in the range of $35 million over five years. The Twins first offer was $12 million over three years. Worse than the dollars per year—our $7 million versus their $4 million—was the discrepancy in contract length—our five years to three. We were $23 million and two years apart.

Still, Kirby and his family wanted to remain in the Twin Cities. Throughout the summer, I kept going back and forth with the team's general manager, Andy MacPhail. Finally, in August, Andy MacPhail brought us a five-year offer of $28 million. This brought them up to $5.6 million per year. The dollars weren't as high as we had hoped, or as high as we believed Kirby's market value to be, but we knew enough about the Twins' finances to know, the club was close to the limits of its resources.

I didn't tell Kirby to take it. I didn't tell him to turn it down. I said, "Kirby, how do you feel about the offer?" Kirby did what he always does with a major decision. He talked it over with his wife, Tonya. After a lot of soul-searching, they concluded they'd take the offer.

But before Kirby accepted, we put in a call to Donald Fehr, the leader of the Major League Players Association. Don has been criticized by some for wanting to squeeze every last dime from every team owner. It so happens, that criticism is undeserved. Don Fehr is determined that each ballplayer be in the best situation for that player. When we called and told Don the Twins offer, he asked only one question. "Kirby, are you happy with it?" Kirby said, "Yes, I am." Don said, "Then you should take it."

Then the unexpected happened. Team owner, Carl Pohlad, overruled Andy MacPhail and retracted the offer. Kirby was greatly disappointed. I was discouraged. Andy was disheartened that the deal he had worked so hard to make had fallen apart. Negotiations stalled. Throughout the fall, nothing occurred to encourage us.

Finally, reluctantly, we went into the free-agent market. Remember, win–win (and certainly WIN–win) isn't lose–win, where you give up everything just to make some kind of a deal. We explored other cities but kept the door open to the Twins front office in case they should have a change of heart. I followed a personal axiom, "Be hard on issues, soft on people." We went to Boston and Philadelphia and learned from the Red Sox and Phillies what we suspected. Kirby Puckett could get a lot more as a free agent, well into the mid-$30 million range for five years, maybe higher.

Financially, things were looking up. However, Kirby and Tonya still wanted to live in Minneapolis. I called Andy MacPhail in late November and told him, "You're going to lose Kirby." To change the course of what now appeared to be almost inevitable would require a change of normal procedure. Standard negotiation was getting nowhere. We suggested an informal meeting with Carl Pohlad, perhaps over a meal. The message came back that Carl and Eloise Pohlad would like to have Kirby and Tonya Puckett, me, my partner, Michael Maas, and Andy MacPhail to dinner at their home. We had no specific agenda and, frankly, we had no expectations.

It was a lovely evening, a great dinner of wine and good food, during which we discussed community involvement, family, priorities—everything but baseball. At the end of the night, Carl turned to Kirby and said, "What do I have to do to keep you here?" Kirby replied, "I just want to be treated fairly." Carl nodded and saw us out.

I went back to the Puckett's house with them. We talked past midnight, well into the morning. Could we work something out? Could we find a way to make a deal in the Twin Cities? Could we do it in time? At this point, we were facing deadlines from the other interested teams. At 3:30 A.M., I called Andy MacPhail at home. We talked about what kind of a deal would work: Something in the range of $30 million, five years, game tickets worth several hundred thousand dollars and other support for Kirby's charitable endeavors. Somewhere between 4:00 and 5:00 A.M., Andy called back, "Deal." Kirby got $30.5 million, tickets for the underprivileged kids he helped, and a pledge of further aid to Kirby's causes. Before he formally accepted, I talked heart to heart with Kirby. "You know, in the next few weeks, someone is going to get $35 or maybe $40 million (and it happened). Think about that before you decide." Kirby looked at me and said, "You're probably right. But no matter how much they get, nobody will be happier than me." We told Andy MacPhail, "Deal."

We negotiated. We got stalled. We explored alternatives but didn't burn bridges. We tried an unconventional approach. We didn't jump at a deal; instead we opted to build a relationship. The Pohlads and the Pucketts had re-bonded. The Twins kept their superstar. Kirby's family stayed in Minneapolis. If that was the total result of building a relationship, it would've been more than worth the effort.

But that wasn't the end of the story. At the beginning of the 1996 baseball season, as Kirby entered the fourth year of his contract, he noticed a problem with his vision. The problem quickly evolved into a serious condition. The sight in Kirby's right eye was fading and fading fast. By July, his career as a major league ballplayer was over. The superstar who couldn't be stopped by 100 mph fastballs, was stopped by the insidious disease, glaucoma.

You have to know Kirby Puckett to appreciate the way he handled this tragic situation. I remember the news conference at which his retirement was announced. Hardened baseball players, callous reporters, and veteran team officials were all in tears. Kirby sat behind the microphone, flashed his big, broad smile and said, "Don't worry about me. It may be cloudy in my right eye, but the sun is always shining in my left eye."

Although he maintained a confident, positive attitude, his life was filled with agony and uncertainty. What would he do? How would they live? What did the future hold? Of course, the agony did not abate but the uncertainty did. Immediately, propositions came in to Kirby for this next phase of his life. He was practically overwhelmed with offers, from individuals and businesses around the Twin Cities, as well as from far away. It seemed that everywhere

and everyone with whom Kirby had "built relationships" reciprocated with opportunities. Among them was a proposal from Carl
Pohlad. He wanted Kirby to work with the Twins. But beyond that,
he asked Kirby if he would participate in other Pohlad business en-
terprises. That dinner in November of 1992 had not only sealed a
baseball contract, it had strengthened a relationship between two
people and two families that lasted through good times and challenging times. The bond transcended the deal. The relationship
outlasted a baseball career. The Power of Nice paid off again.

R·E·F·R·E·S·H·E·R
CHAPTER 11
BUILDING RELATIONSHIPS

> **Bonding leads to relationships which leads to more deals.**

- Don't hit and run—Meet and bond.
- Short-run versus long-run.
- Greater return-on-effort.

How to Bond

Gather Information—Remember Prepare? Use what you already know.

Observe—Office, walls, desk, pictures, momentos, class rings, clothing style, cars.

Talk—Ask questions, conversation leads to more conversation, leads to relationships.

> **No "faux bonding" Pretending you have a shared interest when you don't, will backfire.**

Rules of Bonding

1. *Meet face-to-face:* Can't bond with a stranger.
2. *Go to their turf:* Learn more about someone in comfort of their home/office.
3. *If negotiation breaks down, rebond:* Go back to what you have in common, not where you differ.

Practice Makes Bonding (Exercise)

- Find a stranger.
- Find links.
- Use Pocket Bonder.

> **Never underestimate the value of relationships.**

"You can't talk to him like that, Herman! He makes your salary every time he trots lethargically to right field."

Putting It All Together

12

Most negotiations call for the use of one, two, or even three of the key principles behind *The Power of Nice*. For example, one negotiation may illustrate the value of the 3Ps with the emphasis on preparation, another on utilizing listening skills, another on how bonding can payoff, and another on how to deal with difficult negotiators, plus various combinations of these tools. But once in a while, a negotiation comes along that requires the application of all of the principles of *The Power of Nice*—one challenge that calls for everything we teach. The following is that rare but illustrative case history that brings to bear all the power of *The Power of Nice*.

THE MAJOR LEAGUE BASEBALL OWNERS VERSUS THE MAJOR LEAGUE UMPIRES (AND THE MAJOR LEAGUE UMPIRES VERSUS THEMSELVES)

What's a negotiator's worst nightmare? Too high a price? Too low? Bad terms? No, it's when your negotiation strategy literally self-destructs. Not only does the deal blow up, but so does all of your negotiating leverage and perhaps even the viability of your negotiation team. What do you do? Give in? Give up? Or take an entirely different approach?

The negotiations between the Major League Umpires Association (the "Association") and the Major League Baseball Owners backfired so badly, in a matter of days, the Association lost virtually all of its bargaining power. *In fact, the Association was instantly so crippled, the umpires would first have to negotiate with themselves to regain a measure of unity and a fresh start just to get back to the table with the owners.*

It couldn't have begun worse, a textbook case of how not to negotiate, a win-lose strategy deteriorating into a lose-lose outcome (a loss for the umpires of their bargaining leverage and an eventual loss of umpire talent for baseball). But later, through an eleventh-hour adoption of the Power of Nice philosophy, it became a case study in *how to negotiate,* putting the umpires back into a position to bargain effectively.

The triggering event occurred on July 14, 1999, with Association Executive Director Richie Phillips' attempt to force early renegotiation of the umpire's collective bargaining agreement. Phillips followed the ill-fated strategy of 12,000 air traffic controllers in 1985—when they struck illegally, President Reagan swiftly dismissed them and immediately ordered the hiring of replacements.

When Phillips, a renowned hardball negotiator, advised members of the umpire's Association to tender their resignations to Major League Baseball, the umps met a similar fate to the one meted out by Reagan. Sandy Alderson, Major League Baseball's executive vice president for operations, responded: "This is either a threat to be ignored or an offer to be accepted." Baseball took the latter option and began hiring replacements.

Many of the 50-plus umpires who resigned tried to rescind their resignations, but sadly 22 were left without jobs. Suddenly the Association, which Phillips had helped build, was practically powerless. Although he worked to obtain many benefits for umpires through the years, he may be most remembered for this faulty strategy.

My relationships with umpires go back a long way, both on and off the field. After spending 25 years in baseball and attending hundreds of games, I not only watched the "men in blue" call balls and strikes on my baseball clients, but I got to know and respect them as human beings. In late 1991, I became deeply involved with umpire Steve Palermo. Steve had been shot and paralyzed, while coming to the aid of two waitresses who were being mugged in Dallas. Steve's heroism cost him the profession he loved. Without adequate compensation or benefits, Steve struggled financially as well as physically. On behalf of Steve and his wife, Debbie, I negotiated with then Acting Commissioner Bud Selig to hire Steve as a special assistant in the Commissioner's Office and provide him with needed benefits and compensation. With this professional stability, Steve was able to focus on his physical rehabilitation. Today, Steve's professional role has grown to being a supervisor of umpires for Major League Baseball and his physical rehabilitation has progressed to the point where he can walk without crutches.

Several years later, the personal side of umpires became even clearer during the infamous Roberto Alomar-John Hirschbeck "spitting incident." I knew John Hirschbeck, one of the most respected umpires in the game, having interviewed him on my television show on Baltimore's NBC affiliate. He talked about the loss of his son, John, to adrenoleukodystrophy (ALD), a rare genetic brain disease and the challenge he and his wife, Denise, faced knowing that their other son, Michael, was also afflicted with the disease.

Sometime later, an unfortunate on-field incident brought John and me together again. After disputing a call, the perennial All-Star, Roberto Alomar, shocked the baseball world by spitting on John Hirschbeck. Having dealt with superstar athletes for many years, I expected the media feeding frenzy that followed. John asked for my advice. He made it clear, from the beginning, that he wanted to put the incident behind him and I encouraged him to do so. Rather than holding a lifetime grudge and treating each other with animosity, John and Roberto both ultimately practiced the Power of Nice, extending their hands to one another when they next met on the playing field and maintaining their mutual respect today. In fact, John's young son, Michael, who is responding to treatment for ALD, is often in attendance at Cleveland's Jacobs Field, cheering one of his heroes, Roberto Alomar. Both of these experiences emphasized to me, not only an umpire's dedication to the game, but the human dimension of these "men in blue" that few see when they are on the field.

My role of working with individual umpires like Steve and John actually evolved into a role of helping a larger group of umpires in the summer of 1998. Back then, when some umpires began to feel uncomfortable with their union leadership, Joe Brinkman, another highly regarded umpire, asked if I would lead an election challenge to Phillips. I declined to challenge Phillips for the post of Executive Director of the umpires' union. But I did offer to advise the group (Brinkman had been joined by John Hirschbeck, Tim Welke, and several other umpires) pro bono. I agreed with their feeling that they would be better served with nonconfrontational leadership and sent them copies of the first edition of this book, which had just been published.

In a meeting of the Association in February of 1999, Brinkman, Hirschbeck, and Welke were unable to garner enough votes to prevent the reappointment of Phillips as executive director. Brinkman and Hirschbeck were dejected. They felt that they had tried a new approach and failed. I comforted them with a bold prediction: Within six months, Phillips would do something "so outrageous and so negative, you'll find renewed strength for real opposition." It took only five months.

When Phillips had suggested the "mass resignation" tactic in July of 1999, many of his troops obediently followed. As one umpire put it, "We drank the Kool-Aid." But only hours later, the same ump thought, "What have I just done?" The uneasiness spread; the umpires put their careers in jeopardy. In one case an umpire said that he signed the resignation because of the intense peer pressure at the meeting. When he arrived home, he replayed the strategy and outcome with his most important advisor, his wife. She summed up the thoughts of families, fans, and experts around the country when she exclaimed, "What in the world were you thinking!" Within 24 hours of the mass resignation meeting, umpires were calling me for help.

Practicing what we preach, I began my own preparation. I called distinguished labor lawyers who represented both union and management perspectives in several industries. Their unanimous response was, "What in the world were they thinking!" These advisors told me the umpires' only hope was to rescind their resignations as soon as possible. I conveyed this advice to those umpires who called me, encouraging each to hire his own counsel, pass the word to other umpires to do likewise, and for all of them to weigh the option of rescinding their resignations.

Further, we started to share ideas with other umpires and legal experts in a series of conference telephone calls. Each call became a mini-seminar in *The Power of Nice* negotiation principles: The **3Ps— prepare, probe,** and **propose**—as well as lessons in dealing with difficult negotiators, listening, and bonding (all in contrast to Phillips' combative style).

On September 27, 1999, we conducted a call with a group of umpire representatives in my Baltimore law office and with more than 40 umpires on phones around the country. During that call, several labor lawyers agreed that the first step to rebuilding the umpires' strength would be to decertify the existing union. A new union was the only hope for dealing constructively with Major League Baseball and possibly helping the 22 unemployed umpires.

Thus began a new negotiation—a negotiation within a negotiation—by Hirschbeck, Brinkman, and their allies to obtain the support of enough umpires to achieve decertification of the union. If the previous strategy of the Major League Umpires Association was a case study in *how not to negotiate*, this new negotiation to decertify the union and start fresh would be textbook Power of Nice.

Initially, I led them through the use of the first of the 3Ps, *Preparation*. Learn everything about the current union: its rules, legal documents, and finances. Use the Preparation Planner checklist (following the acronym, **P.A.I.D.S.**): Gather and analyze information about **P**recedents for decertification, as well as the applicable labor law. Find **A**lternatives to Phillips' leadership of the MLUA, as well as alternative approaches to waging a successful decertification campaign. Learn how the **I**nterests of the undecided umpires would impact the process. Become fully familiar with the timetable and **D**eadlines governing the election process. Analyze the relative **S**trengths and Weaknesses of the existing umpires' union and of those of the group being led by Hirschbeck and Brinkman. And finally, set **Goals** for the Hirschbeck-Brinkman group; establish **Team** assignments for the leaders of the group while analyzing Phillips' team; and map out a **Strategy** for a successful election campaign.

Then, together we practiced the second P, *Probing*, patiently asking every umpire for goals, objections, and worries, both rational and emotional. We instructed our leadership team in using another acronym, **W.H.A.T.**, to frame questions: Find out **W***hat* is important to the constituents, **W***hat else* is important, **W***hich* element is most important, and **W***hy* it is important. Then, **H***ypothesize*, by asking questions in the form of "what ifs" rather than direct or threatening questions. To gather additional information, **A***nswer* their questions with your own questions. And, in your never-ending quest for more and more knowledge, encourage respondents to **T***ell me more*. From time to time, I would point out to Hirschbeck (emerging as a leader), the principles they were practicing. "Keep probing; keep asking, and don't hesitate to ask them to tell more and more." "Learn what others want; understand their needs." "The best way to get what you want is to help others get what they want."

Another important call came on Sunday, October 3. Hirschbeck conducted the telephone meeting with me quietly offering advice. The subject was key; it involved asking the other umpires to fund the projected $100,000 expense of a decertification effort at a cost of $3,000 per umpire. If this **P***roposal*, the third P, had been made earlier, it would have likely been rejected. However, because Hirschbeck, Brinkman, and their team had taken the time to *Prepare*, and because they spent countless telephone calls *Probing* the interests of the other umpires, when it came time to make this proposal it was not a bombshell, but instead, a foregone conclusion.

Hirschbeck asked for questions and concerns. A novice at the start of this process, John was becoming a seasoned negotiator, utilizing the lesson of *Listening* by encouraging his leadership team to "let others vent opposing views," "diffuse anger," "listening isn't just waiting to talk." Because the conference calls extended to as much as three hours, some umpires became frustrated with the apparently slow movement. John counseled them to be patient with another Power of Nice principle, **"Negotiation is a process, not an event."** Ultimately, the Sunday call was a huge success. The umpires were becoming comfortable with decertification and creation of a new union.

Support was growing. Forty nine of the 93 umpires joined with Hirschbeck, Brinkman, and the rest of our core group on the next call. The $100,000 decertification fund had been raised. On October 16, the petition to decertify the old union was submitted to the National Labor Relations Board (NLRB). The issue would be put to a vote. All umpires were invited to a meeting in Baltimore on November 2.

On the evening before the meeting, our team met until 10 P.M. The preparation session was interrupted with news that Phillips had filed a defamation suit against Hirschbeck and others. I advised the group that the suit was probably without merit, simply a part of Phillips' strategy of intimidation. When dealing with difficult people, **"Don't take it personally and don't get personal."** Rather than take the bait and get distracted by the lawsuit, I told the umpires, "When people are under pressure, they revert to habits. Richie's habit is to intimidate. Let's make sure our habit is *Preparation.*"

We then reviewed 21 questions, ran our lead umpires, Brinkman and Hirschbeck, through their drill, playing **devil's advocate,** preaching and practicing, "prepare, prepare, prepare." At midnight, Hirschbeck and others were still up making notes.

At a Days Inn Hotel in Baltimore the next day, 52 umpires appeared in person. They walked past a banner reading: "Vote for Our Future—Vote Right," referring to the fact that the new union they were forming, the World Umpires Association (WUA), appeared on the right side of the ballot in the coming decertification election. The atmosphere was highly charged. One staunch opponent fired a steely glare at me and refused to shake my hand when I extended it to him. Looking me in the eye, he told me, "Go **** yourself." Despite the emotions in the air, we reminded ourselves to neutralize our emotions, to maintain self-control, and not to take any of it personally.

Hirschbeck conducted a democratic meeting. He went through the 21 questions; he listened; he probed; he patiently waded through disagreements; he let everyone have their say regardless of their point of view. To umpires who were accustomed to meetings where dissent was squelched, where the floor was owned by the few who could shout the loudest, Hirschbeck's open, approachable, and fair style was a welcome change. Even some of those who vehemently opposed the new union were the first to agree that this meeting had demonstrated the integrity of the people behind it. At the end of the meeting, the umpire who previously would not shake my extended hand, found me, reached his hand toward mine, and said, "Nice job."

The preparation paid off. Skeptics and several opponents were won over. The official vote finally came on November 30. In a crowded hearing room at the NLRB in New York, the umpires' ballots were counted. In an overwhelming victory, the tally was 57 to 35 and the World Umpires Association replaced the Major League Umpires Association as the certified bargaining agent for all major league umpires. The umpires would once again be in a position to negotiate effectively.

Phillips appealed, but the NLRB's decision stood. By this time, I had stepped aside from my volunteer advisory role. The World Umpires Association and its team of lawyers took on their first task, negotiating a new collective bargaining agreement that was completed on September 2, 2000. Phillips and the Major League Umpires Association filed a grievance on behalf of the 22 umpires who lost their jobs and would not relinquish its control to the new umpires' union. Despite the fact that in May 2001, an arbitrator reinstated 9 of the 22, the lives of these umpires and their families had been profoundly altered because of an ill-advised, and ultimately failed, strategy. With that sad exception, the World Umpires Association had achieved its objective—a sound collective bargaining agreement with Major League Baseball. The umpires had learned and practiced one more principle of the Power of Nice: *Building* (or, in this case, rebuilding) *relationships* for more deals and better deals in the future.

Speaking to *The New York Times* shortly after the election victory, John Hirschbeck summed it up, "We learned from Ron Shapiro and from his book, *The Power of Nice*. We were prepared in all respects, from every angle, in every phone call."

Thanks, John. We couldn't have said it better ourselves.

Putting It All Together

Prepare—Research, study, stockpile knowledge, learn everything you can about others at the table. Use the Preparation Planner checklist and **P.A.I.D.S.**

Probe—Ask questions, look for common ground, determine needs, put yourself in the other person's situation. Practice **W.H.A.T.**

Propose—Don't hurry, let others go first, let discussions become offers. Know your alternatives.

Listen—Listening is not waiting to talk. The others are unloading their emotional baggage and, at the same time, telling you what it takes to make a deal.

Negotiation is a process, not an event—Go through the steps. Mix and match steps. Repeat steps when necessary. Don't short-cut.

Dealing with a difficult negotiator—Neutralize your emotions. Don't take their methods personally. Don't get personal.

Devil's advocate—Find someone with whom you can practice your strategy.

Building relationships—Leads to more deals and better deals in the future.

"Okay . . . I'll trade you Cal Ripken's agent and financial advisor for Kirby Puckett's marketing rep and stock broker!"

(By permission of Bob Gorrell and Creators Syndicate.)

The Portable Negotiator

Put the Power of Nice in Your Pocket

Okay, you've read the book. Now how do you remember it all? How do you make sure you practice the lessons every time you negotiate? Repetition. Practice. Habit.

> ### THE POWER OF NICE
>
> The best way to get what you want is to help the other side get what they want.

From now on, every time you negotiate, you want to take along The Power of Nice. The following forms will help you whenever you're making a deal. Read them, fill them out, review them before each and every deal. Pretty soon, you'll see the forms in your mind before you see them on the page. The systematic approach will become automatic. Everywhere you go, the Power of Nice, WIN–win, and the 3 Ps, will go with you.

PREPARE

In **preparing** for my negotiation, I will seek the following **information** *(remember Precedents, Alternatives, Interests, Deadlines):*

_____

_____

_____

I will use the following **information sources:**

_____

_____

_____

The following person/s in my network can help me gather information:

_____

_____

_____

The following person will be my negotiation **coach:**

_____

My negotiating **devil's advocate** will be:

_____

My negotiating **strategy** will be:

_____

I obtained this important information as a result of my **preparation:**

_____

_____

_____

_____

PROBE

The other side's current stated **position** is:

_____

_____

_____

When it is time to **probe,** I will seek the following **information:**

_____

_____

_____

To determine information, I'll ask the other side these **questions:**

_____

_____

_____

I will use the following **probing technique** *(remember W.H.A.T.):*

_____

_____

I will be a more effective **listener** by:

_____

_____

By **probing,** I uncovered the following interests underlying the stated positions:

_____

_____

_____

_____

_____

_____

PROPOSE

I will try to get the **other side to make the first offer** by:

_____

_____

_____

I will **aim high** by asking for:

_____

_____

I'll concede these **less important issues** to obtain items I need:

_____

_____

_____

To generate **proposals,** I will **brainstorm** with these people:

_____

_____

The following creative **proposal** might match anticipated interests:

_____

_____

_____

My approach to **proposing** yielded the following results:

_____

_____

_____

_____

_____

_____

NEGOTIATING FROM WEAKNESS

I will go to the following **objective third parties** to check my assumption that I am in a **weak position:**

_____

_____

_____

If I am in a weak position, I will **expand** my **goals** by *(don't forget Money Isn't the Only Goal, Look for Intangibles, and Make the Deal Bigger):*

_____

_____

_____

To strengthen my position, I will **locate allies** by *(remember to Add to Team, Find an Expert, and Locate Others Similarly Situated):*

_____

_____

_____

Finally, I'll use **brainstorming** to find creative solutions such as:

_____

_____

_____

By identifying **weaknesses** and using the appropriate techniques, I was able to achieve the following results:

_____

_____

_____

_____

_____

DIFFICULT NEGOTIATORS

I am facing a negotiator who is being **difficult** by:

_____

_____

_____

The following **emotional tactic** is being used:

_____

I will **deflect** the emotional tactic and **re-focus** on the issues by:

_____

I'll use these **tacking** procedures:

    I'll **understand their pressures** by:

    _____

    _____

    I'll **acknowledge their concerns** by:

    _____

    _____

    I'll let them **save face** by:

    _____

    _____

After encountering a difficult negotiator and employing the appropriate techniques, the negotiation resulted in:

_____

_____

_____

_____

_____

ASSESSING PERSONALITIES

My negotiation **personality** is:

_____

My identifying characteristics are:

_____

_____

My negotiation **style** is:

_____

_____

The other side's negotiation **personality** is:

_____

The other side's identifying characteristics are:

_____

_____

The other side's negotiation **style** is:

_____

_____

To negotiate effectively with the personality I'm facing, I will:

_____

_____

_____

To negotiate effectively with the personality, I'm facing, I will not:

_____

_____

_____

My assessment of negotiation personality types yielded the following results:

_____

_____

_____

_____

_____

_____

_____

UNLOCKING DEADLOCKS

To break the deadlock, I will **change something** (*remember, Location, Negotiators, or Bring in a Mediator*):

_____

_____

_____

To break this deadlock, I'll use the following **objective mechanisms** (*You cut–I choose, Sealed bids, External criteria, Arbitration*):

_____

_____

No deal may be the best option if:

I've been forced below my bottom line, which is:

_____

_____

The following alternative is better than the one proposed:

_____

_____

The other side can't meet the terms of the deal because:

_____

_____

These long-term problems outweigh short-term gains:

_____

_____

The result of trying to unlock this negotiation deadlock was:

_____

_____

_____

_____

BONDING AND BUILDING RELATIONSHIPS

I will **bond** with the other side by *(remember Gather Information, Observe, Talk)*:

_____

_____

_____

Possible **bonding** interests include *(remember The Pocket Bonder)*:

_____

_____

_____

My common **bonds** with the other side are:

_____

_____

_____

_____

_____

After bonding and building relationships, this negotiation had the following short-term results:

_____

_____

_____

_____

_____

This negotiation had the following long-term results:

_____

_____

_____

_____

POST-NEGOTIATION QUESTIONNAIRE

The best negotiators learn from their successes and mistakes, as well as those of the other side. Use this post-negotiation assessment to analyze your performance and identify ways to improve results in your next negotiation.

Yes	No	*PREPARE*
___	___	1. Was your pre-negotiation preparation thorough?
___	___	2. Did you determine precedents, alternatives, interests, and deadlines?
___	___	3. Did you establish an aspiration level and a walk-away position?
___	___	4. Did you obtain information about the negotiation style of the other side?
___	___	5. Did you formulate a negotiation strategy and put it in writing?
___	___	6. Did you use a Preparation Planner (or a shorthand version)?

PROBE

Yes	No	
___	___	1. Were you able to ask questions to determine the other side's interests?
___	___	2. Was there information disclosed that changed your strategy?
___	___	3. Were you giving or receiving more information?
___	___	4. When you probed, did you utilize *W.H.A.T.*?
___	___	Did you ask *W*hy?
___	___	Did you *H*ypothesize?
___	___	Did you *A*nswer questions with questions?
___	___	Did you *T*ally up information?
___	___	5. Were you an effective listener?

PROPOSE

Yes	No	
___	___	1. Were you able to get the other side to make the first offer?
___	___	2. Did you immediately accept their first offer?
___	___	3. Did you "bid against yourself" before obtaining a counter-offer?
___	___	4. Did you aim high?
___	___	5. Did you lower your sights when you got to the table?

CHALLENGING NEGOTIATIONS

Yes No

1. Was the other side a "difficult negotiator"?
2. Were you able to control your emotions?
3. Were you dealing from a position of weakness?
4. Did you employ techniques such as tacking to overcome your weaknesses?
5. Did negotiations reach a deadlock?
6. Did you employ techniques to break the deadlock?
7. Did you consider "no deal" as an option?

RELATIONSHIP BUILDING

1. Were you "hard on interests but soft on people"?
2. Did you acknowledge the other side's concerns and interests?
3. Did you engage in sufficient bonding during the negotiation?
4. Did you make a one-time deal or a deal that can lead to more deals?

THE DEAL

1. Did you achieve most of what you wanted?
2. Did the other side achieve at least some of what it wanted?
3. What did you do best as a negotiator?

_____

_____

_____

_____

_____

4. What could you have improved?

_____

_____

_____

_____

"The Shapiro Negotiations Institute faculty of certified trainers, including Ron Shapiro and Mark Jankowski, combine a vast array of real-life business experiences with effective, entertaining, and energetic teaching styles.

The Institute provides educational and highly customized negotiation seminars, training programs, and keynote speakers.

FOR MORE INFORMATION

Shapiro Negotiations Institute
3600 Clipper Mill Road
Suite 401
Baltimore, Maryland 21211

Phone: 800-665-4SNI (4764)

E-mail: sni@shapironegotiations.com

Web site: http://www.shapironegotiations.com

INDEX

· · · · · · · · · · · · ·